Reginald Lane Poole

A History of the Huguenots of the Dispersion at the Recall of the Edict of Nantes

Reginald Lane Poole

A History of the Huguenots of the Dispersion at the Recall of the Edict of Nantes

ISBN/EAN: 9783337293376

Printed in Europe, USA, Canada, Australia, Japan

Cover: Foto ©ninafisch / pixelio.de

More available books at **www.hansebooks.com**

THE LOTHIAN ESSAY MDCCCLXXIX
BY R. L. POOLE B.A. BALLIOL COLLEGE OXFORD.

A HISTORY

OF THE

HUGUENOTS OF THE DISPERSION

AT THE

RECALL OF THE EDICT OF NANTES

BY

REGINALD LANE POOLE

London

MACMILLAN AND CO.

1880

[All rights reserved.]

OXFORD:
BY E. PICKARD HALL, M.A., AND J. H. STACY,
PRINTERS TO THE UNIVERSITY.

PREFACE.

An author in his preface commonly sets out with a protest against the disparagement of his predecessors; and, although we seem to possess an invincible capacity for absorbing anything that comes into print, the putting forth of a book is still a matter of reasonable diffidence, as if one should dare to add to the infinite. The existence of a book has to be accounted for; it even needs an apology. The fortunate origin of the following chapters, representing a university essay, relieves me from this demand; and what I shall say about previous histories may be dressed in the modest obliquity of the third person. It is open to enquire what was the deficiency in former treatment that appealed to the trustees of the marquess of Lothian's historical prize when they called for a fresh review of *The Emigration consequent upon the Revocation of the Edict of Nantes.*

The history of the banished huguenots has been written in polemic and anecdote, homiletically, statistically, genealogically. Cut off from these methods by the conditions of space and manner incident to the form of an essay, it was left to me to assume the systematic habit of the bibliographer. To write otherwise had been a task of greater ease, perhaps of more popular interest. But the disorder in which the subject has hitherto been left, while it enhanced the difficulty of arrangement, made a compact index to its literature the more necessary.

What I have called the polemical method is probably obsolete, and its value is almost entirely collateral. The tracts and memoirs of the day, the letters of the huguenot ministers, must be used not for their emphasis but for their allusion, not for the text but the margin. In this sense they have the first importance, on their own side, and subject to check from every less partial source. Beside this literature—and its bulk may be gathered from the catalogue of the special Walloon Library at Leyden—we must range the books of anecdote, of which Mr SMILES's *Huguenots in England and Ireland* is a meritorious specimen. The body of such a work looks back to the authentic memoirs of the refugees, and these it is wiser to consult immediately. What remains of value lies in its stray facts and in its reference to books that might otherwise elude notice.

These indirect and irregular materials have their coëfficient in the minutely elaborate and complete literature of genealogy and statistic for the different countries of the exile. The Refuge in Holland has its historian in KOENEN and partly in BERG and DRESSELHUIS, Switzerland in MOERIKOFER, England in BURN, COOPER, and AGNEW. The German monographs might form a library by themselves; hardly a church but has its separate chronicler. ERMAN and RECLAM, who wrote a century ago, are the most comprehensive and diffuse : but, while all their successors amuse themselves more or less in second-hand generalities, the only manual that takes in the whole of Germany is that presented in the succinct little *Survey of the Migrations and Settlements of the Refugees*, published at Karlsruhe in 1854.

The year before this was doubly notable in huguenot bibliography. It witnessed the one attempt hitherto made to build up out of the fragments scattered among individual treatises a general history of the emigration. It witnessed also the foundation of the Historical Society of French Protestantism. The industry and carefulness of CHARLES WEISS's *History of the French Protestant Refugees* deserve the grateful commemoration of after-labourers in his field: but the materials accumulated in the twenty-eight volumes at present published of the Society's *Journal* make a revision and reconstruction of his History at once necessary and possible. The central institution, moreover, gave an impulse to historical enquiry, which was carried on into a close examination of the local reliques of the old huguenot churches. The special treatises of LIÈVRE, ARNAUD, ROSSIER, WADDINGTON, DELMAS, and many more, are samples of this quickened interest in all things huguenot.

M WEISS was among the first promoters of the Historical Society of French Protestantism : and had he lived to reissue his History, it would certainly have gained much in statistical completeness, as well as in vivid colouring. The book as we have it is deficient in life ; it attempts a completeness of detail often irrelevant to the subject, and through the rigid following of its scheme of arrangement chapters have to be written in which there is little or no matter worth writing, and which have added to the bulk of the book without adding to its value. Moreover, with every striving after candour, there is a constant undercurrent of religious antagonism which gives the book the character rather of controversy than of history.

Many of these objections apply to my essay equally or in a greater degree: some are perhaps intrinsic in the nature of the subject. A writer in the *Edinburgh Review* expressed surprise at M WEISS's failure to seize his opportunity of making 'a living gallery of historical portraits': but those who read the critic's sample of his own collection may congratulate M WEISS on his taste and forbearance. There was all the difference between a history and a review-article, between the permanent and the ephemeral treatment. The history of the huguenots in exile is a history of high interest, but it lacks unity. The starting-point is one and regular; the emigration is at haphazard and diverse; and the heterogeneity of the circumstances is further embarrassed by the immense and multiform compass of the literature. My endeavour has been limited to the indication of the distinguishing lines of the emigration, noting the points of contact with society outside, and supplementing what could not be other than a brief sketch by a fairly exhaustive apparatus of reference to the special text-books of each department of the subject. In this work I am particularly bound to record my thanks to the librarians of two collections not usually accessible to the public, to Dr W. N. DU RIEU, curator of the Walloon Library at Leyden, and to the rev. T. V. BAYNE, librarian of Christ Church.

REGINALD LANE POOLE.

BALLIOL COLLEGE, OXFORD,
    December 1879.

CONTENTS.

CHAPTER I.

THE POLITICS OF CALVINISM: THE HUGUENOTS AT HOME.

Presbyterianism, 1. The Huguenots' Schools, 5. Their Industry, 8.

CHAPTER II.

THE KING.

The Lesser Emigrations, 11. The Policy of Lewis XIV in Church, 15. And in Foreign Relations, 17. The Opposition to Colbert, 21.

CHAPTER III.

THE TYRANNY.

Stages of Oppression, 23. The Great Emigration, 28.

CHAPTER IV.

THE REFUGE IN THE NETHERLANDS.

The Dutch Protest, 34. Friesland, 37. Groningen and the East, 39. Zeeland and the Frontier-Country, 41. The Cape-Colony, 43.

CHAPTER V.

THE FRENCH SOCIETY IN HOLLAND.

The Making Ready at Amsterdam and Haarlem, 45. The College at Rotterdam, 48. The Immigration, 49. The Ministers, 51. The Society of Rotterdam and the Hague, 54. The Industry of the Refugees, 58. Their Influence on Manners, 60.

CHAPTER VI.

THE PASSAGE THROUGH HAMBURG AND THE NORTH.

Emigration to the German Sea-Ports, 63. Denmark, 65. Russia, 67. Poland and Sweden, 69. Mecklenburg and Brunswick, 70.

CHAPTER VII.

THE REFUGE UNDER THE STUARTS: THE FRENCH QUARTERS OF LONDON.

England and the Huguenot Oppression, 73. Attitude of Charles II, 75. James II, 78. The French in London, 81.

CHAPTER VIII.

THE DISPERSION IN ENGLAND AND AMERICA.

The French in Greenwich, 87. By the Coast, 88. At Norwich and Canterbury, 90. Their Industries, 92. The Emigration to America, 95. The Palatine Influx, 99.

CHAPTER IX.

THE FRENCH IN THE ENGLISH REVOLUTION: THE COLONY IN IRELAND.

The Huguenot Regiments, 101. Political Agency of the Refugees, 105. Their State in England, 106. The Colony in Ireland, 109.

CHAPTER X.

THE REFUGE IN SWITZERLAND.

The Passage through Vaud and Geneva, 114. The Society of Geneva, 118. The Refuge in the Cantons, 121.

CHAPTER XI.

THE PASSAGE THROUGH SWITZERLAND INTO GERMANY.

The Charities of Frankfurt, 125. Commerce in Saxony, 128. The Fortunes of the Palatinate, 129. The Colony of Erlangen, 131. Wuerttemberg and Baden, 132.

CHAPTER XII.

THE REFUGE IN AND ABOUT HESSE.

The Colonies of Neu-Isenburg and Hanau, 134. Hesse, 137.

CHAPTER XIII.

THE PLANTATION IN BRANDENBURG.

The Great Elector, 144. The Edict of Potsdam, 146. The Settlement, 148. Agriculture, 156.

CHAPTER XIV.

THE FRENCH COLONY IN BERLIN.

Frederick I, 154. Trade, 155. The Soldiery, 157. The Church, 158. Education and Learning, 160.

CHAPTER XV.

FRANCE AFTER THE EXODUS.

Loss in Population, 165. Commercial Decadence, 169.

CHAPTER XVI.

THE POWER OF THE REFUGEES AND ITS REFLEXION UPON FRANCE.

The Refugees a Military Force, 175. Political, 176. Intellectual, 177. Social, 179. Religious, 180. France All Catholic, 181.

SUPPLEMENTARY NOTES.

I. *Dragonnades*, 185.
II. *Walloon Churches in the Netherlands*, 187.
III. *Some Reports of Count d'Avaux*, 190.
IV. *The Huguenots and the Church of England*, 191.
V. *The Royal Bounty*, 193.
VI. *French Churches in London*, 194.
VII. *Supplement of French Settlements in England*, 199.
VIII. *Statistics of the Diaconate of Frankfurt*, 201.
IX. *French Colonies in Hesse*, 201.
X. *The French Colony in Brandenburg*, 202.

CORRECTIONS.

P. 24, line 3 and notes, lines 1 and 5, *for* réligion *read* religion.
P. 26, line 3, *for* Annis *read* Aunis.
  „   line 18, *for* were *read* was.
  „   note 4, line 2, *for* des *read* de.
P. 36, note 7, line 5, for *Gemeenden* read *Geemeenten*.
P. 40, note 3, line 1, *for* gives *read* give.
P. 47, note 1, line 4, *for* Scheidam *read* Schiedam.
P. 162, note 3, line 3, *for* Bartholomèss *read* Bartholmèss.

CHAPTER I.

THE POLITICS OF CALVINISM: THE HUGUENOTS AT HOME.

The religious movement of the sixteenth century at first produced no further political result than the transfer of spiritual control, in certain countries, from the pope to the temporal ruler. Wyclif's dream of church government seemed to have found its fulfilment. But men were no sooner reconciling themselves to the altered condition, than there arose in an obscure republic, just freed from its bishop's tyranny, another system, taking its colour from the polity of its birthplace, destined in time to transform the national life of Holland, England, and Scotland, and to organise in France an anti-monarchical party only to be quelled by a measure involving the temporary ruin of the country.

The presbyterian theory could not flourish in the face of the absolute views of the sovereigns of the time[1]. Everywhere it aroused or encouraged a frank spirit of resistance: the diffusion of the system is uniformly accompanied by a strenuous tendency towards public freedom. Its workings in the different countries were necessarily varied in their manner and their success. The liberties of Holland were won by the fortitude and the sufferings

---

[1] Cp. W. E. J. Berg, *de Réfugiés in de Nederlanden*, 1. 13; Amsterdam 1845. It is unnecessary to comment on more than the paradox of such an assertion as that of M Guillebert, that the huguenots at Neuchâtel, being used to monarchy, found themselves more happily situated there than under the 'régime républicain' of the Swiss cantons; *Bulletin de la Société de l'Histoire du Protestantisme français*, 3. 623; Paris 1855. This invaluable collection of materials for huguenot history I shall hereafter cite simply as 'the *Bulletin*.'

of a generation. In England, after a transient revolution, the conservative mind of the nation acquiesced in a compromise which elevated a popular aristocracy analogous to the already-accepted protestant hierarchy.

In Scotland and France, on the other hand, the course of events was obstructed by the tendencies of the monarchy in a manner altogether peculiar to these two countries. Here, far more than elsewhere, the political element of Calvinism was bound up with the religious; and religion was not seldom the mere shibboleth of party. Accordingly, we soon find the nobility attached, in a great majority, to the new opinions. The huguenots[1], or the presbyterians, are openly resolved to abjure allegiance unless their claims are allowed[2]. In Scotland their alternate successes and defeats endure through a longer struggle: their final victory is almost simultaneous with the final blow that destroyed the party of their religious kindred in France.

It is necessary to recognise the fact that the huguenots had a continued existence as a political party, in order to render Lewis the Fourteenth's attitude towards them in the least intelligible. Certainly this has been persistently denied by them and their descendants[3], and its assertion is stigmatised as an attempt to vindicate conduct which, judged by its results, is in a supreme degree indefensible. But the truth is, that, from the point of view of the national disaster, the recall of the Edict of Nantes, setting, as it did, the whole world in an attitude

---

[1] The derivation of the name 'Huguenot' is elaborately discussed by M E. Albaric, in the *Bulletin*, 6. 288-309; 1858. Through the form *aignos*, which actually occurs, he traces the word to *eignots*, *Eidgenossen*, 'confederates'; an old etymology newly fortified.

[2] See the Declaration of the Lords of the Congregation, Oct. 23 1559, in Leopold von Ranke, *History of England*, 1. 249 n.; Oxford 1875; and cp. his *französische Geschichte*, 3. 497 f.; Stuttgardt 1855.

[3] Even by impartial writers like M Francis Waddington, who says of protestantism in France, *Son existence, comme parti politique dans l'état, finit avec la prise de la Rochelle*; introd. to *Mémoires inédits de Jean Rou*, vii; Paris 1857: cp. the *Bulletin*, 2. 202; 1854.

hostile to Lewis, stands at so indefinite a height among the
follies of statesmen, that no exaggeration of fact can aggravate
it. And, for this very reason, we should grasp at anything
which, while it cannot palliate, may serve to explain this stu-
pendous mistake. *There is no man,* said Bacon, *doth a wrong
for the wrong's sake, but thereby to purchase himself profit,
or pleasure, or honour, or the like; therefore, why should I be
angry with a man for loving himself better than me?*[1] It will
be time hereafter to dwell on the failure of all that Lewis hoped
to achieve.

Cardinal de Richelieu, who had more in him of the Frenchman than of the priest, and most of all of the statesman, had
from the first seen that the position of the huguenots under
the Edict of Nantes, which practically erected a protestant republic in the midst of a catholic kingdom[2], was incompatible
with that fulness of scope and energy which it was his aim to
assure to the royal authority[3]. The state of affairs in 1629
enabled him to achieve a considerable success. The political
independence of the huguenots, fortified as it had been with a
number of strong places, was at an end. But the strength of
protestantism as a party in the state was not bound up with
these fortresses and these political assemblies. When the
huguenots ceased to be *un état dans l'état*, they remained none
the less *un peuple dans le peuple*[4]. And such an existence was
incompatible with the principles of symmetry and uniformity
which Lewis was sincerely resolute to establish.

For, under the Calvinistic discipline, men felt and thought
and lived in a sphere wholly apart from the catholics. The
Calvinistic reform did not involve merely the destruction of the
hierarchy of caste. The Lutherans also had done this; only,

---

[1] *Essay of Revenge.*

[2] See a lucid study of the subject in S. Sugenheim's *Aufsätze und bio-
graphische Skizzen zur französischen Geschichte;* Berlin 1872.

[3] Frédéric Ancillon, *Tableau des Révolutions du Système politique de
l'Europe,* 4. 288 f.; Paris 1823.

[4] A. Sayous, *Histoire de la Littérature français à l'Étranger,* i. 214; Paris
1853.

in conformity with their theory, the presbyters being appointed by the prince, the practical result was not dissimilar, except in name, to the constitution of the English or of the Gallican church. Calvin had gone further. The minister became not only one of the people, but through their self-elected presbytery he was their own choice. And this was the true essence not alone of their church polity but also of their religion. The sacerdotal despotism was exchanged for an immediate divine rule. No barrier was left standing between man and God. It was a perfect republic; rather, a perfect theocracy. This is the secret of the immense influence of Calvinism: this is why, while the activity of Lutheranism has been confined almost to the country of its birth, Calvinism was able to rise into a colossal power throughout the world.

It is too much the custom to judge this more than human religion by the code of doctrine on which it is ostensibly based; and the reader of the *Institutes* of Calvin is moved to wonder how a theology, which degrades the dignity and the ethical sense of man, which stultifies the justice of God, can ever have created this heroical race, whose strength lay in the very attributes which their dogma contemned, whose excellence was founded upon a high self-respect, and upon a faith in the eternity of truth. It is a commonplace that a moral strength cannot owe its source to a scheme of intellectual formulas: it is also certain that a mere agreement of opinion cannot bind together a people as the huguenots were bound together. Their religion was grounded on something deeper than this. The admission of the baseness of man's nature was saved from leading to apathy or to an abject stagnation by the equal consciousness of a divine presence. The dogmatic confession was little more than an apology for the belief, suited to the scholastic temper which Luther had revived. Hence the spirit of Calvinism has outlived the forms to which it was once wedded. It is yet strong, though it has abandoned most of the fortifications once held essential to its being.

The instinct of his religion attended the huguenot wherever

he went. At home he was by training grave, almost austere. When he appeared in public his manner was marked by an independence, a defiance, acquired by long years of social isolation. He knew that his religion bore the stigma, with the bulk of the people, of being in a minority, and he knew that a minority was a standing offence to the administrative system. The sense of the need of self-assertion was quickened and educated by the free discussion encouraged in presbytery and synod. More than this, it was brought to mature vigour in the schools that had grown up in the heart of the huguenot society, those schools to which the English universities, on the common ground of religion and scholarship, accorded a rank equal to their own[1]. It will not be amiss to dwell shortly upon this influence, which has seldom received much recognition from historians.

The academy which the national synods more than once singled out as a model to the rest was that established at Die in Dauphiné, in 1604[2]. With no more than 120 or 140 students in the year, it was directed by five professors[3], besides the usual complement of classical masters, a staff about equal to that of the far more considerable foundation at Saumur[4]. Its praise stood in the union of liberal tendencies with a strict discipline. Supported by the greater part of the townspeople, the academy was able to make fight against the intruded oversight of the bishop[5] until all its more popular rivals had been extinguished.

[1] D. C. A. Agnew, *protestant Exiles from France in the Reign of Louis XIV*, I. 17; ed. 2. 1871, quarto.

[2] Michel Nicolas in the *Bulletin*, 2. 322.

[3] The chairs were of Divinity, Hebrew, Rhetoric, and two of Philosophy: E. Arnaud, *Histoire de l'Académie protestante de Die*, 112 ff.; Paris 1872.

[4] Die had two classical *régents*, while Saumur in 1637 had five: *Bulletin*, 1. 305; 1853.

[5] In 1682 a Jesuit had planted a cross in front of the *Temple*. The consequent appeal to Grenoble elicited the fact that the academy, having no letters-patent, must come under the bishop's supervision by the Edict of March 4 1666. It was suggested to enforce this right in 1684, but the king superseded its necessity by an Arrêt de Suppression, September 11 1684:

The first to fall was the École de Théologie of Nîmes[1]. We must not be misled by the name: it was the least theological in its characteristic of any[2]. Even theology was taught on different lines to the common[3]. The dominant interest was humanism, whatever was historical, literary, philosophical. There was a poetical school which sought to raise the dialect of Languedoc to the dignity of a written language[4]. Claude Guiraud lived here, the correspondent of Gassendi and Descartes; and natural science was cultivated with the same devotion as natural and moral philosophy. But what is to be especially noticed is the strong common-sense that prevailed in the academy, and its constant contention against the refinements and hairsplittings of the day; a fact which must have had its share, as tending to subordinate the religious to the intellectual, in producing the disproportionate number of 'new converts' in the place where pressure was first put to it[5]. The history of the academy reaches from 1561 to 1664[6].

Arnaud, 105 ff. See the *Histoire de l'Édit de Nantes*, 5. 672; Delft 1693-1695, quarto. The authorship of this book is conceded to Élie Benoît, the B. M. A.D. of the title-page; cp. Bayle, *Lettres choisies*, 2. 427 f.; Rotterdam 1714.

[1] It is unnecessary more than to mention the foundation at Montpellier, which was united with Nîmes in 1617; or the very interesting Royal University of Orthez in Béarn, established in 1566 by Jeanne d'Albret. The latter was conspicuous for the uncompromising vigour of its Calvinism;—one of its professors was Lambert Daneau, the rigid enemy of catholics and Lutherans alike:—but it expired with the Edict of Reunion in 1620. Its one distinguished name is that of Paul Charles, who died in 1649: Nicolas, as above, 2. 321; J. Lourde-Rocheblave, in the same, 3. 280-292.

[2] Jean Claude was here only a short time: Nicolas, 2. 323.

[3] 'When there were two professors of divinity, one was charged with the task of explaining holy scripture in the form of exegesis, and the other paraphrased in three years, after the scholastic manner, what were called the commonplaces of the science': Borrel, in the *Bulletin*, 2. 546.

[4] L. von Ranke, *französische Geschichte*, 3. 500.

[5] Nicolas, 2. 324 f. The duke of Noailles reported the conversion of 60,000 in three days, which probably proves more than the vigour of the dragonnade: L. von Ranke, 3. 521; who draws a different conclusion, 501. A contemporary journal telling of the flight from Nîmes may be read in Ménard, *Histoire de Nîmes*, 5 preuves 18 f.; Paris 1754, quarto.

[6] Borrel, 2. 543.

Of wider importance was the university of Saumur[1], whither students thronged from England, Scotland, Holland, and Switzerland; the school long presided over by Louis Cappel[2], the founder of modern biblical criticism, and illustrated by the names of Caméron and Moïse Amyraut. But, in the view of this essay, its special interest lies in its theological and political influence upon the sister-universities of Sedan[3] and Montauban[4]. For it was here, when the dispute between Arminius and Gomarus was raging, that Duplessis-Mornay procured the acceptance of the remonstrant view of the doctrine of grace. Sedan yielded to the guidance of Saumur[5]. But Duplessis went further: in his pamphlet *De la Mésure de la Foi*, published in 1609, he sought to reconcile the non-catholic Churches by overlooking 'non-essentials'; and his political scheme, supported by the weight of Josué de la Place, whose will governed the opinion of Saumur, obtained the adhesion of the academy of Montauban[6].

In this way, a considerable party in the universities became attached to a belief which overthrew many of the barriers between the huguenots and the catholic church; the sacramental issue, once the test of protestantism, was practically discarded[7].

---

[1] The foundation of Saumur was resolved upon by the national synod held there June 15 1596. The scheme was carried out in 1599, not as commonly stated in 1604: *Bulletin*, 1. 301-316; 2. 306 and n. The academy was suppressed January 8 1684: Benoît, 5. 782.

[2] Conspicuously known as the first to overthrow the authority of the Hebrew vowel-points and of the Masoretic text of the *Old Testament*. He was professor of Hebrew, afterwards of divinity, and many times rector: *Bulletin*, 1. 302.

[3] Sedan was suppressed by Edict of July 9 1681.

[4] Founded 1597 or 1598; removed to Puylaurens 1659; suppressed March 5 1684: Benoît, 5. 783; Nicolas, *l'Academie protestante de Montauban*, 11; Montauban 1872: and in the *Bulletin*, 2. 43-49. The town of Montauban also was a centre of Protestant life; 2. 46.

[5] L. von Ranke, 3. 501. In later times it seems to have returned to Calvinism, if we may judge by the names of Pierre du Moulin and Jurieu; Nicolas, in the *Bulletin*, 2. 328 f.

[6] Nicolas, 2. 325-332.   [7] L. von Ranke, as above.

The opportunity was quickly seized by statesmen; and, while Turenne and Richelieu were planning a reunion of the churches, the Arminian party was growing yearly stronger. But, happily or unhappily, Lewis the Fourteenth in taking up the policy chose the wrong moment for carrying it into action. His ill-will toward the huguenots had already displayed itself, when he proposed a union at the synod of Charenton in 1673[1]. The reaction had begun, and the followers of Gomarus, now in a majority, refused to be admitted to the church on the same suspicious footing as the followers of Jansenius[2].

The free spirit, fostered in the consistories and synods of the protestants, in their schools of learning, found an apt expression in the zest and the success with which they devoted themselves to the improvement of manufacture and the extension of commerce[3]: their training in the administration of their church was recognised by the extent to which they were employed in financial business, in public farming and the negotiation of loans[4].

The history of the huguenots might vindicate the saying of Sir William Petty that *Trade is most vigorously carried on in every state and government by the heterodox part of the same, and such as profess opinions different from what are publicly established*[5]. Certain it is that in almost every branch of industry they surpassed the catholics. Weaving had become one of the principal industries of the country: in 1669 men counted 44,200 wool-weavers in France[6]. And it was almost a monopoly of the

---

[1] The *projet* may be read, with his criticisms, in Jurieu's *Politique du Clergé de France*, 337–343, and ff.; the Hague 1682.

[2] Louis was so conscious of the defeat that he had the proceedings of the synod destroyed: L. von Ranke, 3. 502 f.

[3] Such is surely a truer explanation of the fact than that which Mr Smiles deduces from the comparative exclusion of the huguenots from official and political life, which indeed can barely be asserted.

[4] L. von Ranke, 3. 499.

[5] *Political Arithmetic*, 118, in W. E. H. Lecky's *History of England in the eighteenth Century*, 1. 187; 1878.

[6] Voltaire, *Siècle de Louis XIV*, 391, ed. C. Louandre; Paris 1874.

protestants. Cloth in Champagne and the south-east, as well as in the north; serges and light stuffs in the Upper Gévaudan in Languedoc, yielding a revenue of two to three million livres; the linens of Normandy and Britany, the silks and velvets of Tours and Lyons; glass in Normandy, paper in Auvergne and Angoumois, things of fashion in the Isle of France; the tanyards of the Touraine, the furnaces of iron, steel, and tin, in the Sedanais;—such a catalogue represents far from the complete tale of protestant activity, gives but a slight indication of the work which satisfied the wants of France, and carried her wares into every country of Europe. But no summary, unsupported by statistics, can ever be certainly cleared of exaggeration [1]; and what statistics are to hand will come more fitly when we have to review the commercial loss to France, resulting from the measures of Lewis the Fourteenth. All we have here to insist upon, is the immense vigour with which the huguenots applied themselves to trade, and the excellence which, thanks to their tone of mind and the superior length of their working year [2], they attained in it.

Alone of the government, their value was recognised by Colbert. But Colbert was the only French statesman who knew the value of trade, who by an elaborately organised administration was able to cope with the demand which the king's profusion and vain-glory continually made on the exchequer. 'This great man,' said a later politician [3], 'was too able an administrator to fail of being tolerant: he had learned that civil and religious liberty was the principle of work, of industry, and of the wealth of nations.' Thus he employed and trusted the German protestant, Bartholemaeus Herward, his comptroller-

---

[1] I have relied chiefly, for what assertions appear above, upon the data which L. von Ranke has excerpted from Charles Weiss, *Histoire des Réfugiés protestants de France;* Paris 1853: for the huguenot historians cannot fairly be called as witnesses in a case like this.

[2] They allowed only the Sundays and the two festivals for holidays, of which the catholics had double the number. The former, therefore, worked on 310 days. the latter only on 260: Weiss, I. 25.

[3] F. Ancillon, 4. 290 f.

general of finance[1], and thus he kept the huguenots in the financial departments as long as his influence lived at court[2]: it was not until the king had grown tired of his services that the full vigour of persecution began, not until his death that the Edict of Nantes was revoked and commerce fled from France.

The mercantile importance of the huguenots, their efficiency in the navy and army, need not detain us[3]: like the inland commerce, we can best judge the work hereafter by the loss which the exodus of the workers inflicted upon their country. It is time to pass from the sufferers to the king who planned their ruin.

---

[1] It was Mazarin who first brought him into the administration, in spite of the opposition raised by the commissioners of the clergy: Benoît, 3. 139; G. de Félice, *History of the Protestants of France*, 2. 17 (English translation, 1853); Berg, 1. 15.

[2] 'M. Colbert fut toujours un appui pour les réformés, toujours un ardent défenseur de l'édit de Nantes. Les protestants ne furent attaqués que quand il est perdu la principale influence dans les conseils:' Rulhiére, *Éclaircissements historiques sur les Causes de la Révocation de l'Édit de Nantes et sur l'État des Protestants en France*, 1. 66; Paris 1788. The place and author are notorious, but do not appear on the title of the original edition.

[3] Cp. below, p. 18, n. 4.

CHAPTER II.

THE KING.

The Recall of the Edict of Nantes has been differently regarded as a measure of centralising policy or a means of recruiting the exchequer, a sacrifice to the liberties of the Gallican church or an atonement for the crimes of the royal revoker. Probably there is truth in all these explanations, but none of them singly is adequate to account for the course of action that culminated in the Edict of October 1685. Its springs lay deeper than the immediate cause of the Recall; and it is difficult to fix a date at which that policy, speaking strictly, should begin.

By some the renewal of the emigration which the Edict of Nantes had arrested is placed at the time of the capture of La Rochelle [1]. But this was merely occasional and provoked by no stress or compulsion. Voluntary emigrants, for commercial or the like reasons, no doubt there were: but under Richelieu or Mazarin there was absolutely no pressure. Voltaire has well seized the characteristic of the time when he says:—*Les guerres cessèrent, et il n'y eut plus que des disputes. On imprimait de part et d'autre de ces gros livres qu'on ne lit plus. Le clergé et surtout les jésuites cherchaient à convertir les huguenots; les ministres tâchaient d'attirer quelques catholiques à leurs opinions*[2]. Indeed the confirmation of the Edict in 1652 seemed to open a new period of prosperity for the society whose privileges it

1652.
May 21.

---

[1] H. J. Koenen, *Geschiedenis van de Vestiging en den Invloed der fransche Vluchtelingen in Nederland*, 75; Leyden 1846.

[2] *Siècle*, ch. xxxvi. 478.

assured. The huguenots built more churches, and their political importance was increased as they became admitted to municipal functions, and as their provincial synod was restored [1].

1659.

Rulhière, whose *Éclaircissements historiques* are our most temperate guide through the troubled period following, sees the first decisive step towards the Recall in the Order which placed 'relapsed heretics' entirely at the mercy of the catholics; and to the enforcing of this and a mass of other vexatious ordinances in 1666 he traces the first of the series of emigrations [2] connected with the new policy. Such also was the impression of the elector of Brandenburg, whose ready protest however was met by an assurance of the king's determination to uphold the Edict [3]. On the sincerity of this assurance it is not necessary to dogmatise. It is at all events significant of the attitude Lewis wished for the time to preserve towards his protestant subjects, whom, as he declared in the same year, *Being no less faithful than the rest of my people, it behooves me to treat with no less favour and consideration* [4]. The huguenots did not indeed accept these overtures, which they contrasted bitterly with the appearance of ordinance after ordinance in their despite. Even in 1665 one had written from Paris, *They say that to overthrow the huguenots, the king desires to suppress the Chambers of the Edict and to annul the Edict of Nantes* [5]; and another, with strained intensity, *The members of the reformed religion are so cruelly persecuted*

1666.
April 2.

1665.
March.

---

[1] L. von Ranke, *französische Geschichte*, 3. 498. The occasion of the confirmation was declared in the preamble to be, ' whereas our said subjects of the religion calling itself reformed have given sure proofs of their affection and loyalty, especially in the present troubles, whereof we continue very content'; Benoît, 3. 158 and rec. 38.

[2] Vol. 2. 342. The *Déclaration qui règle les Choses que doivent observer ceux de la R. P. R.* may be read in Benoît, 5, recueil 16.

[3] Adolphe Michel, *Louvois et les Protestants*, 4; Paris 1870.

[4] To the huguenots of Havre, April 1666; *Œuvres de Louis XIV*, 5. 375, in L. von Ranke, 3. 499.

[5] *Lettres de Patin*, 3. 516, cited by H. T. Buckle, *History of Civilisation in England*, 2. 178, n. 5, who remarks with heedless ostentation, ' I do not remember that any of the French historians have noticed that there was a rumour of' the Revocation ' in Paris twenty years before it occurred.'

through the whole kingdom that, if the work go on, it is to be feared that nothing less than a great massacre must be looked for[1].   166. May 29.

What these grievances, hardly more yet, precisely were, we may learn from a contemporary tract attributed to the great minister of Charenton, Jean Claude. In the first place, their public worship was being step by step proscribed[2]. Of a hundred churches in Poitou, Provence, and the Pays de Gex, not twenty were left: half those in Languedoc were closed: only two remained in the whole of Britany[3]. Other restraints must have been nearly as vexatious. [a]The singing of psalms had been prohibited, first on the highways, [b]then even in private houses[4]: [c]next the protestants were forbidden to bury their dead in the open day[5]. [d]Their magistracy was abolished; [e]they were declared incapable of all but rudimentary teaching. At the same time, while conversion to the catholic faith liberated a man from debt, [f]a protestant was compelled to maintain a child whom the advantages offered by conversion had seduced from his father's religion. *These things*, is the comment of our witness, *make us justly apprehensive that in end they will break out in acts of open violence; there being nothing which they are not in case to undertake for accomplishing of our ruine. And unless we be wilfully blind, we cannot but see that they design to drive us (by despair) into some insurrection. (But that we never shall do,*

[a] 1659.
[b] 1661. Mar.
[c] 1662. Aug. and Nov.
[d] 1663. Oct.
[e] 1663. Feb.
[f] 1653. Oct. 1665. Jan.

---

[1] Boreel, despatch, in Berg. 1. 16 n.

[2] The climax was reached when the Edict of Revocation allowed in all France protestant service only in the chapels of protestant ambassadors in Paris; that is, for a long time, practically those of Sweden, Denmark. and Switzerland; the rest being at war: *Bulletin*, 3. 595. A galling intrusion upon public worship had been ordered by an Arrêt du Conseil of February 19, 1672, according to which a 'banc des catholiques' was to be placed in every church 'directement devant le prédicateur, pour pouvoir le réfuter': in the same, pp. 60 f.

[3] *Brief Relation of the Persecution and Sufferings of the reformed Churches of France, translated out of French*, 7; 1668, quarto.

[4] Benoît, 3 rec. 59 f., 65 f.; *brief Relation*, 8 ff.

[5] Thus at Lyons burial could only take place ' in the fields, and without the city; the which was done by night, and not without some jeopardy': MS. among the Hoop papers, in the *Bulletin*, 3. 595, n. 2.

preferring rather to suffer the greatest extremity and our very blood to be shed, then in the least to violate the respect which we owe to our prince.) And if they cannot overcome our patience (as assuredly they never shall), then their resolution is, By continual importunity to prevail with his majesty to drive us out of the kingdom. But we hope that the king is so good and just, that he will never gratifie them in such a thing, without a parallel. And if we should be called to such a trial, we hope God will give us such strength and courage that we may serve him wherever his providence shall call us. And this in effect is the general resolution of all the protestants in the kingdom[1].

In such a spirit enough left the country to excite alarm in the minds of the government[2]: Count d'Estrades, returning in 1668 from his embassy at the Hague, affirmed that as many as eight hundred families had already taken refuge in Holland[3]. The outflow was not allayed until Colbert had procured the withdrawal of the obnoxious Order[4]. But this dread and this flight were due more to presentiment than to any actual danger. The huguenots at this time certainly suffered much inconvenience, much trouble and annoyance, but no real peril[5].

1669. Feb. 1.

Thus the earlier outflow bears no proportion and no immediate relation to that which was forced upon the huguenots by the *dragonnades* of 1681 and the years following. This date therefore seems the fittest to begin our survey. Now at length Lewis the Fourteenth, freed from external complications, found him-

---

[1] P. 22.

[2] Rulhière, 1. 64.

[3] So he told the marquess de Ruvigny: Weiss, 2. 4.

[4] Benoît, 5, rec. 33 ff. An Edict of August in this year forbade the settlement of huguenots abroad. The point of view is curiously perverse, its preamble reciting that 'in the license of the late times many of our subjects, forgetting what they owe to their birth, have passed into foreign lands, work there at all the crafts wherein they are skilled, even to the building of ships, join themselves to navies, settle abroad without thought of return, and confirm themselves there by marriage and by the getting of sundry goods, putting them to serviceable use, against their duty to us and to their country': in the same, rec. 38 f.

[5] L. von Ranke, as before.

self in a position to take in hand seriously the ruin of his protestant subjects. To understand how he was brought to think this work necessary to the achievement of his idea of kingship, it is well to review for a moment the habit of mind by which he was informed.

Although brought up, especially through his mother's training, in the strictest forms of catholicism, Lewis had none of that reverence or devotion, either to the papacy or to the church, which were conspicuous in his pupil James the Second. Had he lived a century and a half earlier, it is hardly rash to conjecture that he would have followed the example rather of Henry the Eighth than of Francis the First. For his presiding instinct was that of a king; and it was this instinct which led him aright oftener than any capacity of statesmanship. He was far more devoted to the dogma of his absolute authority than to the divine power of the papacy, and he early discovered that this power, like that of the clergy, was ever assuming more and more, and in France particularly, an attitude embarrassing to himself[1]. Richelieu had wished to sever France from any dependence upon Rome by the creation of a patriarchate[2]: and Lewis's plan differed only in terms. It is at once evident what an obstacle was raised by the existence of a schismatic body within his dominions. Could he but expel the whole sect, he might claim the liberties of the national church as the reward of his crusade.

Considerations like these[3] naturally aroused hostility at the Vatican, and served to point Innocent the Eleventh's condemnation of the Recall[4]. Mere persecution in the interests

---

[1] Sugenheim, 5.

[2] Aignan, *de l'État des Protestants depuis le 16me Siècle*, 81; ed. 2, Paris 1818.

[3] In more than one instance the same day that proscribed a huguenot church or abolished one of their privileges was marked by the promulgation of an edict depriving the catholics of some old right or institution (as the Sorbonne).

[4] I have not been able to read the pope's letter to the emperor Leopold in the original. It appears in a Dutch version in the *Hollandse Mercurius*

of the universal church could deserve no blame. Lewis's was condemned because it was a sacrifice to the idea of the Gallican church, and French unity[1]. But the national church recognised and supported its benefactor. To the clergy the huguenots owed not a few of the most irritating edicts against them. The king's signature needed but the ratification of public opinion, whether by silence, indifference, or applause, to accentuate the unison of the several ranges of the state [2].

In 1660 the clerical assembly had proposed to make the 'relapse' of converted huguenots a penal offence, and had called for the destruction of churches and colleges: in 1665 it added a demand for the abolition of the Chambres de Mi-Parties of Bourdeaux, Castres, and Grenoble. Five years later the assembly wished to have the license of conversion extended to huguenot children of seven years; and in 1675 it went on to ask, with the exclusion of protestants from the faculties, for a practical recall of the Edict of Nantes [3]. Nor was the hostility of the clergy confined to petition. They took an active share in the direct work of suppressing the religion. The archbishop of Lyons was more strenuous than the intendant M de Berci in this regard [4]; and

---

1688, 39 f.; Haarlem 1689: and bears date February 5 1688. A letter of Queen Christina of Sweden, written from Rome May 18, 1686, appears in *the pastoral Letters of the incomparable Jurieu*, 25; London 1689. 'I pray God,' she says, 'with all my heart that this false joy and triumph of the church, do not one day cause her true tears and sorrows. It must be known for the honour of Rome, that all those that are men of merit and understanding here, and animated with true zeal, do no more lick up the spittle of the French court in this case than I do.'

[1] L. von Ranke, 3. 532. To this extent, therefore, it is impossible to accept the duke de Saint Simon's partisan-judgment of the Revocation as 'without the least pretext or any necessity': *Mémoires* 24, 181; Paris 1853. M Emmanuel Michel indeed is hardly too strong when he says that Lewis 'in declaring war to the death with the religion that called itself reformed, was combating a German importation, was guarding the national beliefs': *Histoire du Parlement de Metz*, 203; Paris 1845.

[2] Auguste Lièvre, *du Rôle que le Clergé a joué dans la Révocation de l'Édit de Nantes*: Strassburg 1853; cited in the *Bulletin*, 2. 398 ff.

[3] Michel, *Louvois*, 8 f.   [4] The same, 261.

the inroads made by the bishop of Amiens on the peace of the huguenots of Picardy since 1669 forced so large an exodus thence to the English coasts that at the synod of Charenton in 1673 the presbytery of Calais declared itself overpowered by the call for relief[1].

One might be tempted to suppose that not the least reason for the energy of the clergy in opposition to the huguenots was suggested by jealousy of the contrast between their own scandalous neglect and the careful order and nice discipline of the schismatics. It is in any case a coincidence that aggression should have begun in Poitou, signal in its ecclesiastical anarchy, where no visitation had taken place for forty years[2]. But the policy which culminated in the recall of the Edict of Nantes was accepted, further, by the clergy because it was strictly a popular policy. We have already seen the disfavour in which the huguenots, as forming a minority, and a vigorous minority, were held. The promulgation of edicts against them was viewed by the rest of the nation with unmixed delight. The Recall was hailed as a monument of sagacity and religion. This might have been anticipated from the unique sympathy that existed between the king and nation, in character and aim, in love and hate, in taste and prejudice. Lewis was preëminently a Frenchman.

In this harmony the huguenots formed the one jarring element: they clashed not only with the temper of the people, but also with the theory of the king. Lewis was set, as has been said, to realise an absolute supremacy. Rather, he took this supremacy for granted, and then with a hard hand he pruned away whatever seemed to withstand his idea. The case of Calvinism was a conspicuous stumbling-block; for to hold a belief other than the king's implied an incipient revolt. Lewis knew well the tendencies of the huguenot's religion[3]; and not

---

[1] L. Rossier, *Histoire des Protestants de Picardie*, 171 ff., 206; Paris 1864.
[2] Lièvre, *Histoire des Protestants de Poitou*, 2. 63; Poitiers 1858.
[3] A curious inversion of reasoning in the interest of a hypothesis may be found in an essay by M E. Albaric, *sur l'Esprit national du Protestantisme*

all their adhesion during the Fronde war sufficed to erase from his mind the memories of the defence of La Rochelle, and the possibility or probability of their again forming an alliance with his enemies. We are told that it was not least these considerations that induced him to hasten negotiations for the peace of Aix-la-Chapelle; and the double fear of an alliance with Holland[1] or of an insurrection within the realm[2] was more potent than the arms of his outward enemies. Long afterwards, but before the active work of terror began, these suspicions revived, and it was ordered that huguenot officers should be gradually and on covert pretexts dismissed the navy[3].

It is indeed curious to remark that in the whole course of Lewis's oppression, until the isolated rebellion in the Cevennes[4], no attempt was made to combat it. The younger and hardier ministers in a few instances suggested an armed resistance.

1668.

1680. April 14.

---

français; Strassburg 1853: cited in the *Bulletin*, 2. 619. 'If the vital principle of protestantism is free enquiry, and if this principle effectually seconds a tendency towards political liberalism, its rule of conduct is none the less the gospel which enjoins respect to the laws and to established governments: it has become in Germany aristocratical, in England royalist, in Holland democratical: everywhere it leagues itself with the government, in so far as it is the expression of public opinion, the symbol of the political faith of the age; and when this symbol has lost its power over nations, when this faith has given place to a new political belief, protestantism, loyal and unshaken, accepts this belief; it bends in conformity with the needs of the age and supports, but never creates, its expression.'

[1] Of such an alliance no actual traces exist: L. von Ranke, *französische Geschichte*, 3. 503. In June 1669 we have a case which M G. B. Depping considers isolated, of a protestant of Nîmes, Claude Roux de Marsilly, being 'broken' on a charge of travelling in England and Holland to excite sedition against France: *Correspondance administrative*, 4. 311–318; Paris 1855. Cp. L. von Ranke, *History of England*, 3. 491.

[2] 'Gli ugonotti in arme' was the presentiment of the Venetian envoy: L. von Ranke, *französische Geschichte*, 3. 503. n. 3.

[3] Letter of Mgr de Seignelay, the minister of marine, in L. Delmas, *l'Église réformée de la Rochelle*, 388 ff.; Toulouse 1870. Koenen notices the impression made on the reluctant government by the loss which resulted to the navy and to commerce, for the preëminence of the huguenots in seamanship was notorious: 61 f.

[4] F. C. Baur, *Kirchengeschichte der neueren Zeit*, 241; Tuebingen 1860.

One[1] went so far as to urge that it was their *Passive submission to all the iniquitous edicts and to all the royal orders*, that *had encouraged the king to aggravate* their *situation day by day. Our obedience*, he exclaimed before the assembled ministers and elders of Cozes[2], *our obedience to one of these edicts has only opened the way to another still more unendurable: our fearfulness is, in truth, to blame for the more part of the evils we have suffered.* To hold our lives and goods to be the king's property was, he said, *to dishonour our fathers' work. For they, sword in hand, won for their children the privileges whereof we are now despoiled.* In their example he appealed *to the God of battles.* But this warlike tone was met only by the charge of carnal-mindedness: the ministers were resolved to suffer for righteousness' sake, how much soever it might be in their power to assert their liberties by arms. *Patient as a huguenot*, became a proverb[3].

On the other hand, the Camisards proved that the old spirit was not altogether extinct. The huguenots of the dispersion did not give evidence by their action that they felt themselves subdued. In speech, indeed, they preserved a dignified moderation[4]; but in writing, or on the field of battle, none could exceed their passionate daring. The irony of Defoe has truly and skilfully put the case for the policy of the Recall. *I agree*, he says, *that in sending away three hundred thousand hugonots he filled his neighbours with much of the wealth of his country, and I may say with some of the poverty too: I allow that he found thousands of them with arms in their hands, strengthening*

1685.
Spring.

---

[1] Jacques Fontaine, *candidat* at Royan, who had already been imprisoned for his opinions. His *Mémoires* were written in French in 1722, published in English at New York in 1853. The English was not accessible to me when I came to read the book: my references therefore are to M E. Castel's version; *Mémoires d'une Famille huguenote;* Toulouse 1877.

[2] The assembly had been convened to take measures in view of the 'cruel circumstances' of the times; p. 143.

[3] Castel, note to Fontaine, 145.

[4] Count d'Avaux tells how duels arose among the huguenots in Holland from a disrespectful speech about Lewis XIV: despatch of May 24 1686, in Charles Read's introd. to *Mémoires inédits de Dumont de Bostaquet*, xxx, ed. F. Waddington; Paris 1864.

the forces of his enemies, and met them in the field upon all occasions. But the king of France could not but know that 't was better for him to see 'em in his enemies armies abroad than to be in apprehensions of them in greater bodies in his own dominions... He also foresaw it would be very often in the power of the hugonots to embroil him at home; and that, backed by the assistance of those foreign powers with whom he was to be engaged abroad, they would be enabled at any time to impose conditions upon him, and check that arbitrary absolute government which he resolved to maintain[1].

But it was just here that Lewis's political sagacity stopped short. He forgot the time when, while his protestant subjects at home had been the heartiest of his allies, the huguenots in Holland, exiles of an earlier date, had maintained close correspondence with the Frondeurs[2]. He forgot that it was in fact to crush the republican press of Holland, strengthened by the talent and experience of the exiles in its resistance to all that savoured of monarchy, that he had devised the war of 1672[3]. The failure of the invasion might have taught him how justly that press represented the tenacity and independence of the little commonwealth. He neglected the lesson, and straightway set himself to a course of policy which, by the emigration it must create, should inevitably change what had been but a harass into a powerful engine of opposition.

If, on the other hand, we are told that the nobility, by means of whom protestantism had first been able to assert its rights, had almost entirely passed over to the catholic obedience; that, since the death of the duke de Rohan, the decay of the house of Bouillon[4], protestantism was without a head; it is sufficient to remember that the lower nobility, the provincial gentry, con-

---

[1] *Review of the Affairs of France.* nr x. 55, April 8 1704. This is not all a jeu d'esprit as Mr W. Minto seems to imply: *Defoe*, 57 f.; 1879.

[2] Capefigue, *Louis XIV*, 3. 9; Paris 1837, 1838.

[3] The same, 1. 200-205. The duke de Saint Simon attributes the war to Louvois' jealousy of Colbert: *Mémoires*, 24. 84 ff. The explanations are not irreconcileable.

[4] Voltaire, 478; Weiss, in the *Bulletin*, 1. 46-50.

stituted by themselves an adequate rallying-point in the event of rebellion¹. Benoît assures us that *The country churches were almost entirely composed of noblesse;* and, though we may reject this as an over-strained generalisation, we may well credit his statement that *In some, one could count from eighty to a hundred families of gentlemen*². Indeed we know that upon the dissolution of a church their houses often formed a centre for the scattered congregation³. The remoteness of court-influence ensured the permanence of once-accepted beliefs. The analogy of catholicism or of toryism among the English country gentlemen at once occurs to the mind; at the same time, the failure of the northern rising under Elizabeth, or of the Jacobite revolts in a later age, may serve to illustrate the fact, that Lewis the Fourteenth misreckoned the importance of the huguenots as a political party. The fear he evinced by the first order to the dragoons in every instance, *Saisir les notables*⁴, was perfectly genuine, but it was stronger than the occasion merited.

It has often been remarked that in France, whenever a collision or even a contrast came into existence between dynastic and commercial interests, the latter were sacrificed. We are not therefore to be surprised that the policy of the Recall was a direct opposition to Colbert's principles. It has not, however, been generally observed how far it concealed a plot by Louvois, the minister of war, to supersede him as well as

---

¹ M F. Waddington insists on this fact in his *Protestantisme en Normandie*, 3 f.; Paris 1862: as also previously in the *Bulletin*, 7. 417 ff.; 1858.

² Vol. 2. 568, quoted with applause by Erman and Reclam, *Mémoires pour servir à l'Histoire des Réfugiés français dans les États du Roi*, 2. 331; Berlin 1782.

³ *Mémoires de Bostaquet*, 40   It is admitted that 'the very great majority of the huguenots of Normandy,' and thus presumably of other provinces, 'conquered by persecution and dragoons, signified a forced adhesion to the cult imposed on them, which on that very account became the more hateful to them. Pursued by the remorse of conscience many of them hoped but to quit the kingdom and to redeem the fault they had committed.' Waddington, *Normandie*, 15.

⁴ Michel, *Louvois*, 36. The other orders were to raze the churche and expel the ministers.

his reforms—in a word, that the Recall was really as much a spoliation as a work of intolerance[1]. Assuming this motive to have had its share in creating the persecution before his death, much more was it recommended when the loss of his guiding hand had left an increasing deficit in the exchequer[2]. Colbert had organised a hard system: while he developed the national strength and prosperity he became day by day less popular. It was natural that, when his fellow-ministers conspired against him, they should seize upon a means of suppressing him which should command the applause of the country. But none the less was the precise circumstance of the Recall, its immediate occasion, determined by changes in the king's private life and that of his court, changes in which the French world at large could take but a remote interest.

---

[1] Bonhomme, *Mme de Maintenon et sa famille*, 340 f.; Paris 1863, cited by Sugenheim, 21.

[2] Cp. the proverb *Rich as a protestant*: Moret, *quinze Ans du Règne de Louis XIV*, 1. 284; Paris 1851, in Sugenheim 20.

CHAPTER III.

THE TYRANNY.

It has been attempted to trace the heat of the protestant oppression to the years of leisure between the peace of Aix-la-Chapelle and the war that led to Nijmegen, between Nijmegen and the formation of the league of Augsburg. A better generalisation asserts that most of the oppressive edicts appeared during the king's fits of illness. But any theory of this sort can only be true in a very limited sense, can only lead to confusion of the point at issue. Thus it is not our intention to run through the shameful annals of Lewis's private life to look for causes: there are enough outside. All that can be of interest in our view, is to notice that a revolution came over the life of the court on the death of the queen-mother in 1666. Every gaiety was supplanted by a missionary enthusiasm. Every one sought to convert the Calvinists: they applauded the success of the divine word[1]. We see here the inauguration of the mercenary, too soon to be followed by the military, stage of propagandism. Here is the overt origin of the first emigration. The sums lavished on this object, how many of the protestants were bought over, and some how many times, are matters of notoriety, and not much to the present purpose.

But another epoch ensued when Lewis placed himself in the power of Père La Chaise, that confessor whose *sweet, mild, pliable* temper is attested by the Brandenburg resident Spanheim[2].

---

[1] Rulhière, I. 97.
[2] Of the other chief mover in the persecution, Harlay, archbishop of Paris, he says similarly, 'Il avait donné des preuves d'un naturel doux,

1681.
August 24.

Le roi, wrote Madame de Maintenon, *commence à penser sérieusement à son salut et a celui de ses sujets. Si Dieu nous conserve il n'y aura plus qu'une religion dans son royaume*[1]. He reviewed his past manners, and thought that, rather than amend, it were easier and more becoming the statesman to hide them in the background by a grand act of merit. But he did not contemplate a holocaust of heresy The method grew within his hands and prevailed with the ascendant of Louvois. In the beginning Lewis had no thought of violence. His first instructions to Michel de Marillac, the intendant of Poitou, are marked by a guarded prudence that well contrasts with the language of Louvois' separate despatch on the occasion[2]. Even to the end he would do his endeavour with one whom his own edicts had condemned to the galleys, and seek by conversion to assure at once his liberty and his spiritual safety[3].

But this must not tempt us to seek, with Rulhière, to prove him ignorant throughout of the horrors with which his work was attended[4]. *Doubtless,* says Sismondi, *he might have been*

---

traitable, bien faisant, et même assez commode envers les gens de la religion' : *Relation de la Cour de France,* in L. von Ranke, 3. 517, n. 1.

[1] 'C'est le sentiment,' she adds, 'de M de Louvois; et je le crois plus volontiers là-dessus que M Colbert, qui ne pense qu'à ses finances et presque jamais à la religion': Rulhière, 1. 206 f. This, however, was not the opinion that caught the notice of strangers to the immediate court-influence. On July 22 1681, the English ambassador, Henry Savile, had said, 'These poor oppressed people are like to suffer all the miseries that can be devised by the malice of the jesuits and executed by the boundless power of the king, who in things of this nature hath put himself so wholly into their hands that their credit with him has given jealousy to all his other ministers, whereof not one doth approve these methods, but are willing upon all occasions to declare they are not the authors of them,'— such declaration being of course to the English representative: *Savile Correspondence,* 210, ed. W. Durrant Cooper; Camden Society, 1858, quarto.

[2] Rulhière, 1. 200-205.

[3] See the case of M de Marolles, in L. von Ranke, 3. 531.

[4] So too F. Ancillon, *Tableau,* 4. 295; and Aignan, *État des Protestants,* 25. The latter pleads, 'Louis XIV avait de la bonté, de l'élévation dans l'âme, et une piété sincere. Jamais ces fureurs ne furent autorisées de lui. Le clergé lui persuadait.'

deceived, might not have known everything; but more watchful than any that had sat on the throne of France before him, more jealous of his omniscience, more quick to resent in a minister the pretension of any concealment, it was impossible that a rude enterprise, pursued by his troops, in every province of his kingdom, against more than two millions of his subjects [1], should ever have been suppressed from his knowledge [2]. At the same time he might gain a colourable justification from the tone of the official reports of the intendants of provinces. When, for instance, Foucault sent word in April 1685, of the conversion of a hundred and fifty families in his district, in June of five thousand people more, in July of sixteen thousand; when at the end of this month he declared that but one, out of twenty-one, thousand protestants remained constant [3]; with all this authoritative evidence of the religious temper of the intendant's work, Lewis might speciously allege ignorance of the other side of the story, might even, in a manner familiar to modern statesmen, plead its improbability or its groundlessness in the face of his official information. That the plea was a subterfuge made it none the less available.

It remains to notice the periods of the oppression, the ebb and flow, years of extreme rigour mixed with times of comparative rest. The first essay in Poitou which gave Marillac [4] the glory of thirty thousand new converts [5] was not so isolated as we are

1681.

---

[1] German pamphlets of the time give 1,800,000; but an official report in Benoît, 3. 639, says 'deux millions' in 1682. An Arrêt de Parlement of December 26 1687, allows even at that date 'près de deux millions.' Probably two millions will be an extreme estimate: L. von Ranke, 3. 500, n.

[2] *Histoire des Français*, 25. 508; Paris 1841.

[3] Baur, 240. L. von Ranke gives further examples: 30,000 converts in a fortnight reported from Dauphiné; 20,000 reckoned by Boufflers in September 1685, in the district of Montauban; 60,000 in the same month in Guienne: 3. 518, 521.

[4] 'The great actor in it,' we read in a broadside of June [16] 26 1681, by *a gentleman of great quality, an eyewitness*, 'is one intendant Marillac, who having from the potent jesuit father Le Chese the promises of the present life, and not caring for those of the life to come, hath laid upon the reformed a most heavy cross': *the horrible Persecution of the French Protestants in the Province of Poitou.*

[5] Lièvre, *Poitou*, 2. 122.

apt to imagine: the same year saw the religious worship proscribed in great commercial centres. Emigration thus followed, not only from the sea-board of Poitou, Saintonge, and Aunis[1], where the chief stress lay, but also from Bourdeaux and Rennes, from Rouen and Havre-de-Grace[2]. Their pursuits, and the situation of their homes, gave the fugitives a natural direction towards Holland and England, and in small part to Denmark[3]. But difficulties were also arising throughout the country. The proscription of the learned professions, the difficulties attached to marriage[4], the terrible facility of conversion allowed to children, the fear that the benefits of catholicism might be too strong for men's faith,—all and each of these had prompted the earlier emigrations[5]. The father who knew that his child must receive the catholic rite of baptism[6] within a day of its birth, that in seven years it would be beyond his religious control, dared not imperil the safety of his family by continuing in France. Exile was a duty, and when the more potent engine of 'missions bottées[7]' were employed it became a necessity[8]. *The heroism of conviction,*

---

[1] Koenen, *Nederland*, 6.

[2] The churches at the two former places, and the ministry at the latter two, were abolished in 1681 by the parliaments respectively of Guienne and Britany, and of Normandy: L. von Ranke, 3. 509.

[3] Lièvre, 2. 116 ff.

[4] This perhaps pressed hardest of all: L. Anquez, *de l'État civil des Réformés des France*, 3 and 28; Paris 1868. For the later stages of the tyranny see the Declaration of June 5 1685, in Benoît, 5. 797, and rec. 173. 3, by which marriage abroad was subjected to a fine of 20,000 livres, or in default of payment to confiscation of property; in either case the wife was banished: cp. also MS. report of an intendant in 1694, cited by A. Michel, *Louvois*, 306; and Waddington, *Normandie*, 32.

[5] See a summary in a sermon of Dr George Hickes, August 1681, cited by Agnew, *protestant Exiles*, 1. 27 ff.

[6] Hence the disabilities of protestant midwives, though the professed reason was the singular one we know from the 20th chapter of *Tristram Shandy*, 1. 103; ed. 1783, duodecimo.

[7] See below, supplementary note i.

[8] This is fairly and earnestly reasoned in the *Histoire et Apologie de la Retraite des Pasteurs*, 147 f.; Frankfurt 1687. The taunt had been: 'The hireling fleeth because he is not the shepherd.' The volume is by Benoît: see Barbier, 2. 799.

it has been truly said, *was now displayed not in resistance, but, if the paradox may be admitted, in flight*[1].

The outflow was for the moment arrested at the remonstrance of Colbert, now for the last time listened to in the royal councils, and by reason of the sympathy aroused by the fugitives in England[2]: but not before three thousand families had left the country[3]. The retirement and death of the great minister were the signal for revived action, wherever an assembly of huguenots larger than usual might warrant or colour a suspicion of rebellion. On such excuses, not yet as an avowed crusade, the troopers of the duke de Noailles were called in at Grenoble, Bourdeaux, and Nimes. Full forty churches were demolished in 1683, more than a hundred in 1684[4]. But the system of military missions was not organised[5] until in 1685 the defence of the Spanish frontier offered the opportunity for a final subjugation of the huguenots of Béarn.

The *dragonnade* passed through the land like a pestilence. From Guienne to Dauphiné, from Poitou to Upper Languedoc, no place was spared. Then it pervaded the south-east country, about the Cevennes and Provence, and ravaged Lyons and the Pays de Gex. In the end, the whole of the north was assailed[6], and the failing edict of Nantes was annulled on the 1st of October[7]. The sombre mind of Madame de Maintenon had postulated the Recall as a preliminary to that marriage which the king had already conceded. On the 21st of the month the great church at Charenton was doomed; and on the 22nd

---

[1] L. von Ranke, 3. 529 f.

[2] A. Michel, 37 f.

[3] Benoît, 5. 500.

[4] Drion, cited by Anquez, 23.

[5] The scheme is said to have been matured in a letter of Louvois, dated October 1 1683: Aignan, 18.

[6] For these stages in the persecution, see *les Plaintes des Protestants*, 57; by Jean Claude: see Barbier, 1. 905.

[7] E. Michel, *Metz*, 201, whose assertion is accepted by Sugenheim, gives this date as that of the appearance of the Edict of Revocation; the common date, the 22nd (Baur, 240), being that of its registration. Cp. L. von Ranke, 3. 525.

the 'unadvised and precipitate[1]' Edict of Revocation was registered in the Chambre des Vacations.

We are not to linger here on the circumstances of the persecution. Even Jurieu, who usually grasped at such materials for the overthrow of catholicism, was forced at length to write[2], *The uniformity of the persecution is the cause that we have less of history to furnish you withal. 'Tis always and everywhere the same. Persons are imprisoned, others are sent to the gallies, women are shut up in cloysters, bodies are drawn on hurdles and thrown to the dunghil; so that it will always be the same thing; there will be nothing but differing names, which may increase the horror you have for the persecution as you see the rage of your persecutors increase*[3]. There is however no trace of blood, no suggestion of suffering, in the calm and gentle despatch in which the king informed his ambassador in Holland, Count d'Avaux, of the achievement of his crusade. *I am right glad*, he wrote, *to advertise you that God having given all the good success I could desire to the care I have long been taking to bring back all my people to the fold of the church, and the tidings I daily receive of a countless multitude of converts allowing no reasonable question that the more stiff-necked will follow the ensample of the rest, I have, by an Edict whereof I send you a copy for your privy instruction, forbidden any exercise within my kingdom of the religion men call reformed. It will be forthwith presented in all my Parliaments, and it will cost the less pains in the carrying out, in that there will be few persons so obdurate as still to desire to continue in error*[4].

The year 1685 is fitly identified with the depopulation of France. And yet, with a blindness that appears to us incredible, the government refused to believe in the desire or the possibility of escape. The penalties attached to capture on the

---

[1] Rulhière, 1. 330.   [2] *Pastoral Letters*, 249.

[3] ''Tis enough,' writes Rachel, Lady Russell, January 15 1686, 'to sink the strongest heart to read the accounts sent over. How the children are torn from their mothers and sent into monasteries, their mothers to another, the husband to prison or the galleys': in Agnew, 3. 4.

[4] *Negociations de M le comte d'Avaux*, 5. 187; Paris 1752, duodecimo.

road,—the galleys or the nunnery,—the vigilant watch at the frontier[1], the frigates cruising by every coast, all these difficulties seem to have persuaded Louvois that few would persist in risking flight. What these measures actually effected was doubtless to diminish the exodus, but in no marked degree [2]. At length, it came to be thought that the emigration was due to its prohibition, as though the huguenots must do a thing from mere perverseness. The watch was relaxed, and a result unlooked for issued. It was the signal of the greatest of the emigrations, that of 1688 [3].

Hitherto every means had been taken to stay the flight. It was published by authority that the fugitives were refused shelter by foreign powers, that they were destitute and without employment. In England more than ten thousand had perished through the hardness of the climate, from the toils of their flight, and above all from misery and starvation. The most part were eager to return [4].

The French ambassadors abroad were enjoined to take every measure to gain information with reference to the emigration, and particularly as to the exportation of money [5]. Count d'Avaux had a well-organised staff of informers [6], whom he

---

[1] 'On fit des battues dans les forêts comme pour tuer les bêtes feroces,' says Aignan, 23.

[2] Thus from Dauphiné, while only about 5000 emigrated between 1683 and 1686, from January to November 1687, 10,300 left the country: report of Bouchu in the Bibliothèque Nationale, cited by Arnaud, *Histoire des Protestants de Dauphiné*, 3. 17 f.; Paris 1876. In October 23 1687, Count d'Avaux wrote, 'It seems that those who are richest now begin to leave the country': in Weiss, 2. 19.

[3] A. Michel, 38.   [4] Rulhière, 1. 349.

[5] The anticipated export did not come up to the actual loss. The *Mercure historique et politique* of November 1686 notices the arrival in Holland of ships containing, of the property of emigrants, 300,000 crowns' worth of gold or precious stones: in Koenen, 89.

[6] The prince of Orange took the step of having the ambassador's house watched. Once in a time of excitement the soldiery attacked the house, and Tillières died in the defence. Other spies, Foran and Danois, were warned in the Amsterdam Exchange by a generous huguenot from La Rochelle, in time to secure their escape: Weiss, 2. 20 f.

kept either in Holland or on the Flemish border. By means of these hundreds of fugitives were decoyed back into the hands of the dragoons who awaited them at the frontier or at the sea-beach. One Tillières employed a more insidious stratagem. This 'giver of advices' was effusively charitable in the reception of the refugees. He gave them money and set them up in trade. He placed a number at Voorburg near the Hague, and built them a church. Having thus wound himself into their confidence he was able to elicit invaluable tidings of the plans of their friends in France.

Within the country it was sought to make every man a spy by laying a price on the capture of fugitives. He who brought one back might expect to gain the half of his victim's goods [1]; whoever secured twelve was for ever free from taxes [2]. In this way general support was added to the regular guards who patrolled the frontier, to the sloops that hovered round the coast. *Lyons, we read, in the winter of 1685, and the other places of transit towards Switzerland are thronged with captives. On the side of Flanders the jails of Valenciennes, Saint Omer, Lille, Tournay* [3], *even through all Picardy till you come to Paris, are filled full of women, children, and men, seized in their flight* [4]. Terrible is the tale of the crowding, the disease, of these prison-houses [5]; and the reckoning, far below the truth, that ten

---

[1] Koenen, 63.

[2] Aignan, 23.

[3] In a single prison at Tournay lay 700 such in 1687: P. J. Wenz, *Reformations-Jubel-Rede, nebst Geschichte der französischen-reformirten Kirche in Emden*, 203; Emden 1819.

[4] *Historie van de wreede Vervolging en Tyrannien gepleegt aan de Gereformeerde in Vrankrijk*, 3. 28; Amsterdam 1686, duodecimo. 'God weet,' is the comment, 'tot wat straffen sy bewaard werden.' This book, though full of exaggeration, is of special value as giving details of the exodus which cannot be found elsewhere. Its precise date of writing is December 1685: cp. 3. 58 with 3. 67.

[5] At Grenoble in 1686 the prisons were surfeited; seventy men in one cell, eighty women and girls in another. And the crowding was the smallest evil: for, the Isère washing the prison-walls, many lost their hair and teeth from damp and chill: MS. of Antoine Court at Geneva, in

thousand lost their lives through failure in escape[1]. Numbers too were sent to the colonies of America. It was like the middle passage of the English slave-trade: a fourth part died on the way, through fever or famine, stifled or otherwise done to death by the press[2].

In the face of all these terrors it is not surprising that a great proportion of the fugitives had recourse to one of two means, politic but questionable, which to a rigid standard may seem vicious alike. They made use of false passports which had perhaps served for a dozen others[3]; or they reconciled themselves to the obedience of the catholic church[4]. Most had the view of securing their goods or carrying them abroad with them[5]: some were led by the nobler motive of rescuing their wives and households from the unutterable violences of the troops forced upon them. *The dread*, says Dumont de Bostaquet, *of seeing so many women and girls exposed to the insults of the troopers, to whom nothing was forbidden, constrained me to subscribe, between the hands of two men, ugly as devils and as full of spite and cruelty, my engagement in obedience to the king's will to embrace the catholic religion at the ensuing Christmas*[6].

Arnaud, 3. 15 f.; cp. Benoît, 5. 895. On July 2 1686, wrote one from La Tournelle, 'We lie here three and fifty of us in a place which is not above five fathom in length and one and a half in breadth. There lies on my right hand a countryman sick, with his head at my feet, and his feet at my head, and so it is with others. There is not one among us which do not envy the condition of many dogs and horses. There were ninety-five of us yesterday condemned, but there died two on that day, and we have yet fifteen or sixteen sick, and there be few escape': Jurieu, *pastoral Letters*, 116 f.

[1] Thus the count de Boulainvilliers, in Aignan, 84.

[2] Benoît, 5 passim; and the *Bulletin*, 6. 382 ff.; 1858.

[3] One, Mariet, a Paris wine-merchant, made good his escape to Holland, with a fortune of 600,000 livres, by means of a passport of which fifteen others availed themselves: Weiss.

[4] Most of the Norman families, received in such 'astonishing numbers' in the church of Threadneedle-street, had abjured before leaving France: Waddington, *Normandie*, 17 n.

[5] 'J'ai damné mon âme,' said one, 'pour sauver mes biens': Fontaine, 164.

[6] *Mémoires*, 107.

But many abandoned their possessions without wavering[1]; and the crowd, hunted from their church and hearth, hurried to the frontier, or paid their last livre to the Dutch or English shipmaster, careless whither they went, now they had nothing left to lose.

The English seaports were thronged with fugitives[2] who had risked the passage, without provisions, in the most miserable boats[3]. Many passed the frontier afoot[4], in the guise of pilgrims, shepherds, beggars; many were aided with money by the catholics of the border: but far more were led just without the kingdom by the very guards set with the object of stopping them, who found the work of help more profitable, as it was kinder, than the work of arresting. It must have been not least these bribes which reduced the mass of the fugitives to that state of pitiful destitution which left so great a multitude at the charity of the churches whither they fled.

---

[1] Of these was the marquess de Bordage, who held an estate worth 50,000 livres. Unhappily his devotion did not save him from capture, at Mauberge, just before he reached the frontier: L. von Ranke, 3. 530. The gain accruing to the exchequer through such reversions may be conceived from two examples. By 1686, 405 families were officially reported to have quitted Normandy, leaving effects behind them to the value of 198,780 livres: Waddington, 21. A document of 1687 relating to the emigration from Picardy gives the number from the elections of Amiens, Doullens, Abbeville, and Péronne, as only 101 persons, but the sale of their property as realising 29,512 livres: Rossier, *Picardie*, 245.

[2] It is estimated that 200,000*l* sterling were expended in fees to English shipmasters in the means of emigration: pref. to *les Plaintes des Protestants*, 9; London 1707, duodecimo.

[3] Sismondi has condensed into an eloquent passage (25, 521 f.) the materials which extend through many pages in Benoît (5. 946-957).

[4] I have not found any confirmation of a singular fact mentioned in the *Oorsprong van de Biwoonders van de Sevennes*, 42 f.; Amsterdam 1703:— namely, that some fugitives went across the Pyrenees into Spain, 'so that many died or ever they reached Holland.' Its truth, however, may be argued from the way in which a statement in the same sentence, that others went by sea to Italy, is supported by a correspondence between Mgr de Seignelay and the French consul at Genoa, with a view to their extradition: A. Michel, 188.

How they came and they settled, we have now to see. We shall trace them, through Holland, to the northern countries of Europe; then in England; then the emigration through Switzerland, into South Germany; and lastly the great colony in the electorate of Brandenburg [1].

---

[1] I find no confirmation of the vague assertion of Napoleon Peyrat, that some of the French exiles went to the delta of the Ganges and to the Indian archipelago: *Histoire des Pasteurs du Désert*, 1. 93; Paris 1842.

CHAPTER IV.

THE REFUGE IN THE NETHERLANDS AND AT THE CAPE.

The long siege which Lewis, with his artillery of edicts and ordinances[1] and his assaults of *dragonnades*, carried on against the stronghold of protestantism, was counterworked by a movement no less decisive on the part of Holland, prompter than any other state in the defence of freedom, and now fighting with advantage. For, while Lewis was attacking piecemeal the outworks, and then mining the walls in detail, a battery was ready in every Dutch province, in every city, to reply with a concentrated fire that might be sustained as long as the perseverance, and longer than the materials, of the king could last. For it is always to be remembered that the contention of Lewis was not with the protestants but with their faith. He hoped to storm protestantism, and he believed the tale of the deserters was approaching the numbers of the garrison. Their fellows in religion abroad knew the temper of Calvinism better, and the common feeling empowered them to make full use of the knowledge. Far from bounding themselves to single or desultory action, they worked with a calm precision that illustrates well the close ties of the reformed commonwealths.

When Louvois opened his missionary career by an attack upon the churches of Poitou, it was in Friesland that popular

---

[1] The abbé Caveirac enumerates four to five hundred: see the *Bulletin*, 2. 398 ff.

passion was soonest excited[1]. The instructions to Marillac were despatched on the 18th of March 1681; they were published on the 11th of April[2]. Within six weeks the Estates of Friesland resolved that, *inasmuch as the welfare of countries and cities doth herein consist, that the same be populous*, it behooved them to grant to *all foreign families*, whom stress of religious oppression had forced to leave their homes, every right enjoyed by natives[3]. Before commenting on the reasons of this guarded language, it is well to notice the considerations that induced so immediate a recognition of Poitou by this particular province. In each, the countrymen busied themselves with husbandry and with the breeding of cattle: *in other respects*, says the encyclopedist, of Poitou, *its traffickings are small*[4]. Even as to the outward aspect of the country, an exile from the level lands of Poitou would suffer no great change in settling on the flats of Friesland; though it is to be remarked that the immigrants for the most part set themselves in the choicest district of the province[5], recommended by its wooded hills, its rich meadows and goodly cornland, and abounding in wild fowl and game of all sorts.

Community of taste was here stronger than the dictate of political interest. The representatives of Friesland had previously been the staunchest supporters of the French party in

1681.
May [7] 17.

---

[1] Benoît is incorrect when he says 'le roy d'Angleterre commença': 4. 491. The English proclamation was nearly twelve weeks later.

[2] Rulhière, 1. 201–205.

[3] G. F., baron toe Schwartzenberg, *groot Placaat en Charter-Boek van Vriesland*, 5. 1193; Leeuwarden 1793, folio.

[4] *Encyclopédie*, under the word; Neuchâtel 1766. See also Lièvre, *Poitou*, 2. 152: 'The people of Poitou were chiefly agricultural, and the fruits of the land more than supplied its wants.'

[5] The eloquence of the geographer Schotanus a Sterringa is exhausted upon the beauty of Gaasterland: 'It is in part mountainous and hilly. You see no mountains or hills in all Friesland save here and at Hemelum. Wherefore this district is pleasant for all kinds of sport, as of hares, pheasants, quails, and the like:' *Beschryvinge van Friesland*, 225; s. l. aut a. (? 1680), folio. In the present day Gaasterland maintains its character as the finest part of Friesland.

the Netherlands. They with their colleagues of Groningen¹ took the same attitude of opposition to the prince of Orange in the Estates-General as the deputies of Amsterdam maintained in the Estates of Holland. The French ambassador, Count d'Avaux, was constantly intriguing with them. Yet, in the face of party traditions, Friesland was the first to utter its protest against the tyranny;—the reference was plain enough though the Resolution avoided stating it:—and, when the Edict touching the huguenot children appeared, Count d'Avaux had to warn his sovereign of the threatening change of feeling in the very men on whom he most relied ². The *alteration* he had observed was not transient: on the contrary, it inspired a fresh encouragement to immigrants in the autumn of the same year ³, and a frank and hearty welcome when they came.

1681.
June 17.

July 24.

Oct. 16.

In this place it will save repetition to note the points in common between the invitations given, and the privileges accorded to the French by the different authorities in the United Provinces. They were, first, relieved from all 'extraordinary burthens or taxes⁴' for a term of years; in Friesland, ᵃHolland⁵, and ᵇUtrecht⁶, twelve; in ᶜGroningen fourteen⁷. By some cities,

ᵃ Sept. 25.
ᵇ 1685.
Nov. 16.
ᶜ 168[5]6.
Feb. [5] 15.

---

¹ Count d'Avaux, *Negociations*, 1. 152 f., 162, 178, 181.

² Vol. 1. 152 f.; compare the similar warning of Barillon, May [6] 16 1686. On the 7th of September Count d'Avaux again reminded Louis that 'Mm de Frise et de Groningue avoient changé de sentiments à cause de la religion,' 1. 173. The duke de Saint Simon places the revival of the party of the prince of Orange earlier, as one of the issues of the Dutch war; *Mémoires*, 24. 84 ff.

³ G. F. toe Schwartzenberg, 5. 1197 f.

⁴ In Friesland and Utrecht the immunity covered the poll-tax; in Friesland also the hearth-tax. Groningen extended it to a variety of detail, to the horn-money and horse-car-money.

⁵ Berg, *Réfugiés in de Nederlanden*, 1. 32.

⁶ Koenen, *Vluchtelingen in Nederland*, 48.

⁷ Berg, 1. 39. The city of Amsterdam at first gave a provisional exemption for three years: *Resolutien der Vroedschap*, September 12 & 23 and October 7 1681; in Koenen, 76. Similarly Haarlem, January 30 1683: Berg, 1. 41. The relief given by the city of Middelburg extended to ten years: J. ab Utrecht Dresselhuis, *de waalsche Gemeenden in Zeeland*, 46 f.; Bergen-op-Zoom 1848.

as Amsterdam[1], Haarlem, Arnemuiden[2], the immunity was extended to the town-excise. Secondly, collections were ordered to meet the wants of the new-comers[3]. Thirdly, master-workers were declared free of guilds, admissible but not compelled to enter; in any case they might practise their crafts without fee. Advances of money were commonly promised, and an engagement added to purchase the produce of their manufactures until such time as they should be firmly established. Lastly, ministers were supported by a state-pension, and allotted to the places where the refugees came in greatest number.

Their material and religious comfort being thus secured, the French in the Netherlands had no such anxiety to obtain an Act of Naturalisation as they had in England. They owned the privileges, more than the privileges, of natives: they were in no haste to take upon themselves also their burthens. Moreover, until the conference of Gertruidenberg, the peace of Utrecht, they held their hope of a return home. Their condition however grew into prosperity and affluence; and the Estates on their part saw the benefit and the fairness of such denizens assuming the responsibilities of natives. Resolutions for this purpose were passed by the Estates of Gelderland and Holland in 1709, of Zeeland[4] in 1710: and the Estates-General five years later harmonised the diversities of provincial usage by a national Act of Naturalisation[5]. [1715. Oct. 21.]

The reply to the call of the Frieslanders should seem to have been promptly given[6]. By the summer of 1683 the

---

[1] Berg, 1. 33.
[2] May 22 1686: H. M. Kesteloo, *Geschiedenis van Arnemuiden*, 81; Middelburg 1875.
[3] Thus at Haarlem, October 1 1682: Berg, 1. 41. By the Estates of Holland December 3: Count d'Avaux, 1. 258. In Friesland, February 1 1686: G. F. toe Schwartzenberg, 5. 1249.
[4] Dresselhuis, 84 f.
[5] A limited right was still reserved to the burgomasters of Amsterdam, of granting exemptions to new refugees: Weiss, 2. 33.
[6] Vol. 2. 9.

number of immigrants, more or less persons of consideration [1], gentlemen who had possessed lands in France, and husbandmen following them [2], was large enough to elicit fresh privileges from the Estates accompanied by extensive grants of land; the Resolution for the first time, and now necessarily describing the settlers not in vague terms, but expressly as French [3]. This is the date of the colonisation of the district of Gaasterland. The village of Balk, already, from its order and its look of well-being, the praise of strangers [4], became the centre of a cluster of little farming settlements [5]. It had its church as early as 1684, and was of sufficient importance to be chosen as the meeting-place of the national Walloon synod in 1686.

1683. Aug. 4.

But the activity of the Frieslanders did not end here. In the winter of the Revocation, not content with repeating their former welcome, and taking thought for the *sore plight* of the *great throng and multitude of great and small* [6] daily making their way into the Netherlands, the Estates at once set about organising new churches for the refugees. Thus were formed the French churches at Sneek and Franeker [7]; about the same time rose the community at Harlingen, and two years later that at Bolsward. The only French church previously existing

1686. Feb. 1.

Sept. 11.

---

[1] The case, for instance, of Le Noir de Monfreton, with a few others, having lent a million to the Estates on common interest is cited by Weiss, 2. 22 f., from a despatch of Count d'Avaux of March 15 1686, which does not appear in the printed *Negociations*.

[2] Koenen, 79.

[3] G. F. toe Schwartzenberg, 5. 1214 f.

[4] 'Een cierlijcke ende neerighe plaetse': Schotanus a Sterringa, 225; who commends the fish of the adjacent Balkster Meer.

[5] Koenen notices for instance the French names found on gravestones in Harich churchyard: 79. n. 2.

[6] G. F. toe Schwartzenberg, 5. 1248 ff.

[7] Ratified by art. x. of the synod of 1686 at Balk: *Articles synodaux* 1592–1687; MS. at Zierikzee, now in the Walloon library at Leyden. This express notice should apparently exclude Weiss's statement that the French now joined the Walloon communities at these places: 2. 28. Such can only have been the case at Leeuwarden; and even there the church was never strictly Walloon.

was at Leeuwarden ; so that the immigration in Friesland took the form, to which the rest of Holland affords no parallel, of creating an entirely new settlement, small no doubt and unpretending in its numbers, but not without importance in the sparsely peopled province.

The city of Groningen was not remiss in accepting the example of the Frisian Estates. In the autumn of 1681 the municipal board declared that Germans and French might freely exercise their religions in the town, and dwelt at great length on the advantages offered by its situation and climate for the establishment of a variety of manufactures and crafts [1]. The Estates of Groningen and the Ommelanden [2] did not follow with any invitation or grant to the huguenots until after the Recall [3]. When, at last, in the winter following, the arrival of some fugitives pressed them to a decision, they seemed anxious to surpass every one in the large extent and the minute details of their bounty [4]. In fine, to attract in the example of emigration those who still remained at home, the Resolution was ordered to be printed and extensively circulated [5]. The effect answered reasonable hope: some were drawn to the country by the encouragement offered to dyers and fullers; by others a new impulse was given to the linen-trade, so that before the end of the century Groningen and Overijssel, where a like immigration took place, could be particularly remarked

1681.
Sept. 5.

---

[1] Berg, 1. 194 n., where it is printed at length, as only previously known through an academical dissertation of Feith *de Gildis Groninganis,* 93; 1838. And Berg is, so far as I am aware, the only writer on the subject who has noticed it.

[2] The official name of the province, as distinguished from, and coördinate with, the city of Groningen.

[3] Unless indeed we are to understand their calling Jurieu to a chair in their university in 1681 as an effect of the first *dragonnades; Mémoires de Jean Rou,* 1. 185 f.: see below p. 48.

[4] Berg, 1. 193.

[5] It was at the time published in French; *Recueil de Resolutions,* &c ; Groningen 1686: its principal provisions are given by Berg, 1. 39 f., who lays special stress on this advertisement.

for their excellence in this industry[1]. But in neither province were there entirely fresh colonies formed as elsewhere. In Overijssel decaying Walloon churches were indeed revived at Deventer and Zwolle, and a new community sprang up at Dwingelo[2]; but the temperament of the people of Groningen, then as now exclusive and local in their sympathies, jealous, and vain of their city, was unfavourable to the social progress of the French[3]. The Walloon church itself did not admit them to their community until near a century had passed[4]. The Estates could accord the exiles eleven ministers, but they could not ensure their welcome by the very body whose sympathy might anywhere else have been taken for granted[5].

Besides Groningen and Overijssel, Gelderland received a good number of linen-manufactures, and five new churches were formed in the province. Utrecht saw the beginning of that most valuable silk-trade, which the policy of her burgomaster drew to the capital[6], and which created the prosperity of Amersfoort. Their velvets and watered silks made so high a name that the original manufacturers at Amiens were driven to call their wares 'Utrecht' in order to hope for a sale[7].

Reserving to a separate chapter the influx into the great and influential province to which the natural tastes and pursuits of the huguenots led them instinctively to turn their steps, it will be convenient here to pass in review the places of refuge in the south of the country.

---

[1] Savary, *Dictionnaire universel de Commerce*, 1. 2. 395, in Berg, 1. 185.

[2] Now of course in the province of Drenthe.

[3] The criminal reports of 1732 give no pleasant impression of the relations of the two societies.

[4] F. H. Gagnebin, note to the memoir referred to below, supplementary note ii.

[5] One of the points of issue between the Walloon and French churches was the triple or the simple aspersion in baptism. In the case of Bergen-op-Zoom the Walloon synod of 1686 enjoined the latter: art. xxxvi.

[6] Koenen, 84.

[7] Berg, 1. 207 f.

The Walloon church in Zeeland was, at the time we are concerned with, in a failing condition[1]. Since 1682, when the land was wasted by a flood, no ministers had been appointed at Goes or Zierikzee[2]. The exiles of the Recall revived the interest, and founded several new churches. The largest proportion came in 1685 and the following year, and from 1688 onwards[3]. Middelburg alone from 1685 to 1693 naturalised 562 of the new-comers. Three fresh ministers were appointed there, and a like number at Flushing; two each at Veere and Zierikzee; one at Tholen, at Goes, and at Bergen-op-Zoom[4]. At Veere, a grange, La Maison de la haute Montagne, still preserves a memory of 1694[5]. Besides these places fugitives sought shelter in some number at Arnemuiden and elsewhere, always to meet with unrepressed kindness. But what is to be specially noticed is the cluster of French churches in the tract of land south of the Scheld, now attached to Zeeland, but under the treaty of Munster the 'peculiar' territory of the Estates-General[6]. *Staatsvlaanderen* or, as they still distinguish it, *Zeeuwsch Vlaanderen*, was by its position the most accessible of the western part of Holland. Canals from Ghent led to Hulst and Sas-van-Gent, from Bruges to Sluis. Hence the district was thronged by refugees: most passed on to Flushing and Goes, and the greater towns of the north; but enough stayed to form no less than nine French congregations by the year following the Recall. Nor is this number a fair index of the size of the immigration. Groede and Sluis, for instance, we know to have been overcrowded,

1682. Jan. 26.

1686. Mar. 6.

1648.

---

[1] Dresselhuis, *Zeeland*, 35-38.
[2] Dresselhuis, observing that the Dutch establishment was equally cut down, justly resents the comparison which Berg, 1. pref. vi, from one side of the case, institutes in disparagement of the Walloons.
[3] Dresselhuis, 45 and 57.
[4] Pp. 49 ff. and 87.
[5] Henri Havard, *la Hollande pittoresque*, 3. 214; Paris 1878.
[6] The territory was annexed in 1644: Baron de Pufendorff, *Introduction à l'Histoire de l'Univers*, 4. 117; Amsterdam 1732, duodecimo.

though their churches were not multiplied. The large addition was in fact to the farming classes, scattered throughout the district, at places like Schoondijke, and particularly in the barony of Sluis and in the Land of Kadsand[1]; and the families were too much isolated to constitute a proportional number of churches.

Adjacent to Zeeland was the barony of Breda, the patrimony of the prince of Orange. The intrusion of the armed evangelists of France into the territory beside the Rhône from which he bore his title[2], called forth the stadhouder's first declared menace to the power of Lewis; *whereby*, wrote home the amazed ambassador, *the exiles* in Holland *lost all desire of returning to France*[3]. It was William's aim, as will appear later on, above all things to keep these valuable supports to his party: he wished also to create a new Orange in the territory he could call his own. Accordingly he invited the exiles of his principality to share his barony, and took careful thought for the welfare of these husbandmen, his special subjects.

Like the south of Zeeland, the fortresses of Dutch Brabant were rather places of transit than of permanent residence; but one new church was formed, at Grave. The instance of Maastricht may give a picture of the surprises of these frontier-towns and of the stir of the times.

When the protestant service of Sedan was proscribed in June 1685, the huguenots in a mass fled here. *They hurried*, says a writer a few months later[4], *to the forest of Ardennes, furnished with nothing; in the journey whither they endured the most extreme misery and famine, in such sort that many even of*

---

[1] Dresselhuis, 66 and 69.

[2] Pressure was again brought to bear upon Orange in the first years of the eighteenth century. But now the chief direction of the 1600 emigrants was to Bern and Zuerich, partly to Prussia: K. F. Koehler, *die Réfugiés und ihre Kolonien in Preussen und Kurhessen*, 29; Gotha 1867. See also a paper by M Gaitte in the *Bulletin*, 19. 337-353; 1870.

[3] Count d'Avaux, 5. 233.

[4] *Historie van de Vervolging*, 1. 76 f.

the Romish faith in Maastricht were fain to have compassion on them. There were more than three thousand of these unhappy fugitives hither come, and more come yet. They hoped to go on to Holland, but some stayed among the kindly Maastrichters [1], and being aided by alms from abroad, even from Cassel [2], they permanently raised the congregation of their little church, which the French occupation of 1672 had once abolished, not to be reopened till the peace of Nijmegen [3], to near six hundred households [4].

1687.

The settlement in the Dutch dependency by the Cape of Good Hope might point a peaceful contrast to the state of things at home. In 1684 the Council of Seventeen offered a free passage to any huguenots who were willing to apply themselves to husbandry or handicraft in the Cape Colony [5]. About eighty families [6], under the guidance of a nephew of the great Duquesne [7], availed themselves of the proposal, and were established by the governor at Drakensteen, some forty miles north of the cape.

Shut in by the wild and barren ranges of what they came to know as the French Mountain, they found a fair valley, well watered by the several streams of the Berg river. It lent itself readily to the active toil of the settlers, and was observed by travellers in the last century for the excellence of its husbandry [8]. This is the Paarl district, once La Perle; the village with

---

[1] They collected 16,300 gulden for the exiles: vol. 3. 54.
[2] Koehler, 58.   [3] Koenen, 80.
[4] Tillières, despatch to Count d'Avaux, February 12 1687; in Weiss, 2. 29.
[5] Weiss, 2. 154.
[6] M G. Goguel says 150: *Bulletin*, 15. 159; 1866.
[7] Aignan, *État des Protestants*, 21 f.
[8] John Barrow's *Travels* in 1797, in Mavor's *general Collection*, 21. 315; 1813, duodecimo: Anderson's *Relation* in James Cook's *third Voyage*, in the same, 8. 107: M de Pagès, *Travels round the World*, 3. 15 f.; English translation, 1792. Francis Masson, 'one of his majesty's gardeners,' is less favourable: 'Though but a poor settlement, being a cold moorish soil, it produces corn enough for its inhabitants, sour wine and some fruit:' in the *philosophical Transactions*, 66. 271; 1776, quarto.

thatched church and houses scattered down a street a mile long, was surrounded with a croft of oaks, their trunks ten or fifteen feet in girth, and their firm and erect tops witnessing to the calm and sheltered region in which they stand.

The other settlements were at Great and Little Drakensteen [1] and at Fransche Hoek [2], hard by. They were formed of detached farms, sprinkled over the valley, remote one from another. Everywhere they sowed wheat and set sundry kinds of fruit-trees, and the special labour of the people of the Paarl was devoted to the growing of vines [3].

In this remote seclusion the huguenot planters have preserved the faith and the virtues of their fathers in a singular degree, and outwardly, although their language was proscribed by the government in 1732, they were long distinguished by their dark hair, which broadly contrasted with the light shade of that of the other colonists [4]. Until a recent date they kept also the custom of directing their home-affairs through one of their elders, deputed for the office. The colony has always borne a primitive complexion, and this patriarchal rule is not its least curious trait. With the memory of their faith, even in this day four thousand people tell their French descent [5].

---

[1] Anderson, as above: I know not whether to identify with Little Drakensteen the village called Charron by the French historians of the Refuge; as Fransche Hoek seems to have been also called Petite Rochelle: Masson, 66. 271 n.

[2] Lord Valentia's *Travels*, in Mavor, 28. 6, commemorate the residence here of a branch of the family of Jean Jacques Rousseau.

[3] C. P. Thunberg's *Voyages* in Mavor, 11. 281. Voltaire says they introduced them, and is of course followed by Lord Macaulay, *History of England*, 2. 16; ed. 9, 1853. So too R. Montgomery Martin, *History of the British Colonies*, 4. 5; 1835. Anyhow we owe them the vintage known from the slope of Constantia: Weiss, 2. 156.

[4] Le Vaillant, *Travels*, 1782, in Mavor, 21. 74.

[5] Goguel, as before.

CHAPTER V.

THE FRENCH SOCIETY IN HOLLAND.

THE province of Holland had always guided the politics of the United Seven: in national affairs it was commonly ruled by the opinion of Amsterdam. And Amsterdam was the camp of the resistance to the house of Orange. The direct issue of the measures of Lewis the Fourteenth in the overthrow of Calvinism was gradually but decisively to loosen his foothold in the city, and to demolish every barrier to the success of the stadhouder[1]. It is more than a coincidence in this regard that Amsterdam, like the Estates of Friesland, soon set the example to the rest of the province of opening its immunities to the *oppressed protestants of other countries*[2]. This was in the autumn of 1681, and it was effected by the motion of the chief-burgomaster van Beuningen[3].

The Estates of Holland followed closely in his path[4]; and, within a week of its publication, their decree of privileges was in every one's mouth to the end of France[5]. Multitudes were decided to invoke its benefits. In the winter of the ensuing year, when the rare hardness of the season gave them a thoroughfare by the ice, but the more increased the troubles of the travellers, they found themselves the objects of a large

1681.
Sept. 25.

---

[1] See Count d'Avaux, *Negociations*, 5. 231 f.
[2] Cp. above, pp. 35 f. France is not expressly named until after the Recall: cp. p. 38.
[3] Koenen, *Vluchtelingen in Nederland*, 76.
[4] Berg, *Réfugiés in de Nederlanden*, 1. 32.   [5] Benoît, 4. 493.

charity; for the prince of Orange had prompted, and the Estates had enjoined, a general almsgiving on their behalf[1].

Meanwhile two men had come to Holland eager to prepare the way for them. One, Amonet, left Paris with the view of sustaining the excitement which the persecution had roused on their account, and of finding them homes and employ on their arrival. He came to the Hague, and there, in concert with a resident minister named Scion, he drew up a memorial on the subject addressed to the Amsterdam corporation, which was perhaps the immediate cause of their resolutions above noticed[2]. The other exile had an aim less wide but, from its special object, more productive of good results. The marquess de Venours[3], after courageously pleading the cause of the Poitevins against the aggressions of Marillac, — he and his son, says an eye-witness, *have been great sufferers for speaking the truth to the king*[4],—was forced to take refuge in Holland. He had not been long at Haarlem before he thought of a plan for giving shelter to gentlewomen on their escape from France[5]. The magistrates received the proposition readily[6]. They granted a site for the Société hard by the church, allowed a temporary house, and sundry immunities. Such was the origin of the Société des Dames Françaises[7], which formed a pattern to the

---

[1] Count d'Avaux, I. 258 f.; Berg, I. 36 n.; Koenen, 77.

[2] Koenen states this positively; but on what ground I know not. The case of Friesland shows that the French troubles were already working in men's minds, and working signal results.—Scion's letter is in the municipal collection at Amsterdam, prefixed to a list of French settlers and their industries from 1681 : p. 77 n.

[3] He died at last fighting for the Orange dynasty in the Irish campaign of 1690.

[4] *True and perfect Relation of the new invented Way of persecuting the Protestants in France*, 2; 1682, folio.

[5] A. J. Enschedé, *Geschiedenis der walsche Kerk en der fransche Dames-Sociëteit te Haarlem*, 30 ff; Haarlem 1878, quarto.

[6] The committee of relief, empowered to lend money to the exiles and to supervise their establishment, was appointed November 27 1682: Berg, I. 41.

[7] *Bulletin*, 27. 563; 1878.

other houses of refuge that rose afterwards at Schiedam, the Hague, Utrecht and Rotterdam¹, and which subsisted until 1770². It was supported as well by the hearty encouragement of the princess of Orange as by a subsidy from the Estates of Holland of two thousand gulden a year and by liberal contributions from Amsterdam, Dordrecht³, and other cities⁴. Nor was it designed merely as a *pension:* it had also an educational object. Dutch girls might enter, and learn French and the French needlework⁵. But the main intent of the marquess was to furnish a home, under the direction of his daughter Madame du Moulin⁶, for girls or widows who could else hardly find a protector⁷.

His efforts were not limited to this one object: he proposed at the same time to introduce the manufacture of druggets from his native province, and in particular to entice a colony from the village of Sesmaissan to Haarlem to make stockings and aps, an industry of no little benefit to the city afterwards. The burgomasters were as liberal in this as in the other case. They issued a Declaration inviting workpeople, especially of manufactures *that are not yet made here:* they also furnished

1686.
Jan. 23.

168[2] 3.
[Jan. 30]
Feb. 9.

---

¹ The first two were governed at the beginning by Mme de Danjeau; the others by the marchioness de Thor and Mme de Soustelle: Berg. I. 47, n. 27; Erman et Reclam, *Mémoires*, I. 251, n. 2, who alone mention the *pension* at Utrecht. With Scheidam, however, it lived long enough to educate the princess of Reuss who was alive in 1782. Another house of refuge is mentioned at Harderwijk in Gelderland: Koenen, 87.

² *Bulletin*, 27. 563; 1878.   ³ Koenen, 88, n. 1; Berg, I. 46, n. 3.

⁴ These sums replaced the original scheme that each girl should bring with her 4000 gulden, which the prohibition to export money rendered impracticable.

⁵ Especially we are told *points de Venise et de France*: Enschedé, 32. It was stipulated that teaching should be given gratuitously to the children of the orphanage.

⁶ Charlotte (or Marie as most wrongly give the name) de Venours became in course of time general superintendent of all the analogous *pensions* in Holland. See Berg, I. 47, n. 2.

⁷ We know also that the princess of Orange, our Mary the Second, chose certain of the huguenot girls to be about her person and brought up at her charges: Koenen, 87 f.

money and a house to establish the marquess de Venour's proposal[1].

These efforts in North Holland in favour of the French exiles were seconded, in a way far beyond its originator's design, by the foundation of the École Illustre at Rotterdam in 1681. It arose, as we have it at first hand[2], somewhat thus: in a chance conversation, the well-known Jean Rou was asked by a wealthy Rotterdam merchant, Paets, whether it were likely that Pierre Jurieu would come as a minister to that city. *Nay*, replied Rou, *Mr Jurieu is at present in a renowned academy*, that of Sedan, *where he holds without controversy the foremost place; he is called to Groningen, another illustrious university, where an eminent position is offered him; he has refused the ministry of Rouen, ... with every hope of very great honour: I could not therefore propose to him the office of plain minister at Rotterdam.* Paets at once offered to found[3] an École Illustre, for his support, *to-morrow, if you will*, added the sanguine Dutchman; but he must have a second chair, for philosophy. Rou answered by suggesting Pierre Bayle, *One of the ablest men*, he said, *in all branches of letters that could be found in France or perhaps anywhere else; for, as touching philosophy, Mr Bayle has distinguished himself with so much renown, ... and, as concerning the humanities, he speaks and writes so purely as well in Greek as in Latin, that I suppose not in both these articles his equal could readily be seen*[4]. A happier choice could not have been made. Almost immediately, before indeed they knew of their invitation, Bayle and Jurieu found their academy at Sedan suppressed.

1681.
July 9.

---

[1] A stipulation appears here also of the apprenticing of the orphanage children. Their earnings were however to be devoted to the support of the manufactory for a year or two: Enschedé, 33.

[2] *Mémoires de Rou*, 1. 184 ff.

[3] The foundation was really made by the corporation; but in this body the influence of Paets was omnipotent: see a letter of Bayle's in Sayous, *Littérature française à l'Étranger*, 1. 239 f., which suggests that Rou has given himself more than his just share in the calling of Bayle to Rotterdam.

[4] This account must correct the arbitrary notice of Sayous, 1. 221, that he and Jurieu took refuge in Holland 'chercher leur pain.'

The winter of 1681 saw them established at Rotterdam[1]; Bayle drawing round him a circle of ambitious followers, Jurieu devoting himself to controversy and politics, and soon the protector of a crowd of fugitives[2]. Other seemingly disconnected events, such as the coming of the great preacher of Metz, Jean Polyandre, to Dordrecht[3], conspired, were it necessary, to support the enthusiasm of the country. *1681. Dec. 5.*

Thus in different ways all Holland was making ready for the great inpouring of the winter of 1685. The persecution had by this time been brought home to the Dutch in a peculiar manner; their fellow-citizens in France, though living in a strange country as aliens, had not been free from the common tyranny. Terrible tales ran from mouth to mouth of the cruelties offered them[4]. It was added, and this appealed specially to the Dutch instinct, that they were not allowed to quit the country or to remove their goods[5]. A speech before the Estates by Fagel, their raadspensionaris, raised the excitement to a white heat. There were menaces of reprisal[6], and the catholics awaited fearfully a panic such as had convulsed England within recent memory. Happily the good sense of the people prevailed, and their representatives contented themselves with demanding passports from the French king[7]. *1685. Sept. 20.*

The Recall almost immediately afforded the means of a more effectual revenge, in the giving fresh encouragement to his

---

[1] Cp. Bayle's letter of June 16 1682: *Lettres choisies*, 1. 147. Each had a stipend of 500 gulden: Berg, i. 37, n. 2.

[2] G. de Félice, *History of the Protestants of France*, 2. 135; English transl., 1853: a fact not well enough known. Sayous alludes to it, 1. 291.

[3] Weiss, 2. 5.

[4] Instances such as the outrages inflicted on the Dutch consul at Nantes, and on many aliens, English and Dutch, in La Rochelle, may be found in the *Historie van de Vervolging*, 1. 48 & 56, which tells much of the vehemence of public feeling in Holland in December 1685: cp. above, 30, n. 4.

[5] Count d'Avaux, 5. 144.

[6] See below, supplementary note iii.

[7] *Historie van de Vervolging*, 2. 55 f.; Count d'Avaux, 5. 166 f., 209 ff. The remonstrance was sent through the minister at Paris, Starrenberg: Lewis's explanations should seem to have been readily accorded.

exiles. Throughout the province subscriptions were eagerly collected; anabaptists, Lutherans, even Roman catholics[1] gave their help[2], and the Jews of Amsterdam contributed as much as 40,000 gulden[3]. The sympathetic enthusiasm was without bound.

In the south the fugitives were welcomed with a characteristic warmth. At Dordrecht, we are told, 'the burghers received them as kinsfolk into their houses, cared for them as for their children, and put them in the way of earning honourably their bread,' while the magistrates loaded them with privileges and pensions[4]. At Rotterdam so great was the inflow of people utterly destitute as to tax the resources of the almoners beyond their power; and the town officials nobly met the need by maintaining great numbers out of their public salaries[5]. Rotterdam indeed seems to have been the chief resort of the poorer emigrants, and the number it received was exceptionally large. Count Saint Didier told of five thousand coming within a month of the Recall[6]. These were above all the exiles of Normandy. *This beautiful and great town*, wrote Dumont de Bostaquet in 1687, is *become well-nigh French by the flight hither of a mass of the people of Rouen and Dieppe*[7], a flight of which the memory was long preserved in the name of the Hôtel de Rouen[8].

1685. Nov. 15.

The French in Amsterdam are said to have numbered two thousand in 1684: by the end of the century[9] they may have approached fifteen thousand. For many years the Walloon diaconate, which the burgomasters established in 1688, constantly maintained two thousand people, and expended an

1684. March.

---

[1] Thus at Haarlem the catholics contributed above 2886 to a total collection of 8430 gulden, December 22 1686: Berg, 1. 42.

[2] Koenen, 85.   [3] Erman and Reclam, *Mémoires*, 1. 251.

[4] Schotel, *Dordrecht*, 2. 178; in Berg, 1. 40.   [5] Koenen, 89.

[6] Weiss, 2. 26. The *Historie van de Vervolging* gives but 4000 a month later: 3. 67.   [7] *Mémoires*, 161.

[8] Waddington, *Normandie*, 17.

[9] Thus Weiss, 2. 27. It is surely a mistake in M J. P. Hugues' report of a MS. in the Amsterdam archives which allows but 5156 in 1695: in the *Bulletin*, 5. 479; 1857.

average revenue of forty thousand gulden. And, although the statement of Benoît that the magistrates resolved to build the refugees a thousand houses at a forty-gulden rental[1], is apparently to be discredited[2], there can be no doubt that such a proposal might well have been debated and more than justified by the result[3].

We have to be content with such bare statistics, and can tell but little of more than the beginning of the immigration. For in February 1686 the Estates of Holland, urged by the Estates-General, forbad all mention in the public prints touching the refugees, above all as to the manner of their escape; and this order, kindly intended, to disappoint the activity of the French spies and informers, has hidden from us most of the contemporary narratives[4].

1686. Feb. 14.

As winter followed the Recall, the increasing necessities of the immigrants were met by more than proportional liberality on the part of the provincial Estates. They granted an annual sum first of 12,000 and then of 25,000 gulden for the French ministers[5]. Sixteen[6] were assigned to Amsterdam, eight to Leyden and to Rotterdam, seven to Haarlem and to Dordrecht, six to Delft, five to Gouda, three to the Hague, three to Gorinchem, and two each to Schiedam, the Briel, and Schoonhoven[7].

1685. Dec. 18. 1686. Jan. 23. Jan. 25.

---

[1] *Histoire de l'Édit*, 4. 269.

[2] See the minute particulars in Berg, 1. 33, n. 2.

[3] By 1725, according to the official list, the number had fallen to 8001: Berg, as above.

[4] Koenen, 89 f.; Berg, 1. 31, n. 2. Cp. above pp. 29 f.

[5] Berg, 1. 45.

[6] The original staff of three ministers had been already raised to eight: Count d'Avaux, 5. 185, October 19 1685. In 1686 it was again increased to twenty; Koenen, 82. In 1688 there appear to have been actually thirty-eight: see a contemporary MS. cited by M J. P. Hugues in the *Bulletin*, 5. 371 f.

[7] *Hollandse Mercurius* 1686, nr xxxvii. 128; Berg, l. c. These sixty-nine ministers were pensioned with 400 gulden if married, 200 if single: Koenen, 85. In Zeeland they were fairer to the bachelors, and allowed them ¾ instead of ½: Weiss, 2. 14.

And the ministers were perhaps the poorest class among the exiles. While the working man, with his fewer wants, could immediately turn his hand to some craft, the minister had no livelihood apart from his office. Moreover they came to Holland in vast numbers compared with the other classes. They relied,—and their trust was not misplaced,—upon the kindred feeling of the nation: but besides this, while all were the exiles of conscience, the minister was also the exile of a proscription. Others, if they pleased, might stay in France; nay, they were forbidden to leave: but to the minister delay meant prison, disease, death. Six weeks then from the Recall[1] found one hundred and eighty in Holland[2]. At the synod held at Rotterdam in the following spring two hundred and two were present[3].

<small>1686. April 24.</small>

But it is not the number, but the intellectual and spiritual eminence, of the ministers of the Refuge in Holland that above all attracts our attention. Here was Jean Claude, whose position in France was felt to be so menacing to Lewis's aims that the edict of Recall allowed him, in marked exception to the rest of his order, but twenty-four hours to quit the country, and who was watched by the king's servants as far as Brussels[4]. He was to Bossuet the only huguenot divine who could do battle on equal terms, who was alone his match in lucid order and resounding dignity of language[5]. Let him be compared with his comrade in the campaign Pierre Jurieu, and his excellence will at once appear. Jurieu, the grandson of Pierre du

---

[1] Before the Revocation thirteen new comers, including Pierre du Bosc and Isaac Beausobre, were welcomed at the synod of Delft. Sept. 5-8, 1685: *Livre synodal*, MS. formerly at Naarden, now in the Walloon library at Leyden, volume 1.

[2] *Historie van de Vervolging*, 3. 69.

[3] Enschedé, 18. And the attendance does not represent the entire number of ministers: thus the junior minister of Middelburg was absent; Dresselhuis, *Zeeland*, 54 f. The common estimate indeed asserts that in the year of the Recall 250 had come to Holland: Erman and Reclam, 1. 192.

[4] *Historie van de Vervolging*, 2. 33.   [5] Sayous, 2. 76.

Moulin, had doubtless an hereditary genius for controversy[1]; he was also a better scholar than Claude; but his temper, naturally hasty and soured by opposition[2], rendered him incapable of pursuing an argument with calmness or precision. The rigour of his theological belief, unsoftened by the charity of Claude, led him to make enemies of those who, in a time when union was beyond all things necessary, should have been his heartiest fellow-workers; and the rebound from the presence of what he held scepticism drew him aside into an excess of superstition[3], and left him a prophet and a visionary.

History has placed Jurieu in the front rank of the French apologists in Holland, because the voice of the hour so pronounced him. In controversy, as in other warfare, it is the bitterest reasoner, the hardest hitter, that wins the public applause. Jurieu the fanatical pamphleteer is, no more than Wilkes, the just representative of his time. It was of only a small class that he reflected the sober judgment. But none the less was his influence fraught with mischief to the religious and social tranquillity of his companions in exile. When he accused Bayle of deism[4], Saurin of Socinianism, his success, had it been permanent, would have tended to snap the link that united the French protestantism of the past with philosophy and culture, with spiritual religion, and to bring in a reign of bare dogma and polemic.

The true exponent of the better thought among the French in Holland is Jacques Basnage. *Fitter*, as Voltaire said[5], *to be*

---

[1] Vol. I, 221 f.

[2] Perhaps to such a cause is due the habitual acrimony of the *History* of Élie Benoît, who, having escaped from the terror at Alençon, came to suffer under a lifelong tyranny at the hand of his wife. But the tale against Madame Jurieu is at least doubtful; and the testimony of the great Saurin may clear Bayle from the common slander. For the facts, see Sayous, I. 297 and 368.

[3] Cp. his long talk about the 'voices in the air,' *pastoral Letters*, 143-165.

[4] This charge cost Bayle his chair and even the liberty of taking pupils in private: *Besluit van de Vroedschap*, October 30 1693; Berg, I. 37. n. 2.

[5] *Écrivains du siècle de Louis XIV*, under the name.

minister of state than minister of a parish, he was above the petty quarrels in which Jurieu lived [1]. In his house at Rotterdam he gathered round him all that was best in the ingrafted society. There he might argue with Bossuet on a large ground of Christian moderation, sparing of unworthy epithets, willing to see the good in his opponent's motive, never forgetful of his high breeding. The intellect of the town, while it delighted in his converse, acknowledged him as master: the devout side, if it was not rather the guiding principle, of his nature endeared to him such men as Pierre du Bosc, the orator of Caen, the courtly and gentle Daniel du Superville, the appreciative and hospitable burgher Paets.

In Rotterdam the connexion between the banished ministers and the men of letters, who felt that the Edict of Recall struck equally at the root of liberal thought, was of the closest kind. The two classes were united by the friendship of their leaders Basnage and Pierre Bayle, an old friendship dating from their university years at Geneva, and now strengthened by the sympathy of exile [2]. For Bayle represents in a peculiar measure the new huguenot spirit of enquiry, of scepticism in the honourable sense, which the suppression of their colleges had forced to seek another home abroad [3]. But, besides this, Bayle had much of his own; and the impress of his teaching turned his pupils' thought into a fresh channel, running parallel, but seldom blending, with the accepted current of Calvinist tradition. His personal history is the best index to his religious position. The son of a minister [4], he was trained and he acquiesced in the views of the huguenot schools: but as he grew up, a hard worker, well grounded in the learning and

---

[1] That Jurieu became his enemy was in his own despite. His liberal tone naturally led the bigot to suggest a charge of heresy.

[2] Sayous, I. 230.

[3] See J. G. von Herder, *Adrastea*, i. i. viii; *sämmtliche Werke*, 9. 83; Karlsruhe, 1820.

[4] He was born in 1647 at Carlat-le-Comte in the county of Foix: Sayous, I. 224.

penetrated by the philosophy of his age, he came to distrust the attempt, which no system favoured more than the Calvinistic, to harmonise the doctrines of positive religion with the dictates of human reason. He sought to keep the two asunder, and fled to the church of Rome[1]. But the change, he soon felt, involved the sacrifice of his reason: he became once more a Calvinist; but he retained to the end the essential separation between faith and reason[2]. How it was that he did not go on from this divorce to the virtual or entire exclusion of religious opinion, as his successors the French encyclopedists did, is explained by his doubts of the competency of reason. To the questions, could we believe sensuous experience, the reality of external phaenomena, he replied with Descartes in the negative. He went further, and not only the absolute truth of mathematical demonstration, but also the value of consciousness, became to his mind matter more or less problematic. Reason, he declared, is strong in detecting error, but weak to discover truth without assistance: the belief in truths that are opposed to reason is what we want as spiritual beings, just because it implies a victory over ourselves. With Tertullian he would say sincerely *Credo quia absurdum*[3].

1669.

Bayle laid bare the chasm, as he held it, between reason and faith; but his feet were planted on either side. No blame to him that his disciples chose to abandon the one in their tenacity of the other. Rather let him have our praise for the manner in which he drew from his principles a toleration not yet bound up with indifferentism. Morality, he taught, being the child of reason, had no kinship with religious belief; and by consequence the moral worth of a man was a thing apart from his

---

[1] W. Windelband, *Geschichte der neueren Philosophie*, I. 357; Leipzig, 1878.
[2] Thus, in his *Pensées diverses sur la Comète de* 1680, he endeavoured to shew that the doctrines of the creation of the world by a benevolent deity, of providence, and of original sin, could never be brought into agreement with the physical and moral evils of this world, and with the sense of responsibility: Windelband, I. 359.
[3] Cp. L. Feuerbach, *Pierre Bayle*, 132; ed. 2 Leipzig 1844.

theological allegiance [1]. The state and the church, the temporal and the spiritual interests of the world, were by their very essence divided one from the other. Men might quarrel with the arguments by which he guarded this position [2]: but its fairness gradually won the favour of most who were unshackled by the surroundings of office or the traditions of routine.

Bayle's authority over the mind of independent students was prodigious. We shall hardly find its like unless in that of Voltaire or of the encyclopedists of the eighteenth century. And of these Bayle was the lineal ancestor. Beyond his philosophy, he was the pioneer of that type of culture which we associate with the term *Aufklärung* or *Illumination* [3]. The *Dictionnaire historique et critique* which he issued between 1695 and 1697 is not merely a monument of sterling, marvellous labour and erudition; it lets us see as well the secret of his later influence. Meanwhile he spoke to the educated society at large through his periodical *Nouvelles de la République des Lettres* [4], the forerunner of our modern literary and scientific journals; a work which overlived his activity, and under the hands of Henry Basnage de Beauval, brother to the great Jacques, maintained, with a less ambitious scope, a useful and considerable importance for many years.

The tenour of the society of Rotterdam may justify the length at which I have dwelt upon it. It has an additional value as an evidence of what Berlin will shew hereafter, that

---

[1] His own experience had shewn him that his ethics had been unchanged by attachment to the Roman or to the protestant church: Windelband, 1. 361.

[2] Thus he affirmed that Christianity had left the moral aspect of the world unaltered: nay, that it had led to fanatical atrocities unknown to the heathen. If it be said that Christianity is not responsible for these, neither, he replied, can it be credited with any moral good that may have followed its introduction, for such existed prior to its origin: vol. 1. 361 f.

[3] Vol. 1. 357.

[4] See in J. G. von Herder, 9. 83 n., a great list, ending with a comprehensive &c., of the journals and *Bibliothèques* to which Bayle's works gave example.

the huguenot emigration was not solely a religious factor added to the countries of the world; that it was also a prize to universal culture leading even to issues with which the old huguenot temper had little in common [1].

Rotterdam was not the only centre of this ingrafted civilisation. *The Hague*, we read in a letter of 1688 [2], *is too beautiful a place not to be filled with men of letters. The ministers hold their own there,*—and Élie [3] and afterwards Jacques Saurin were no unworthy arbiters of the opinion of the place ;—*but we have also among our exiles plain private persons eminent for their knowledge and integrity. Of these is the illustrious Mr Rou* [4] : *his Historical Tables have made so much noise in France that one ... will scarcely say he knows not in what part of the world their author lives. But that you may speak thereof with the more certainty I acquaint you that he makes his sojourn at the Hague, known, loved, honoured, by whoever has a mind fair enough to judge of good things after their merits.* This society was closely connected with the court. Ménard was chaplain to the prince of Orange and chaplain-general to the French forces in time of war [5]: Claude was chaplain to the prince, and also historiographer to the Estates of Holland [6]. William was not without a taste for letters; far less did he lack the religious sympathies of his country. But the pressure of the politics of the day made him regard and employ the work of Lewis the Fourteenth as an instrument

---

[1] Cp. Capefigue, *Louis XIV*, 3. 10 & 6. 35 ff.

[2] A. R. d. L. [de Ladevèze], *Apologie des Réfugiés*, 107, the Hague 1688; in Waddington, intr. to *Mémoires de Rou*, xxiii.

[3] Élie Saurin, like so many of the famous refugees, was a Dauphinois, having been born at Usseaux in 1639: Arnaud, *Dauphiné*, 3. 24. J. G. von Herder traces to this southern origin their prevailing tendency to oratory and polemic, rather than to exact science; and the rush of sermons and books of controversy at this time may support the inference: 9. 83.

[4] Jean Rou, born in 1638, had graduated at Saumur, taking his legal licentiateship at Orléans. He became advocate in the parlement de Paris in 1659, and, after a residence in England, withdrew to Holland, where from 1689 to 1711 he was secretary-interpreter to the Estates-General. His *Mémoire* are of a high and most genuine interest.

[5] Berg. 1. 45.

[6] Koenen, 91.

mainly to the achievement of his own schemes. It will appear hereafter how he used the refugees in this other character, as a moral and a material force to aid him against the arrogance of France, and in his designs upon the English crown.

But if Holland was at this time busy with political enterprise it had not abandoned its pursuit of industry and commerce. We have seen how men made ready at Haarlem for the arrival of the huguenot fugitives. Even earlier the town had no small sprinkling of Walloons from Valenciennes and Saint Quentin [1]. So that anyway it came about that 'those who fled at the Recall found here, not only their countrymen, sometimes even their kinsfolk, but also their manufactures in full bloom [2].' *They came*, it is true, as we read their tale in the municipal records, *in a sorely desolate state, lacking ... the means of life and in no wise able to sustain their families*. But it was not for long that they needed town support [3]. Their woollen manufacture increased till the town became too small for them, and they built the Nieuwe Stad [4]. Besides cloth, druggets, and such woollen stuffs, the French introduced into Haarlem a variety of silk fabrics, velvet, plush, and the like, which, though coarser than the original manufactures at Lyons, Tours, and Paris, were long in great demand abroad because cheaper by fifteen or twenty per cent.[5] Their bleaching-grounds were also of the best repute in Holland.

In the matter of the woollen trade Haarlem was soon outstripped by Leyden, where the French made the finest cloth, the best serges, that could be got in the country [6]. The number of

---

[1] Enschedé, 17 f. [2] Berg, 1. 41 f.

[3] The magistrates promised aid for two years from December 1 1685: Enschedé, 19.

[4] The Nieuwe Stad had indeed been founded in 1672; but hardly more than founded. In 1687 the French had seven ministers; in 1688, nine; in 1690 the number was reduced to six. The baptisms from 1671-1680 had numbered 102; from 1681-1690 they were 257; from 1691-1700, 380; Enschedé, 23 & 27.

[5] Savary, in Berg, 1. 186.

[6] The same, 1. 185.

workmen pushed out a suburb of the town, the present Nieuwe Hoogewoerd ; and we are told that the comfort of the immigrants was so enviable that even catholic soldiers would leave the regiments of Lewis the Fourteenth to settle here [1].

But, as might be expected, Amsterdam was most of all sought for [2]. Here, as early as 1683, a whole quarter of the city was peopled by the workmen of Pierre Baille, the richest manufacturer of Clermont-Lodève [3]. Before this time Amsterdam had been almost exclusively busied with her maritime commerce. Now, industries were rising everywhere in silk and wool and linen : a new part of the city was built for the comfort of the workers, and almost entirely occupied by manufactories of hats. Paper mills abounded, especially in the neighbouring town of Zaandam. The book trade also, through which so much of French literature was soon given to the world, was greatly increased [4].

Even before the Recall Amsterdam could spare from her new population a colony of some hundreds for the settlement at Surinam. Chiefly craftsmen, with a few farmers, they established themselves, under the auspices of the proprietor Aersens van Sommelsdijk [5], at Paramaribo; and increased by a new shipload in 1686 they formed the clearing of La Providence and planted sugar [6].

The instances of Haarlem, Leyden, and Amsterdam are

---

[1] Letter of Louvois, January 20 1686, in Count d'Avaux, 5. 231. The story is still current in the town.

[2] Four or five hundred came from La Rochelle alone : L. Delmas, *l'Église réformée de la Rochelle*, 277.

[3] Berg, 1. 33, says they filled the Nordsche Bosch, including the Reguliersgracht, the Vijzelgracht, Noorderstraat, Noorderdwarsstraat, and Looijersstraat : names which recur with a strange diversity in Weiss and his translators, English and American.

[4] One Gaylen, a bookseller of Lyons, made good his escape hither with a fortune of a million livres : Weiss, 2. 19.

[5] Whose character, the praise of preceding historians, has not gained by the publication of the appendix to Rou's *Mémoires*.

[6] Weiss, 2. 160.

typical of the impulse given by the refugees to trade. It is perhaps needless to trace this activity in the other cities of Holland[1]. We may only notice, in passing, the great hat-manufacture the French made in Rotterdam, their vigour at Dordrecht in pursuing the Greenland fisheries[2], their varied industries in these and other places, as Gouda, Schoonhoven, and den Bosch. But before quitting the subject it will be well to comment on the social influence of the Refuge, the estimate of which has been embarrassed by several confusions.

The visitor to Holland, struck by the great prevalence of French names, words, and all that speaks of a conquest or an overrunning, is apt to refer to the immigration of the Recall that which, in by far its largest extent and most pervasive action, belongs to a date three centuries earlier. It was then that the Welsh,—'Walloons' we call them,—made the indelible mark upon Dutch society[3]. The inroad was too strong to be resisted, and the natives could only see with a murmur their genuine life transformed or at least transfused by the strong current of French vitality[4]. *Al, wat walsch is, valsch is,* became then the saying: but the reproach was rather to the outward complexion than to the more real virtues of the new population.

On the other hand, many Dutch writers[5] have confounded the entry of the huguenots, a high and strenuous race, with the later influx of adventurers, of 'every one that was in distress, every one that was in debt, and every one that was discontented,'

---

[1] The subject has been elaborately and minutely investigated by Jonkheer Berg in the volume I have constantly cited, with a regret that its fellow has never appeared.

[2] See also the list of industries at Dordrecht in Berg, 1. 209.

[3] The cause was a fearful plague in Flanders, the famous Dood van Yperen. It is said by scholars that it was this inflow which gallicised the sound of the Dutch vowel *u*, adding so to say an Umlaut to the German vowel.

[4] The domination of French manners was lamented long before the Recall by Antonides: Koenen 2.

[5] Among them even Luzac, the well-known author of *Hollands Rijkdom*: Koenen, 4.

whom the easy freedom of the country attracted to it. By this confusion a writer of too large influence, in the *Neder-landsche Spectator* of 1750[1] was led to do wrong to truth and history by applying to the emigration of the Recall the words of Horace: *Hoc fonte derivata clades in patriam populumque fluxit.* The survey he makes, with much of just criticism, is vitiated, as criticism written with a view to public applause commonly is vitiated, by a strain of overcharged invective; it paints in broad colours the collected results of centuries, as though they were the single product of a generation.

'This people,' says the *Spectator*[2], 'oppressed and hardly handled, came over to us in so great swarms, that it seemed about to equal the number of the inhabitants, and scarcely to be provided with places to live in. Not alone were they received cheerfully as brothers and fellows in faith; but people of every diverse sect lavished abounding gifts upon them: and everywhere, as guests, free from the charge of scot or lot, they were furnished and favoured with rare immunities.

'The engaging joyousness, which no tyranny could quench, the courteous grace which could gain an entrance by its modest tact everywhere, soon made so much impression here on the more and better part of the people, and so used its mind to their manners, that it came to be reckoned an honour the most to resemble the foreigners, and to exchange the old laudable customs of the nation, the true and just mark of the constant Batavians, for the mobility, the lax bearing of the French. The language even not only grows debased, . . . but he who will pass as courtly must ill speak his mother-tongue and win praise for the French he speaks with the excellence of a native[3]. . .

'Uprightness, simplicity, faith, thrift, modesty, is turned to craft, flattery, assurance, excess, luxury[4], distinction of persons;

---

[1] Nr 45. 145 ff.   [2] P. 150.

[3] At this day, to say the king speaks French to such a one is a synonym for marked and familiar favour.

[4] 'Our state, by hospitality large-hearted and open-handed, had grown

and civic converse has lost its bond with people of rank[1]. Children can talk of fashion, can dance, fence, as soon as may be; a good carriage, a French idiom, an etiquette to ladies, this is the staple of French school-training: knowledge, learning, industry to fit one for affairs, such things are left to pedants or to those who must make their living by them.'

And so the essayist passes in review the havoc brought in by the entry of 1685. The judgement became a fixed position with patriotic writers: it even grew in violence when the discontent of the 'Batavian Republic' reverted to the huguenots as the prime cause of the evils under which the nation laboured. Its very untruth may serve to shew how strong was the influence which could support a fabric of such dimensions without caring to deny or to remonstrate.

---

and waxed mighty: but so have many vices stolen in and quickly spread, and harmed exceedingly these ancient virtues:' p. 152

[1] Koenen however probably goes too far when he speaks of king-worship among the results of the French immigration: 94.

CHAPTER VI.

THE PASSAGE THROUGH HAMBURG AND THE NORTH.

THE fugitives of a persecution are not apt to be nice about their destination. It is enough for them to have escaped. Moreover, in a general flight like that of 1685, there were multitudes who could not afford to choose their future. If, where they found themselves, they were provided by charity or their handiwork with the means of subsistence, they were content there to stay, in spite of small annoyances from the religious or local mistrust of the inhabitants. Such places were, for the most part, the cities of transit on the German border to the north. It will be convenient to treat, together with these, all the places in this direction whither the huguenots came as it were occasionally and by chance, together with the organised settlements in Denmark, Mecklenburg, and Brunswick.

The little East-Frisian port of Emden, now as in the early days of the reformation *the Lord's hospice*[1], was especially flocked to by fugitives from Metz and other places[2]. Most of them, however, passed on into Brunswick or Brandenburg. Indeed, willing as the town was, it was incapable of receiving very many. The first minister that arrived was at once attached by the magistrates to the French church, where he stayed until

1686.

---

[1] An inscription on the church door used to run, *Heer bewaere de Herbarg diner Gemeene.* Another still exists,—*Godts kerk vervolgt verdreven Heeft Godt hyr trost gegeven: Schepken Christi*: Wenz, *Emden*, 46, 48.

[2] Koenen, 66.

twenty-two years later he was appointed ordinary minister[1]. Little more is heard about the refuge in Emden: the like may be said of Bremen and Luebeck. We should hardly know of the existence of a French colony at Luebeck but for an incidental notice of the 'difficulties' it encountered from the Lutheran burghers and of King Frederick the First's good offices on their behalf[2]. To Bremen, indeed, Charles Icard, the translator of Calvin's *Institutes*, is said to have led a band of exiles, who were well received by the townspeople and whose church lasted for a century[3]: but it is unlikely that their position was pleasant or less free from embarrassment than that at Luebeck[4]. For, while the Lutheran states did not close their gates to the banished Calvinists, they still refused an entry to guilds and all civil functions: in many cases, as indeed everywhere in England, the settlers were disqualified from holding land[5].

Under similar conditions, but far different in respect of number, was the immigration to Hamburg, overwhelming to the resources even of that great city[6]. Most of these refugees, again, went on into Brandenburg; but the residents were not few. Many of them were persons of quality[7], but the more part manufacturers of coarse linens, an industry which, by its export to England alone, had brought France an annual revenue of 200,000*l.* sterling, but which was for ever lost to France from its establishment in Hamburg in 1692[8]. The people of the city were at first cordial to the fugitives, and ample col-

---

[1] About this Samuel Allart, see Wenz, 132; who notices the additional benches set in the church on account of the immigration, 133.

[2] Erman and Reclam, *Mémoires*, 1. 262.

[3] Vol. 1. 257.   [4] So I infer from Weiss, 1. 229.

[5] Erman and Reclam, 1. 257 ff.

[6] *Uebersicht der Wanderungen und Niederlassungen Religionsflüchtlinge nach und in Deutschland*, 77 f.; Karlsruhe 1854.

[7] *Historie van de Vervolging*, 3. 114.

[8] These 'lockrams' and 'dowlas' had been one of the chief industries of Normandy and Britany: Macpherson, *Annals of Commerce*, 2. 650; cp. Burn, *Refugees in England*, 19.

lections were made in the different churches¹: but the exclusive spirit of Lutheranism forbad them, with the Walloon community to which they attached themselves, the free exercise of their religion, until a century had elapsed from their first arrival². All this time they were forced to attend the French service at Altona³, where, as at Glueckstadt, every liberty was allowed to the reformed congregation. In these towns the French found prosperity and engaged themselves with profit in commerce and in the whale-fisheries, then greatly the vogue in the duchy. Holstein also furnished a road into Denmark: but the readier passage was by sea.

1686.

The invitation from Copenhagen was among the first answers to the crusade of 1681. In September⁴, King Christian the Fifth, moved by his queen, who united the blood and the charity of the princes of Brandenburg and of Hessen-Cassel⁵, offered to receive a hundred or a hundred and fifty banished families *Willing to reside in his dominions,* and promised *To grant them lands and build them churches with full religious freedom.* The added pressure of the queen and her known goodness induced a small number, in all amounting to a few hundreds⁶, to direct their flight towards Copenhagen. Two of

---

¹ These churches alone contributed 1100 rixdollars; *Historie van de Vervolging,* as above.

² Erman and Reclam, I. 261, 265 f. The chapel *auf der hohen Bleichen* was built in 1785; *Uebersicht der Wanderungen,* as above.

³ The Walloon community here dates from 1582; the church that served as well for Hamburg was built shortly after 1686: Erman and Reclam, I. 264; *Uebersicht der Wanderungen,* 78.

⁴ This seems to be the date of the Public Letter: Benoît, 4. 492; Koenen, 57; D. L. Clément, *Notice sur l'Église réformée française de Copenhague*; Copenhagen 1870.

⁵ Queen Charlotte Amalia was the daughter of Wilhelm VI, landgrave of Hessen-Cassel, and of Hedwig Sophia, sister to the Great Elector. She died in 1714.

⁶ The abbé Jean Novi de Caveirac, who divides by six all figures of the emigration, allows 50 families or 200 souls: *Apologie de Louis XIV,* 84 and 87; Paris 1758: for the authorship see Lelong, *Bibliothèque historique de la France,* I. 403 b, ed. 1768, Paris, folio. From the lists of Clément we

F

the ministers first called hither were among the most illustrious in France. Philippe Ménard had served the metropolitan church of Charenton[1] and was afterwards French chaplain to William the Third[2]; Jean de la Placette, 'one of the profoundest moral philosophers of his day[3],' had been for five-and-twenty years minister at Orthèz in Béarn, and he chose his new post above the more ambitious field opened to him by the Great Elector[4]. The French community met for some years in a private house[5]: the church for them and their German friends[6], near the Rosenborg Palace, was opened in 1689, and a new one on the burning of the first, in 1731[7]. The succession of its ministers inaugurated by Ménard and La Placette was maintained unbroken until 1812; since when the church has been content with one minister.

1689.
Nov. 10.
1731.
March 4.

The Lutheran clergy had resented the tolerance of Christian the Fifth[8], the more when it was extended to residents of the Dutch and German reformed societies, and even to the Jews. Their opposition checked the inflow, and rendered the king's support half-hearted. His death in 1699 changed the face of things. Frederick the Fourth, the willing fellow-worker with

1685.
Jan. 3.

---

get a minimum of 274: pp. 8-13, 36 n. In 1731 the congregation numbered 800: p. 15.

[1] He came to Copenhagen, November [8] 18 1685: *Bulletin*, 7. 30.

[2] He succeeded his brother Jean on the latter's death in 1699: see a memorial of M Ménard 'le cadet' (son of Jean), dated May 31 1716, among Archbishop Wake's papers in the library of Christ Church Oxford, vol. 28.

[3] Spittler, *Kirchengeschichte*.

[4] He was offered at first to be the minister at Koenigsberg. He ultimately retired to Utrecht, where he died in 1718: Clément, 37.

[5] Where since 1688 they had their presbytery.

[6] For the reformed Germans shared the privilege; they had previously availed themselves of the service in the queen's private chapel.

[7] Leave for building a church was granted in 1685. A new, the present, site was given by letters-patent of July 27 1687; and the church was founded April 20 1688: pp. 4 f.

[8] When the French jubilee-service was offered in 1789, the presence of the bishop of Seeland and of many other Lutheran parsons might point an instructive comment: p. 13.

his mother, not only saw to the comfort of many new immigrants, but also let the influence of his envoy at Versailles be happily exerted in the rescue of huguenots from galleys and jails, and of their women from nunneries. Of these last the French at Copenhagen long commemorated the Douze Confesseuses by this means saved and brought to their city[1].

In 1720 a church was established for reformed French and Germans at Fredericia in Jutland. They seem to have come chiefly from Brandenburg. Others are said to have introduced flax and hemp into Iceland[2].

The Refuge in Denmark included a few military officers; of whom was the ancestor of the Irish earls of Lifford, Frédéric Charles de la Rochefoucault, count de Roye and Ronci, who was worthily welcomed as grand marshal and commander-in-chief of the Danish forces[3]. But the bulk of the settlers were occupied in husbandry, and here most of all in the cultivation of potatoes, of the tobacco-plant, which they introduced[4], and of wheat, which they improved.

The settlement in Russia[5], such as it was, was effected by the interest of Friedrich the Third of Brandenburg, who in 1688 directed his special envoy at Moscow, J. Reyer Czapliez, to persuade their imperial majesties to receive the huguenots

---

[1] Clément, 6.   [2] Peyrat, *Histoire des Pasteurs du Désert*, 1. 93.

[3] The marshal died at Bath 1690. He had been a lieutenant-general in the French army: *Bulletin*, 2. 662; Samuel Smiles, *the Huguenots in England and Ireland*, 515; ed. 2, 1868.

[4] They also introduced turnips and cabbages; Weiss, 2. 298.

[5] Weiss, 2. 316, has taken from the travels of a suspicious writer, Count Lagarde, an account of a French colony vaguely described as 'on the banks of the Volga,' a specification which admits a considerable range to conjecture It is said to be commercial and agricultural. The inhabitants preserve the complete dress of Lewis XIV, with large-skirted coat and voluminous peruke: 'they still express themselves in the classic idiom of the contemporaries of Corneille and Racine.' This remarkable people go yearly to the fair at Makarieff to traffic with the Hindoos. In the absence of authority and in view of the absurdity of the tale,—gross as a mountain, open, palpable,—I shall content myself with giving a denial of such an existence from the mouth of a native of Makarieff.

into their territory. In consequence of this action a letter of Grace was issued in the following year[1], giving free entry to the empire,—and, characteristically enough, free exit as well,—to any emigrants of the evangelical faith who might choose to come: their religious liberties were secured, and the government-service was opened to them. This leave seems to have attracted a few refugees: but it is curious that none apparently availed themselves of the general privilege, preferring the more immediate protection of individual licenses[2]. Those who settled at Moscow had the advantage of the Dutch church, so called, which, as the Dutch language was no longer needed, was devoted to the common worship of the French and German reformed communities[3].

Their position was firmer at Saint Petersburg. When Tsar Peter built this city he seems to have taken a certain pleasure in outraging the prejudice of the orthodox church by giving all encouragement to Lutherans and Calvinists. The imported population gave a new tone to the rising capital, different in manners and civilisation to the rest of Russia. Among the rest a French society grew up; whose church, built in 1723[4], and closely dependent upon the mother-church at Geneva[5], was frequented as well by the Swiss, English, and Dutch residents.

Much has been said of an imagined military effect of the Recall in Russia. A Dutch writer of repute[6] affirms that, had

---

[1] See the *Copia des Passes, welchen beyde tzaarischen Majestäten in der Moskau auf sr churfürstl. Durchl. zu Brandenberg beschehene Recommendation*, in Moritz Posselt, *Franz Lefort*, 1. 466 ff.; Frankfurt-am-Main 1866: and cp. J. M. Kemble, *State-Papers and Correspondence*, 388 f.; 1857.

[2] Posselt, 1. 469.

[3] In 1699 it employed the services of three ministers: Edward von Muralt, *Chronik der vereinigten französischen und teutschen reformirten Gemeinde in Sankt Petersburg*, 7; Dorpat 1842.

[4] Since 1746 it has had a ministry united with that of the reformed German community: p. 10.

[5] The church was in part perhaps built at the charges of the Genevese: Weiss, 2. 315.

[6] N. C. Lambrechtsen van Ritthem, *korte Beschrijving van Nieuw Nederland*, 49 f.; Middelburg 1818.

it not been for this measure of Lewis the Fourteenth, 'the military training of Europe, brought in by French emigrants and eagerly taken advantage of, would never, or at all events not at so important a juncture, have been introduced among the troops of Peter the Great.' Such a statement needs a double limitation. François Lefort, to whom the real credit of the reform is due, was no doubt of French descent, but his family had lived for two centuries at Geneva. Voltaire, who observes this [1], adds on the other side, 'What is to be noted, and should well refute the hasty blunder of those who pretend that the recall of the Edict of Nantes and its issues cost France but few men, is the fact that a third part of this army, this regiment so called,'—it numbered twelve thousand,—' was composed of French exiles [2].' But here also the case is uncertain. Voltaire gives the authority of Lefort's manuscripts: but we are hardly to suppose that the general took pains to ascertain such matter of detail. How many of these four thousand were actually French, whether more than three hundred [3], must still allow reasonable question [4]: and on either hand the source of the impulse given to Russian discipline remains uncertain.

Sweden and Poland can scarcely be said to have formed asylums for the scattered French. In Poland, since Sigismund the Third the ascendant of catholicism had even restored to the older faith many of the protestants who saw themselves else excluded from honourable positions in the state [5]. The only place where the huguenots gained a foothold was Dantzig, and

---

[1] *Histoire de l'Empire de Russie*, ch. vi.; 1. 121; Paris 1759.
[2] Vol. 1. 125. The assertion is adopted bodily in Baumgarten (Semmler), *Uebersetzung der algemeinen Welthistorie*, 29 (div. 2. vol. 11), ch. iii. sect. iii. §§ 344, 345; 1765.
[3] This number is given by W. Tooke, *History of Russia*, 2. 59; 1800.
[4] The suspicion is shared by the author of the *Uebersicht der Wanderungen*, 67, and by the not usually overcritical Professor Weiss, 2. 314 f.
[5] See a notice by B. D. Cassius in N. C. Kist and W. Moll's *kerkhistorisch Archiev*, 2. 429-441; Amsterdam 1859.

here but few¹. Some Parisians managed to reach Sweden with part of their property, by entrusting it to the Swedish ambassador, Count Lilieroot, or to his secretary Palmeguiste, who restored the value on their arrival in Holland. King Charles the Eleventh permitted a subscription to be raised for them in Stockholm, and gave the exiles certain privileges and encouragement. But the order to have their children baptised by the Lutheran ministers prevented any number from availing themselves of the king's bounty ².

In 1698, however, the Estates-General begged his successor Charles the Twelfth *To take charge of any new emigrants that might come, and to give them lands in his German provinces; for our land*, they wrote, *shut in by such narrow boundaries, is so crowded by the French exiles for the faith, that it can now support no more* ³. And some hundreds were admitted to Royal Pomerania ⁴.

Of the same date was the settlement in Mecklenburg, in tardy response to an invitation which Duke Christian Ludwig had put forth so early as 1683. In a Declaration of October 24, 1698, his successor Friedrich Wilhelm provided for the establishment of some families in the town of Buetzow ⁵, where they settled in May 1700. The colony was not longlived: a fire in the following year spread the French community among their neighbours of the German reformed discipline; and it needed a fresh effort on the Duke's part and an offer of increased privileges to recall them ⁶. Meantime others had been more happily entertained at Schwerin and in the village of Tarnow.

In Brunswick, likewise, and from the first, the French met with cordial welcome. The dukes of Braunschweig-Wolfenbuettel and Braunschweig-Bevern aided those who came to the town of Brunswick, at the same time, perhaps in company, with

1686.

---

¹ Their church however is noticed as still existent by Erman and Reclam, I. 281.

² Weiss, 2. 312.   ³ Koenen, 96 n.   ⁴ Weiss, as above.

⁵ Extended immunities were given by a Declaration of August 1 1699: *Uebersicht der Wanderungen*, 77.

⁶ Declaration of September 14 1703: as above.

their fellows who went on to inhabit Magdeburg and Halle [1]. By the first years of the eighteenth century they had a church, and the community was known for its trade and industry.

The elder house of Braunschweig-Lueneburg had for some time been strongly influenced by French, and protestant, manners. For Duke Georg Wilhelm of Celle had married a noble lady fled from the desolation of Poitou. Eléonore d'Esmiers brought with her many of her country-men and women, and, as the tyranny at home increased, she attracted to her court an entire society of exiles of rank [2]. The brother, Ernst August of Hanover, eagerly followed this example and that of the elector of Brandenburg. Like the latter, in the month after the Recall, he issued a Proclamation closely modelled on those which the hospitality of Holland had suggested. In this he elaborately set forth the advantages offered to such huguenots as should enter his dominion [3]. At the frontier they should be charged with no duties (art. i); they should pay no taxes, except excise, for twenty years upon their settlement (vi). The duke secured them protection for their persons and freedom for their faith: he engaged, when necessary, to provide a minister [4] and a school (ii–v): the houses they lived in were to be tax-free for ten years; if built by themselves for twenty-five (vii, viii). A simple oath of fidelity should involve the rights of citizenship without its burthens [5] (ix, x). They might take apprentices, and look for all support from the duke in establishing their business. Even should any quit the country during the twenty years of immunity, they should at their return be received on the old footing (xv).

1685.
[Nov. 21]
Dec. 1.

---

[1] Erman and Reclam, I. 276; *Uebersicht der Wanderungen*, 80.
[2] Erman and Reclam, I. 274 f.; *Uebersicht der Wanderungen*, 79 f.
[3] It may be read in the *Historie van de Vervolging*, 2. 58 f.
[4] He postulated a congregation of but one hundred.
[5] Immigrants were to be admitted to guilds at reduced charges (x). While they became natives in the eye of the law (xii), they were at liberty to name an arbiter for their own suits (xiii), and to dispose of property as they pleased; only the property of intestates was necessarily to follow the law of the land (xiv).

The Declaration immediately drew fugitives to Hameln and Hanover. In the former town, unlike any other in Germany, the Lutheran community opened its church to them [1]: the influence of the duke was for once stronger than the traditions of sect [2]. In Hanover the duchess built a church in the Neustadt [3], and the duke, by a liberal admission to the civil and military services [4], secured a greater importance to the colony than its numbers alone might warrant. It shortly gained also a certain political significance in the dynastic arrangements of England, by the intercourse it held with the exiles in this country and in Holland [5].

It was at these courts that the French first proved that gracious and civilising power afterwards conspicuous in the society of Berlin. At Celle and Hanover French was spoken as purely as in Paris; and a refinement altogether new began to inform the relations of the German principalities [6]. *The court in general*, wrote Toland in 1705, *is extremely polite, and even in Germany it is accounted the best both for civility and decorum* [7].

We have now reviewed the leading circumstances of the dispersion to the north. Its course lay roughly by sea or through the Netherlands; so that its character is doubly northern, and of a different feature altogether to that, mixed up with vaudois, which poured in upon Germany from Switzerland and down the Rhine. The colony in Brandenburg shares the characteristics of both, and calls on every ground for a separate treatment. Before passing to these, the history of the Refuge in England must have its place; and it will not unfitly follow that in Brunswick.

---

[1] Afterwards there was a separate French church: *Uebersicht der Wanderungen*, 79.

[2] The only parallel I can recall is that at Carlshafen in Hesse, where the same building was used by both sects: Koehler, *Réfugiés in Preussen und Kurhessen*, 70.

[3] J. Toland, *Account of the Courts of Prussia and Hanover*, 56; 1705, quarto.

[4] Erman and Reclam, 1. 273.   [5] Weiss, 1. 230.

[6] Kemble, 386.   [7] *Prussia and Hanover*, 53.

CHAPTER VII.

THE REFUGE UNDER THE STUARTS: THE FRENCH QUARTERS OF LONDON.

THE huguenot migration to England was complicated in a signal degree by political considerations. Not only was this government deeply compromised in regard to France, but there was also a constant tendency to see in the persecution itself a reflexion of their own measures affecting the catholics; and from this sense of being in a sort responsible, and not liking to admit it, there grew a desire to wash their hands of the unwelcome consequences. A few extracts of the time will make this clear.

Even in the spring of 1668 Thomas Thynne had written to Lord Clarendon from Stockholm, *The French, whose cause wants many more colours than it will bear, endeavour to make his majesty the author of the horrid persecutions the reformed religion undergoes in France; and that that king does it only in retaliation of the late proclamation against papists*[1]. With this remark at the beginning, we may compare that of Bishop Burnet at the end, of the tyranny; he was in Paris until the August before the Recall. *As far as I could judge*, he says, *the affairs of England gave the last touch to that matter*[2].   1667/8. [Feb. 27] Mar. 8.

1685.

Meantime, in 1679, Henry Savile, the English ambassador at the capital, wrote in a like tenour: *The archbishop of Paris and the père de la Chaise do all that they can to prevail with this*   1679. June 5.

---

[1] T. H. Lister, *Life of Clarendon*, 3. 446 f.; 1837.
[2] *History of his own Times*, 1. 655; 1724, folio.

king to make him revenge the quarrel of the English catholics upon the French protestants, who tremble for fear of some violent persecution, and are ready to go into England in such vast numbers as would be a great advantage to the nation, if you would by easy naturalization make it in the least easy to them. I find those who are rich are afraid our king should meddle with their concerns, but the crowd and the number talk of nothing but the necessity of his declaring himself protector of the whole protestant religion, and live upon the hope of seeing that glorious day [1].

<small>1679. June [2] 12.</small> The reply of his brother, Lord Halifax, was a cordial expression of approval. *I am sure,* said he [2], *we must renounce all good sense if we do not encourage them by all possible invitations. It hath ever been so much my principle that I have wondered at our neglecting a thing we ought to seek; and those that have not zeal enough to endeavour it for the preserving of our religion, might have wit enough to do it for the increasing our trade.* No step was however taken. Probably Charles the Second felt that the heat of the Exclusion Bill was scarcely a prudent juncture to select for risking an estrangement from Lewis [3]; and the matter lapsed until the edict of July the Fifth, 1681, empowering children of seven years' age to change their faith, was <small>1681. July 5.</small> issued. On the day of its appearance Savile reported [4]; *These poor people are in such fear that they hurry their children out of France in shoals .. I will confidently aver,* he added, *that had a Bill of Naturalization been passed in England last winter, there had been at least fifty thousand passed over by this time.* A little

---

[1] The despatch goes on to say, 'All protestants are turned out of all places except just the gens de robe, but all in the finances, and all the common soldiers in the guards are cashiered, which would be no disadvantage to you in a dispute with this crown, for you would have them all if you pleased': *Savile Correspondence,* 93.

[2] Pp. 97 f.

[3] Similar considerations seem to have prevented the measure of naturalisation being brought forward next year: Halifax, as before, 176. Its defeat, when introduced in 1681 and 1694, was due purely to the protective spirit of boroughs and corporations: Agnew, *protestant Exiles,* 1. 36.

[4] *Savile Correspondence,* 201 n.

later he again insists [1] on the number of seamen and persons of wealth anxious to emigrate. [1631 July 22.]

At length the spirit of the government was roused. Sir Leoline Jenkyns, in his despatch, said [2], *What you write of the poor protestants of that side is great sense and a noble compassion. On this day se'ennight there was a memorial, drawn by some of them already come over, read before his majesty in council. His majesty ordered letters to be immediately prepared for his royal signature to my lord of London and my lord mayor* [3] *for the making a speedy collection to answer in some measure their present necessities . . Besides this collection, there is a brief directed to be issued out all the kingdom over; and his majesty hath this day agreed to everything in the report and advice of the committee.* [July 28] Aug. 7.

The Proclamation [4] referred to offered to the immigrants *Letters of denization under the great seal without any charge whatsoever, and likewise such further privileges and immunities as are consistent with the laws for the liberty and free exercise of their trades and handicrafts.* The king further promised to submit to parliament a general Bill of Naturalisation [5], while he placed the exiles for a time on a level with home-born subjects in regard to taxes and admissibility to schools and colleges. Lastly, with the view of securing their immediate relief, so far as might be, he named the archbishop of Canterbury and the bishop of London [6] *To receive their requests and petitions.* [July 23] Aug. 7.

---

[1] *Savile Correspondence*, 210; L. von Ranke, *französische Geschichte*, 3. 523, gives the date as the 11th.   [2] *Savile Correspondence*, 213 f.
[3] Printed at once as a broadside in folio: *his Majesties Letters to the Bishop of London and the Lord Mayor.* They bear date July 22, and commence, 'Whereas we are given to understand that a great number of persons and whole families of protestants in the kingdom of France have lately withdrawn themselves from thence,' &c.
[4] Benoît, 4. 491 f.: Bishop Kennett, *complete History of England*, 3. 403; 1706, folio, where the date is once misprinted *August* 28. L. von Ranke is a month more inexact, giving September 28. The proclamation is printed at length in Cooper's preface to his *Lists of foreign Protestants and Aliens*, xviii. f.; Camden Society 1862, quarto.
[5] Cp. above, p. 74, n. 3.
[6] At a later date, January 15 1696, these dignitaries were placed at the

1681.
Aug. 20.

This concession, hard won as it was, is of the first importance in the huguenot history of the time. *You cannot imagine*, wrote Savile, from Paris, *the joy here upon the news of the care the king is pleased to have of the protestants who seek refuge in England. No question but he will soon be sensible of the good effects of it.* One effect of the Declaration is full of moment [1]. When, says Rulhière [2], the noise of it reached Lewis, Marillac was at once recalled from Poitou; and the terror was for the time suspended.

It was not too soon. The English pamphlets of the day [3] are full of notices of the number and the need of the fugitives, and of their especial influx into England. *They come hither*, we read in one [4], *in troops almost every day, and the greatest part of them with no other goods but their children.* Another [5] tells

---

head of the French Committee to add weight to its endeavours against the proselytising activity of the French ambassador; but, on the remonstrance of the French church in London, the king refused his consent to the arrangement: *Mémoires envoyés de Londres*, 68 f. & 83 ff.; Cologne 1699, duodecimo. This curious little volume throws an unpleasant light on the internal affairs of the French society in London. In the form of a history of the French Committee, it clothes a bitter attack on the honesty and public spirit of some of its members, the ministers Satur, Brocas, and de la Mothe, mere placemen, in the view of the tract, and employing every artifice to maintain their position of influence: 10–14, 86.

[1] *Savile Correspondence*, 214 n.

[2] Vol. 1. 221; A. Michel, *Louvois*, 37 f.

[3] To those cited in subsequent notes may be added such tracts as *the great Pressures and Grievances of the Protestants of France*, by E. E. [Edmond Everard] 1681, folio: which translates the Edict of Nantes and the Declaration of April 2 1666, with a running, and no friendly, commentary.

[4] *The present State of the Protestants in France, in three Letters*, 4; 1681, quarto. Compare the notice of Narcissus Luttrell, July 20 1681, *brief historical Relation of State-Affairs*, 1. 112; Oxford 1857: and *an Harangue to the King by a Minister of the French Church in the Savoy*, October 19 1681; a broadside.

[5] *True and perfect Account of the new invented Way of persecuting the Protestants in France*, 3 f.; 1682 folio: where we learn further that since September 1681 fugitives had been forbidden to take with them any goods at all. According to Johann Beck this prohibition was at work earlier, and ships and houses were searched at Dieppe, Havre, and Honfleur:

how *The people, being thus perplexed, begun in July to draw towards Rochelle, and seek a retreat into the protestant princes' countries, in England chiefly, under the right defender of the faith.* Their joy at the issue of the Declaration [1],—*A masterpiece of providence* they called it,—knew no bounds: *We love you,* exclaimed a huguenot pastor, addressing Charles, *we love you as a God on earth, for such you are* [2].

The political storm of the time unfortunately did not leave them long in this ecstasy. The rumour went abroad that the king intended to devote the money collected for them to the support of those hated foreigners his catholic agents. Men came to look askance at the refugees; suspicious of their true character, they refused to subscribe for their necessities [3]. Though Charles went so far as to publish an Advertisement with the express view of shutting out the calumny, the standing of the French was for some time anything but pleasant; they had constantly to procure letters testimonial to their *sober, harmless, innocent* [4] way of life, and were seldom received on the equal footing of religion by the working men into whose company they were for the most part thrown.

1681.
Oct. 29

Relation, June 28 and July 5 1680 and April 11 1681 ; in L. von Ranke, 3. 517.

[1] 'The refugees ought to be most sensible of the extraordinary favours they daily receive here in England:' P. L. *true and faithful Narrative of the late barbarous Cruelties and hard Usages exercised by the French against Protestants in Rochel*, 4; 1681, folio.

[2] *Harangue*, as above. 'The French ministers,' says the historian Paul de Rapin de Thoyras, 'thought themselves under such obligations to the king, that they were amongst the most forward to display his virtues in their sermons... I myself remember to have heard a preacher in the church of the Savoy launch out into the profanest flattery:' *History of England*, 2. 760 f., English translation, ed. 3, 1743, 1744, folio. Was he present at this *Harangue*?

[3] *State of the Protestants in France*, 4; Agnew, 1. 26.

[4] Letter signed by the vicar and principal people of Rye, April 18 1682: 'we believe them to be falsely aspersed for papists and disaffected persons, no such thing appearing unto us by the conversation of any of them:' cited by W. D. Cooper, in the *Sussex archaeological Collections*, 13. 201; Lewes 1861.

The king's regard for his new subjects was, however, plain. His double manifesto served as a warning to Lewis; and the Edict of Nantes continued in name to subsist. It is upon the death of Charles, partly no doubt as an incitement to his successor's aims, that we see the more sustained defiance, the final recall, of the huguenots' charter. Domestic reasons, indeed, produced the last measure at a moment inopportune for James the Second: his own concerns were for once left unconsidered, and he was now placed in a situation of peculiar embarrassment. Just as he was about to ask of his Parliament concessions to Roman catholics, his hopes were arrested by the firm sense of the people that the Recall, to them the most unsufferable tyranny, was the legitimate outcome of the very system by which they were themselves menaced. James saw the ground cut from beneath his feet: he was driven to take up a new position [1]. So, when the huguenots poured into England, *The king was the more bountiful to them, that he might seem to condemn their persecution for conscience; the liberty whereof he professed to be his principle and practice* [2]. He promised a collection in all churches for their support [3]; *And the people of England were more especially liberal on this occasion; because they began to think it might be their own case, and must be everywhere the effect of popery and arbitrary power* [4].

1685. Autumn.

But public feeling was soon divided, in suspicion of the king or of the exiles he made a show of welcoming. It was whispered that the royal Briefs *Were designed by the court for*

---

[1] Lingard ascribes the change to the wise and conciliatory endeavours of Cardinal Adda: *History of England*, 10. 102; ed. 6, Dublin 1874.

[2] Kennett. 3. 472.   Agnew, 1. 59.

[4] Kennett, as above. How this argument was insisted upon afterwards to prevent the refugees from taking advantage of the Declaration for Liberty of Conscience, may be seen from such tracts as *a Letter from several French Ministers, fled into Germany upon Account of the Persecution in France, to such of their Brethren in England as approved the King's Declaration*, 6 f., s. l. aut a., quarto, [translated by W. Wake, according to Anthony a Wood]. Cp. also Bishop Burnet's *Letter to Mr. Thevenot*, &c., 56, dated from the Hague, September 10 1688; London 1689, quarto.

the maintenance of French papists, that were invited over to serve the king's designs¹; or else *That it was but a piece of policy in order to curry favour with his protestant subjects*². The first rumour was soon disappointed: the collection was not ordered until several months had elapsed from the date of James's ostentatious promise. The popular mind was excited³; but the king's policy remained obstinate. When the count de Bonrepaux came at the close of 1685 charged, among other commissions, to entice back the huguenots to France⁴, he was received at the court with effusive display⁵; and it was chiefly through his influence that the Brief on which the collection hung was not issued until the following spring⁶. It could indeed be deferred no longer; but the king did his best to reduce it to a perfunctory ceremony. He told the archbishop of Canterbury to forbid any reference to the occasion of the national almsgiving, in the sermons before it was made⁷; the order was to be read without comment⁸.

1686.
March 29.

April 23.

James had by this time sufficiently shewn his reluctance to shelter the exiles. He had withdrawn the proclamation in their

---

¹ It will hardly be believed that men recurred to this charge even in 1699; yet we have the word of Isaac de Larrey for it: *Histoire de l'Angleterre*, 4. 342; Rotterdam 1713, folio.
² Quoted by Kennett, as above: see also P. de Rapin, 2. 760.
³ The silence of the *Gazette* with reference to the French troubles was the theme of angry comment: see Evelyn's *Diary* as early as November 3 1685: cited by Mr Agnew, as above.
⁴ Macaulay, 2. 51 f.
⁵ Agnew, 1. 30.
⁶ 'By the interest of the French ambassador,' says Evelyn, April 25 1686, ambiguously. Mr Agnew adds that of Lord Chancellor Jeffreys, by whom the Brief had to be signed: 1. 59 f.
⁷ Mr Agnew, as above, cites from the Brief the destination of the fund now collected, to 'persons of quality and all such as through age and infirmity are unable to support themselves and their families'; and compares the notice of Evelyn, April 15 1688: 'The persecution still raging in France, and many very considerable and great persons flying hither produced a second great collection.'
⁸ Barillon, [February 22] March 4, in Macaulay, 2. 78 n. Cp. supplementary note iv.

May 5. favour¹; and now, at the call of Barillon, he condemned a tract of Jean Claude's, which in telling of their overthrow sinned rather in the completeness of its facts and the conviction of its reasoning than in any false bias, to be publicly burnt². But even Barillon saw he had gone too far: Lewis, he hinted in his despatch, must regard such demands for the future as inexpedient, the feeling of the people never having been so greatly roused since James's accession³. The very means, in fact, that had been taken to discourage public sympathy on behalf of the refugees, worked together with the steps of home-policy to produce an entirely contrary effect. The nation raised a splendid fund of relief, and left no opportunity unused of shewing the exiles the kindness they sorely needed.

These had come over certainly in great numbers: *Some few, only, brought or had privately sent over sufficient effects with them; but far greater numbers came in a true state of persecution, empty and naked, to depend on the hospitality and charity of this good-natured kingdom*⁴. It is true that the mission of Bonrepaux was not entirely without fruit, and that several hundred refugees⁵ were seduced into trusting themselves once more to the mercy

1686. July 24. of Lewis the Fourteenth. *The king*, we hear in July 1686, *is said to be inviting back his subjects from all parts, especially the handicraft part of them, whose departure is said to have much prejudiced his revenue, and promiseth them his toleration; though it doth not appear that they are forward to believe that an Order of Council can preserve what the Edict of Nantes could not*⁶. On the contrary London became fuller every day; and free Letters

---

¹ Macaulay, 2. 77.

² The order to burn *les Plaintes des Protestants* appeared in the *Gazette* of May 8: Cooper, *Savile Correspondence*. 28 n. 2.

³ Mr Agnew states, on the authority of the memoirs of Sir John Bramston, that the book was burnt in the French, as well as in the English translation: 3. 22; cp. 1. 30, and Macaulay, 2. 77 f.

⁴ Kennett, 3. 472.

⁵ Weiss reckons 507 in the spring of 1686; 1. 292: Mr Agnew gives 253 on May 5; 1. 30.

⁶ Letter in the Ellis Collection, cited by Mr Agnew, as above.

of denization were granted with growing frequency and to increasing numbers[1]. The religious wants of the French population in the City had hitherto been satisfied by the London Walloon Church in Threadneedle-street[2]: now a new one was established in Aldersgate[3] by Letters under the great seal, and made subject to the direction of the English primate.

1686.
July 16.

The following year saw two churches spring up in the Spital Fields[4] beyond Shoreditch, and one in Hungerford-market by the Strand[5]. The official account of the relief-committee[6] reported in December that 13,500 refugees had been helped in London during the year, as well as 2000 at the sea-ports[7]. They were all artificers, labourers, and the like[8], excepting 143 ministers, who received a fixed support, and whose children were apprenticed or placed in household service, at the expense of the committee, and some 283 families of persons of quality[9],

1687.

---

[1] See the lists in Cooper, *foreign Protestants*, 39–59, or more completely in Mr Agnew's first volume.

[2] As early as 1549 the French had shared the Dutch church in Austinfriars: in the following year they obtained this one of their own. Having been destroyed in the fire of 1666 it was quickly rebuilt, and opened for service April 2 1667: Burn, *foreign protestant Refugees*, 24.

[3] The migrations of this church are many. From its first site in Jewinstreet it was removed, November 8 1691, to Brewers' Hall: then from February 26 1693 it had only a room in Buckingham-house, College Hill; and it did not settle down to its final place in S Martin's Lane, S Martin-Ongar, until April 20 1701, its new lease having been confirmed by act of Parliament, February 3 1699: pp. 153–155.

[4] The Église de l'Hôpital received the king's license August 11, while that of S Jean, Swan Fields, seems to date from October 2: pp. 165 ff., 178 f. Cp. Waddington, *Protestantisme en Normandie*, 17 n.

[5] Smiles, *Huguenots*, 342.

[6] For the history of the Royal Bounty see supplementary note v.

[7] *Extract out of the Books of Account*, &c., a folio of one sheet among the Ashmolean tracts, numbered F. 1. xxxv. in the Bodleian catalogue. This copy is without date of year: the report however was published March 19 1688 according to Weiss, who consulted the original in the State Paper office: 1. 286.

[8] Such were set up in their occupation, furnished with tools, and taken care of.

[9] Of these alone the number was 140 families, 'constantly supplied by

1688.
Sept. 4.

lawyers, physicians, merchants, and tradesmen. Besides the three in London twelve churches had been established at the committee's charges in the several counties. Such was the charity of one year. In the next, the French ministers in and about the city of London were incorporated, with power to purchase lands and build houses; the same Letters-patent providing for the erection of three new churches, in the Spital Fields [1], Soho [2], and Leicester Fields [3].

These names bring to mind three of the most palpable monuments of the immigration. The peopling of the waste Spital Fields [4] was entirely due to the French: in a generation nine churches had arisen there [5], and the workmen were so

---

weekly allowances.' Their children were sent ' to the best trades,' or 'into his majesty's troops,'—the latter to the number of about 150,—others into Germany or the northern parts.

[1] This church, distinguished from that in Soho as La Nouvelle Patente, first met in Glovers' Hall, January 30 1689: moving into Paternoster-row, Spitalfields in 1707 and into Crispin-street ten years later, it was ultimately fixed in Brown's Lane: Burn, 168-173.

[2] On September 4, says Kennett, M Daillon ' solicited a patent for the erecting a nonconformist and independent French church in Sohoe-Fields; which was readily granted: and from hence it is that the French call that meeting-house La Patente to this very day:' 3. 472. This was of course after the Declaration of Indulgence: cp. Macaulay, 2. 211 f.—The church was opened in 1689 in Berwick-street, nearly opposite Fryingpan-alley, but permanently settled in 1694 in Little Chapel-street, Wardour-street. It had a consistory of its own, but ten ministers served in common also for its fellow in Spitalfields: Burn, 149 ff., 168 n.

[3] The suspicion is forced upon me that this church, which is known to have existed first in Glasshouse-street, was that same wooden chapel which James II had first set up on Hounslow Heath. Strype records its removal thence in his edition of Stow's *Survey*, 2. 1337; 1720, folio. A new building for the French church was opened in Leicester Fields in 1699: Burn, 134-137, 138 f.

[4] We may see the Fields in their open, but partly wooded, stretch in such prints as Cornelius Dancker's *Londini Epitome et Ocellus*, Amsterdam 1647,—a panoramic view.

[5] See below, supplementary note vi. Spitalfields did not become a parish until 1727, when Christ-church was completed: *England illustrated*, 2. 47: 1764, quarto. The date represents a considerable activity in this part of the suburbs: about the same time Stepney also lost S Ann's, Limehouse;

many and so busy that the silk-manufacture of London was multiplied twenty-fold[1]. It is hard to realise in the dense alleys of to-day the lanes bordered by hedgerows and shaded with elms[2] in the latter years of the seventeenth century. Yet the population of Bethnal Green, part of the same colony, which, from its centre, we name after Spitalfields, but which extended from Aldgate and Bishopsgate far into east and north, bears even now evident marks of its foreign descent[3].

1713.

The settlement westward of Temple Bar had assumed considerable proportions by the first year of James the Second, when two Acts of Parliament (cc. 20 & 22) carved the new parishes of Saint Ann, Soho; and Saint James, Piccadilly, out of Saint Martin's-in-the-fields[4]. It is not of course pretended that this growth was wholly or even mainly due to the French immigration. But judging from the churches and from the notices of the foreign complexion of much of these parishes, it is impossible to disguise the prominence of the new comers in their formation. Before this, indeed, the services in the chapels of Somerset-house[5] and of the Savoy-palace[6] had been found inadequate, and new congregations had been

1685.

S George's-in-the-East; and S Matthew's, Bethnal Green: and S Luke's was carved out of S Giles's, Cripplegate: S. Lewis, *topographical Dictionary of England and Wales*, 3. 121; 1831, quarto.

[1] It is usual to regard as a creation of the immigration of 1685 the district of Petty France, which occupies nearly the site of New Broad Street: see W. Maitland, *History of London*, 2. 795; ed. J. Entick, 1775, folio. It occurs however as 'a large place and generally well-built' in the 1603 edition of Stow's *Survey*, 62; reprinted by W. J. Thoms, 1876.

[2] As in Petticoat-lane, where once the ambassador Gondomar is said to have lived: Burn, 179 f.

[3] Isaac Taylor, in Agnew, 1. 64 f.

[4] Macpherson, *Annals of Commerce*, 2. 620.

[5] The presbyterian service in the chapel of Durham-house in the Strand had been moved here when the former was burnt down in 1653: it was not exchanged for the Anglican office until 1711: Burn, 108 f.

[6] An Order in council of March 10 1661 had established a French congregation in the refectory of the Savoy with an episcopal service and subject to the jurisdiction of the bishop of London. It was carried into

formed in Castle-street, near Leicester-square[1], and in Spring Garden, Whitehall[2]. But in the generation following the Recall no less than ten churches sprang up in these parts. From 1689 the Cock-and-pye Fields in Saint Giles's began to be covered with clusters of houses, their names as yet untainted with the squalid associations of the Seven Dials[3], scattered down the fresh slope than ran to the Strand from Saint Giles's church and the fields above High Holborn. Westward the hamlet that had gathered round the duke of Monmouth's palace grew into a town, as it encroached upon its site, the now deserted Soho Fields, and in time engrossed it. To the south the French had their market at Hungerford[4] and then in what is now Little Newport-street, still conspicuous for its un-English look. Separate from Covent Garden, it was better suited as well to their means as to their tastes, and the inventive genius of the race taught them to make use of, and

---

effect July 14. In June 1675 the king granted to the dean and chapter of Westminster 60*l.* for 'the preaching ministers of the French church of the Savoy... in addition to what is already allowed them from the same church according to his majesty's Order in Council.' In 1731 the building became ruinous, and the people dispersed to the chapel of Spring Garden or to Les Grecs; in 1737 it was finally abandoned. This episcopal congregation, oddly enough, traces its origin to the inconvenient distance of the strongly Calvinistic church in Threadneedle-street. Hence from 1641 the duke of Soubize maintained a service in his own house, which he opened to his countrymen of the neighbourhood: Burn, 109–113. When situated in the Savoy, it came to be the fashion for the English nobility to attend, just as the English church is affected by the upper classes at the Hague: Smiles, 341.

[1] The chapel was built on the east side of Castle-street, a little above Hemming's-row, at the expense of the government: it afterwards was moved to Moor-street, Soho: Burn, 151 f.; Smiles, 342.

[2] It should seem to have been a chapel-of-ease to the Savoy; whence it was also known as the Little Savoy. Its rebuilding, after a fire in 1716, opened a new epoch of prosperity for the church, and it replaced and survived the Great Savoy: Burn, 137 f.; cp. J. Armand Dubourdieu, *Appeal to the English Nation*, 81; 1718.

[3] Lewis, as above; Macpherson, 2. 644.

[4] The topography of this part of the then suburbs may be recovered from some papers in the *Gentleman's Magazine* of 1829 and 1831.

even bring into vogue, food which the habit of the time discarded[1]. The church hard by was fondly named La Charenton,—*simulataque magnis Pergama*,—a humble image of the superb mother-church. Very soon, indeed, the annoyances of the catholics near drove the community to seek a different abode, where this memory was forgotten: but another was stored up in La Tremblade, this new church of theirs in West Street[2], which kept in mind the seaport on the coast of Aunis, the *little town well peopled* of Jacques Fontaine's narrative[3], whence so many of the fugitives from La Rochelle embarked.

Of the churches in Soho the Greek church in Hog-lane[4] in time swallowed up all the others, and remains alone in the west of London[5], still flourishing in its new place in Bloomsbury-street. 'Les Grecs' should claim a notice, were it but that it lives for us in Hogarth's picture of *Noon;* as Lamb reminds us when he tells of 'those heroic confessors, who, flying to this

---

[1] The case of the ox-tails, which the French rescued from the fell-mongers, is notorious: Burn, 258.

[2] The register of La Charenton extends from 1701 to 1704 or 1705; that of La Tremblade, otherwise known as La Pyramide, carries it on from 1706 to 1741 or 1743. But the congregation was older. 'The church in West Street,' we read in a letter addressed to the bishop of London, in Burn, 144, 'is not new, although it meets in a new place. It was first established in Weld-house more than ten years ago, with the express permission of my lord bishop.' So that 1696 is its latest date; while the reference to the 'insults of papists' might place it even earlier than the Revolution. Cp. Smiles, 467.

[3] *Mémoires*, 161–173.

[4] The register, according to Mr Smiles, extends only from 1703 to 1731; but an earlier beginning may be inferred from the archbishop of Samos's *Account of his building the Grecian Church in So-hoe Feilds*, a broadside of 1682, which relates that Charles II had made a grant for this church in 1674, that the archbishop had carried out the work in 1676, but that its services, through their distance from the city, were unavailable to his countrymen, and by the date of the account had been disused. The permanence of the name should argue an immediate or at least a speedy transfer of the church to the French.

[5] For that in Westbourne Grove is a new-fangled church, unconnected with the early immigration, and unlike them partly propagandist.

country from the wrath of Louis the Fourteenth and his
dragoons, kept alive the flame of pure religion in the sheltering
obscurities of Hog-lane and the Seven Dials [1].' We are now
to trace them at the sea-ports and spreading their work and
example of work throughout the country.

---

[1] *Essays of Elia,* ' The South-sea House.'

CHAPTER VIII.

THE DISPERSION IN ENGLAND AND AMERICA.

OF the French who came to the English coast, like those who reached the German sea-ports, many left their destiny to the sea that furnished them a road, and where it landed them they stayed; but others, of a higher rank in social estimation, gathered about some known protector, whose influence might gain them the means of exercising their religious offices, and whose house, if need were, might furnish them a shelter. Conspicuous among these was the marquess de Ruvigny, the aged chief of the huguenots, once their guardian at the French court, now at the English, whose sons were also to appear prominent in the history of the Refuge in Ireland; the younger, La Caillemotte, by his command at the Boyne, where he fell, opening the way for the colonies which his brother Henry, earl of Galway, planted at Portarlington, and encouraged everywhere in the island. The father gained for his friends at Greenwich the goodwill of the people and the privilege of worship in the parish church[1]; and he assembled round him his old comrades in war, with statesmen and men of letters; so that the village was sought after as a first and natural resort by fugitives of rank or position, until the removal of his son into Hampshire carried the more part with him, or scattered them about Westminster, Soho, and Marylebone. What remained were chiefly the sea-folk, shipwrights and provisioners.

---

[1] Evelyn records a service here in 1687, which about a hundred attended. It was the English service done into French, succeeded by a sermon: the French church in London-street is mentioned in 1709: Burn, 116 f.

Southampton thus received a circle of persons of consideration, of which the centre lay hard by, at Rookly, Lord Galway's house. The colony he attracted long preserved the high-bred characteristic which he imparted to it, and which was worthily maintained by Philibert d'Hervart, baron of Huningen, once William the Third's Envoy at Geneva[1]. But these were not the only French society here. Southampton, since the days of Edward the Sixth[2], had received an unbroken influx of refugees from the channel islands[3], from Valenciennes, Lille, and the sea-ports of northern France. Now their numbers were swollen by the emigrants of Normandy, Upper Languedoc, and, above all, Poitou. The church of God's House near the harbour had of old been their property, and it still preserves the record of former exile and its refuge here[4].

Colonies of a like origin are found lining the south coast, and reach from Severn to Thames. To the west, churches grew up at Bristol[5], Barnstaple[6], Bideford, Plymouth[7], Stone-

---

[1] He died here in 1721: Smiles, 348 & 476. His father's name I have before, p. 9, spelt Herward, the original form, but doubtfully; for I cannot ascertain when the word became French. [2] Burn, 80.

[3] These in their turn served as a refuge to the exiles of the Recall: *Mémoires et Observations faits par un Voyageur en Angleterre*, 363; the Hague 1698, duodecimo. The author is Misson de Valbourg; Barbier, 3. 222: and his christian name, Maximilian (not Henry); Agnew, 2. 11.

[4] This chapel of S Julian, as it was otherwise called, was a foundation of Henry III, which Edward III had given to the Queen's College at Oxford: Burn, 82. Its French register begins in 1567 and runs to 1797: an interesting choice of its entries may be read collected in Smiles. With the adoption of the Anglican liturgy in 1712 the style of the church was changed to the Protestant Episcopal French Church: Smiles, 134-140 and 471-481.

[5] Service was held in the mayor's chapel of S Mark the Gaunt, its register beginning May 29 1687; until a new church was built for the French in 1726: Burn, 123 ff.

[6] The service in the high school-room is not certainly traceable before 1705 or perhaps 1703: pp. 131 f.

[7] The Eglise Française Conformiste standing in How-street is mentioned in 1701. Its congregation melted into that of Stonehouse about 1778: pp. 125 ff.

house¹, Dartmouth², and Exeter³. From the outset of the dispersion — from those few *who resided outside Rochelle*, and who came in the autumn of 1681⁴ downwards—we have repeated notices of ships arriving at Plymouth filled with fugitives. Some of these brought industries with them: there were workers in silk and cotton at Bideford⁵, tapestry-makers at Exeter. But coming as most did from Poitou, Saintonge, and Guienne, from Nantes and La Rochelle⁶, their main interest lay naturally in shipping and commerce.

1681.
Sept. 6.

At Bristol in 1682 it was proposed to give the French just settled there the fines levied on the dissenters of the city⁷, and in other grotesque ways we may learn the distressed state of the new comers, and the kindly feeling with which they were received. *The good folk of Barnstaple*, said Jacques Fontaine⁸, who had made his escape in an English ship, and reached the Devon coast at Appledore, *shewed themselves full of compassion in our regard: they made us welcome in their houses, and entreated us with affectionate care. Thus has God given us fathers, mothers, brothers, sisters, in this strange land.*

1685.
Nov. 30.

---

¹ An old building at the end of Shute-street was granted by the lord of the manor to a French congregation about 1692, and their worship there lasted for a century: pp. 127 ff.

² The church at Dartmouth is at least coeval with that at Stonehouse, but it is not heard of after 1748: p. 131. Its nonconformist character is shewn by a letter of July 5 1723 among the Wake papers, 27. nr 119.

³ S Olave's church, for which the parishioners had no use, was appropriated to the French shortly after the Recall: Burn, 129 ff.

⁴ *Gazette* cited in the *Ulster Journal of Archaeology*, 3. 214; Belfast 1855, quarto. The *Historie van de Vervolging* reckons 300 refugees in the town by the winter of 1685: 3. 62. Their poverty and number appealed above most to the national charity.

⁵ The French silk-manufacture had existed here since 1650. The congregation was broken up about 1760: Burn, 132 f.

⁶ This suggestion of the corporation,—verily ἄλλων ἰατρὸς αὐτὸς ἕλκεσι βρύων,—is quoted from a periodical publication in Smiles, 349 n.

⁷ Letter of Mme de Soyres, widow of the last French minister at Bristol, March 7 1838; in Burn, 124 f.

⁸ *Mémoires*, 173.

Cordiality however soon turned to jealousy as the denizens clashed with or excelled in the crafts of the people. Fontaine, for instance, removing to Bridgewater and Taunton, caused the townsmen no small displeasure at his interference with their business. He was once brought before the mayor of Taunton to prove his right to carry on his trades: for this ready worker applied himself indifferently to the occupations of preacher, grocer, and wool-carder. He remained but on sufferance until an opportunity offered of going to Ireland. This instance is typical of the difficulties that troubled the French immigrants, quick in finding out means of livelihood in the midst of the slower, more conventional English people.

Isolated settlements were therefore more or less temporary; and the history of those at Winchelsea, Rye[1], Dover[2], Sandwich[3], Faversham[4], and Yarmouth[5], would be only a recital of what has been said of the western sea-ports. They were thoroughfares by which the refugees for the most part went on their way to some known colony, and especially to the old establishments of their kindred at Norwich and Canterbury. To Norwich[6] their arrival was peculiarly welcome; for earlier

---

[1] The Walloon community at Winchelsea was formed as early as 1569 or even 1560: that at Rye is probably contemporary. The latter had the use of the parish church for two services of a Sunday, from April 18 1682; *Sussex archaeological Collections*, 13. 202. Winchelsea had at one time a cambric manufacture: Burn, 96 f.

[2] Founded in 1646, this church is described by its minister, L'Escot, in a letter of January 12 17[19]20, as ' une église petite à la vérité, mais paisible, et composée de fort honnêtes gens, parmi lesquels je jouis d'une grande satisfaction.' Dover was even then a great place of passage for the French, and their church was much in need of help: Wake papers, 27. nr 115.

[3] The congregation dates from 1568: its services were held in S Peter's church. It is not heard of after 1737.

[4] This congregation appears in 1696 and 1706: it was a cure 'worth little': Burn 98.

[5] A Walloon settlement of 1568: Smiles, 123.

[6] The Flemish colony seems to date from 1336, the Dutch and Walloon from 1564: Burn, 59 ff. It was in this year that the Walloons were given the bishop's chapel, afterwards the church of S Mary Tombland: Smiles, 133 f.

in the century the rigour of Bishop Wren had induced numbers to leave the country, *to the lessening the wealthy manufacture there of kerseys and narrow cloths, and, which was worse, transporting that mystery into foreign parts* [1]. The damage was undone by the new influx, which restored the trade to its former prosperity, and brought in many branches of industry previously unused there [2].

Different was its effect upon Canterbury. The Walloon weavers who had settled in this city in the time of Henry the Eighth, increased by various later emigrants from France, numbered about thirteen hundred in 1665: in 1676 they were incorporated as a company of the city [3], with a hall at the Blackfriars [4]. The first result of the exodus of 1685 was a great accession to their numbers: in 1694 they had a thousand looms, and thrice as many workers. But the great manufacture that had grown up by this time in Spitalfields, gradually withdrew the industry from Canterbury, which soon came to suffer as well from the importation of silks and calicoes from the East Indies [5]. In 1719 two-thirds of the looms had stopped; at the end of the century only ten master-workers remained.

But the French population did not diminish with equal rapidity [6]. In 1709 it had sufficient vitality to form a secession [7]

---

[1] Clarendon, *History of the Rebellion*, I. clxxxiv.

[2] Such were lustrings, paduasoys, brocades, and tabinets; also cutlery and clockmaking: Smiles, 336. In 1703 the export wool-trade was said to excel that under Charles II by a million a year: *Conference of the House of Lords with the Commons concerning the Bill to prohibit occasional Conformity*, 24; in the pref. to *les Plaintes des Protestants*, 23. But a boon above the reckoning of financiers was the settlement at Norwich in 1685 of a Dieppe surgeon, Gaston Martineau, the ancestor of a family known in every side of our literature.

[3] The number was then reckoned at 2500; but this must include English apprentices.

[4] Noticed in 1687: Burn, 39.   [5] P. 41.

[6] It had other occupations besides weaving. Burn enumerates, from Hasted's *Kent*, 421, such handicrafts as clockmaking, cutlery, and hardware, and the manufacture of surgical instruments: p. 17.

[7] Some fifty or sixty families, says their minister, Jean Charpentier, in a

from the presbyterian congregation that had worshipped since the days of Elizabeth in the undercroft of the cathedral, and to set up a 'uniform' or episcopal service in a malt-house near by[1]. The two communities lived on side by side for some thirty-six years: the Anglicans returned to the Calvinistic body[2], and ended by converting their brethren to the formularies of the English church at the beginning of the present century. The members now did not exceed the number of eighty communicants, but tradition has continued the service to this day.

The French have left their impress on most parts of southern England. Some joined the Walloon lace-makers at Buckingham, Newport Pagnell, and Stony Stratford, whence the manufacture spread into several of the neighbouring counties[3]. The old settlement at Wandsworth[4], then slowly disappearing, was called into fresh life by a large number of furriers and manufacturers of beaver hats, chiefly from the town of Caudebec, which gave a name to its most famous industry. For forty years, until a theft restored the art, France was reduced to import all the best goods of this kind from England; even the cardinals of the Holy College fetched their hats from Wandsworth[5]. And at the end of last century the works in the village,

---

letter of May 7 1716, among the Wake papers, vol. 28. The congregation originated, according to a letter of one of its members, of about the same date, 'par la haine et les fausses accusations de ceux du milieu desquels nous sommes sortis.' Yet the rev. Pierre le Sueur, who succeeded Charpentier in the following October, speaks of the 'bonne correspondance' existing between the two communities: in the same collection.

[1] Burn, 51. A second independent body seems to have existed about 1716, according to a letter in the volume of the Wake correspondence above cited.

[2] About 1745: Burn, 54.

[3] The counties of Oxford, Northampton, Cambridge, Bedford, and the borders of Bucks and Herts are mentioned: Smiles, 337.

[4] Its chapel, nearly opposite the parish church, was opened in 1573, and enlarged in 1685. Its restoration between 1809 and 1831 proved only the prelude to its extinction: Burn, 117 ff.

[5] Weiss, 1. 334: cp. Macpherson, 2. 650; Waddington, *Protestantisme en Normandie*, 36 n.

though much reduced, were still existent[1]. Less successful was the attempt of one Passavant to revive the decayed Walloon tapestry manufacture[2] at Fulham: he soon moved to Exeter, but the remnant of the colony he had brought seems to reappear afterwards in the three congregations at Chelsea and in that at Hammersmith[3].

Other trades were created by the exiles of the Recall. The fine linens and sailcloth of Ipswich, as of Hamburg, are among these. The English ambassador at Paris, in view of a war, coveted the addition of sailcloth to the national industries, and his wish was fulfilled in 1681[4]. The growth of Spitalfields pushed many of its weavers into the country to north and east; to Hoxton, Stepney, and Bow[5]. Some went to Bromley in Essex to print calicoes[6]. The glass-makers left their shops in the Savoy to find cheaper fuel in Sussex[7]. Paper-mills were set up at Laverstoke on the Itchin in Hampshire, by Henry de Portal, still the chief of paper-works[8]: others were established in various parts of Kent, at Maidstone, and along the Darent; one at Glasgow, the first in Scotland.

---

[1] Lyson, *Environs*, 1. 503; 1792: in Burn 118, who remarks the permanence of name of The French Burial-Ground.

[2] It had received encouragement from Charles II, who carried an Act to promote the immigration of tapestry and linen-cloth manufacturers (15 Car. II. c. 15): Burn, 260.

[3] The chapel in Cook's Grounds, Chelsea, is noticed in 1714: another was in Little Chelsea. Dubourdieu, writing in 1718, mentions a third: *Appeal*, 53 f. Of these one, certainly, survived until 1729. That at Hammersmith emerges in 1701 and 1706.

[4] It was at first maintained at the charges of the London Walloon diaconate: Smiles, 337.

[5] The increase on this side of London may be indicated by the growth of Wapping into a parish, that of S John, in 1694; Macpherson, 2. 655.

[6] There was in 1690 an establishment of this sort at Richmond in Surrey: Burn, 259.

[7] Smiles, 331. The glass was introduced by Abraham Thevenart in 1688: Burn, 253.

[8] The Portals retain to this day the monopoly of Bank-of-England notepaper: Smiles, 332 ff., from Baron Frederick de Portal's *Descendants des Albigeois*; Paris 1860.

Edinburgh received a number of cambric-workers. The burghers built them a large house on the common north of the Green Side, long known as Little Picardy[1]; and in 1693 the city was charged to the amount of two thousand marks for the support of the manufactory. Others worked in silk, and planted mulberry-gardens on the slope of Moultrie's Hill[2]. Helped by a public alms[3], these Picard exiles fared prosperously, and maintained their native speech and manners, in a house itself of French fashion, until the middle of the eighteenth century[4].

1689. April 11.

Manufacturers formed the bulk of the French immigrants to this country[5]. The agricultural classes preferred Germany or the less peopled districts of Holland, as Friesland and Zeeland. Few only came to England. Poitevin exiles settled in Essex, at Thorpe-le-Soken[6]; others, perhaps, at Thorney Abbey and Whittlesey in Cambridgeshire, but of these the traces are faint and uncertain[7]. The reasons for this small ingress are to be

1683.

---

[1] W. Maitland, *History of Edinburgh*, 215; Edinburgh 1753, folio: who mentions the existence of a French chapel in the city. Cp. Agnew, 2. 313.

[2] Smiles disposes of the fancied Bourdeaux colony at Burdy House in Edinburgh: 338; as against the *Ulster Journal*, 1. 211 n.

[3] In the Proclamation of the Scottish Convention-Parliament, collection was to be made for Irish as well as French refugees: Agnew, 1. 60.

[4] They came from Cambray, Tournay, and Amiens: Rossier, *Protestants de Picardie*, 250 f.

[5] 'To the immigration,' says Macpherson, 3. 618, 'England owes the improvement of sundry manufactures of light woollen stuffs, of silk, linen, paper, glass, hats; the two last since brought to the utmost perfection by us. The silks called alamodes and lustrings were entirely owing to them; also brocades, satins, black and coloured mantuas, black padua-soys, ducapes, watered tabbies, black velvets; also watches, cutlery-ware, jacks, locks, surgeons' instruments, hardware, toys, &c.'

[6] On June 4 1683 the bishop of London licensed a French service in the neighbouring church of Beaumont. It was begun July 1, but the French of Thorpe-le-Soken preferred to worship in their own village, and were allowed to do so July 29. In 1685 they had leave to build a church, and this was opened March 4 1688. In 1726 it was closed 'for want of members:' Burn, 121 ff. Cp. Lièvre, *Protestants du Poitou*, 3. 359 n.

[7] See supplementary note vii.

found more in the intricacy and, as foreigners thought it, the insecurity of the English system of renting land [1], than in the special hazard of James the Second's reign. Hence it was not the farmer, but the craftsman, carrying his means of support in his hands or in his brain, that came to settle here; and rather than the country he chose the towns or large villages, where he could at once occupy himself in his handiwork, or whence, if need be, he could at once remove.

If the agricultural classes came in small number to England, they more than made up the deficiency by the great proportion they formed among those who crossed over to the continent of America. The history of this settlement has yet to be written, and it is not likely that its materials will be found on this side the Atlantic. I cannot therefore pretend more than to indicate a bare outline with little colour [2].

From the French coast there came but few directly, for their craft could rarely risk so long a voyage. Most on starting went to London, where they got their letters of denization [3], or they travelled through Germany into Holland [4], before they set sail for the new world. On their arrival they commonly met with cordial welcome, for the exiles of Lewis the Fourteenth were not the first huguenots who had taken refuge in America; and in several ways they found their social position arranged for them without any of that jealousy which troubled them in other countries.

One company, which left France in 1684 or 1685, was well received at Boston. The General Court of Massachusetts gave

---

[1] Georges le Sage, *Remarques sur l'Angleterre*, 1710 & 1711, 303 f.; Amsterdam 1715, duodecimo: whose explanation is accepted by Sayous, *le dix-huitième Siècle à l'Étranger*, 1. 23 n.; Paris, 1861.

[2] I have taken a few data from a supplementary chapter to the American translation of Weiss, 2. 283-333; New York 1854. But it would be hard to find a worse literary specimen or a more confused and contradictory set of statements than this appendix.

[3] See a letter written in the winter of 1687 by an exile at Boston in Massachusetts, in the *Bulletin*, 16. 69 ff.; 1867.

[4] Bancroft, *History of the United States*, 2. 180; ed. 3, Boston 1846.

1686. them eleven thousand acres where the village of Oxford now stands¹. There they all went, leaving but twenty households behind²; and they quickly changed the wilderness assigned them into an orchard of pear-trees, and a garden of roses and currant-bushes. They built a fort against the attacks of the

1696. Indians, who at one time almost destroyed their labour and drove many back to Boston³; but in spite of danger and difficulty, the little colony grew and became strong. It was not now isolated, for a French church had by this time arisen at Boston⁴.

1664.
Jan. 24.   New York was earlier peopled by the French. In 1664 a Dutch merchant there had informed the government of letters from La Rochelle telling of the wish of some to emigrate; and a Resolution was passed promising to help them and to grant them lands without charge⁵. So the already existing French settlement in Staten Island received its second foundation, and had its clergyman as early as 1675⁶. But the greatest influx into the city of New York dates from the Recall; and this is also the origin of the new colony in Long Island. Some six thousand acres obtained by purchase not by free grant, were the lot of the refugees; and the planters of New Rochelle

---

¹ Abiel Holmes, *Annals of America*, 1. 324; ed. 2, Cambridge, *U. S. A.* 1829: R. Baird, *Religion in the United States of America*, 165; Glasgow 1844: Weiss, [app.] 2. 318 f.

² *Bulletin*, 16. 79. Holmes, indeed, says only thirty families colonised Oxford: they were aided by contributions from Boston, Salem, and other places; 1. 417 and n. 5.

³ This date is given as that of the foundation, not the revival, of the plantation, in *the Huguenots in France and America*, 2. 62; ed. 2, Cambridge, *U. S. A.* 1843.

⁴ Vol. 2. 68; where the date is given as 1704: the brick church in School-street is however mentioned in 1696; Holmes 1. 417.—There was a certain strictness in the admission of the French since an Order of the governor and council in 1692. It had been observed that 'many of a contrary religion and interest' had intruded themselves among the huguenots into the privileges of the state: vol. 1. 441 & n.

⁵ Weiss, [app.] 2. 303.

⁶ In Richmond county: [app.] 2. 315.

bestowed anxious pains on the reclaiming of the wild country. For many years they could not support a church, and these zealous people, after labouring hard the week through, spent much of the nights of Saturday and Sunday in walking the sixteen miles to and from the nearest church, at New York [1]. Their clearing and their industry repaid them in time, and in 1704 they had reached a measure of prosperity which allowed them to build their wooden church of Le Saint Esprit [2]. In a country of so mixed a race as New England, and of a bent so identified with Calvinistic traditions, the huguenots became readily absorbed into the older population: the Act of Naturalisation of 1703 [3] seemed rather to formulate a fact than to involve any alteration in their standing.

The southern states called for a more organised settlement. In 1679 Charles the Second had embarked a number of refugees in two ships, to plant vines and olives in South Carolina; and in 1690 William the Third sent out new colonies into Maryland and Virginia [4]. In Virginia they were placed on James River, about twenty miles from Richmond [5]. Here they planted the Monacan settlement, increased in 1699 and the following years by perhaps six hundred new huguenot families [6]. Monacan was made into a parish in 1700, and

---

[1] Weiss, *Histoire*, 1. 377.

[2] It was afterwards rebuilt in stone and adopted the episcopal order. To the first Queen Anne gave the church plate: Weiss, [app.] 2. 304 and 309.

[3] Baird, 165.

[4] In these states naturalisation had been allowed since 1666 and 1671 respectively: as above.

[5] Pp. 166 f. *Account of the Settlements in America*, 2. 216, ed. 3. 1760; by Edmund Burke. It is in Virginia that we get the last glimpse of the family of Jacques Fontaine, often before referred to: his four sons, the eldest, Pierre, having been ordained in the English church, went across in 1715 and 1717. They were accompanied by their sister, who married a M Maury and became the ancestress of a distinguished Virginian family: *Mémoires*, 340 and 343.

[6] Holmes mentions the arrival in 1699 of some three hundred huguenots, 'soon after followed by others,' who settled twenty miles above the falls of James River: 1. 472.

exempted from the usual assessments for seven, then for another seven, years. Its 'model' farms were the admiration of the state, and everything was tending to prosperity, when an unhappy dispute caused a secession to Trent River in North Carolina. These last were ultimately forced by the Indians into South Carolina, which already was the most flourishing of the French settlements. From the ports of Holland alone there came almost a thousand fugitives[1]. The climate and the soil naturally attracted them; and we may be sure that, of the six hundred whom the English committee sent to America[2] in 1687, by far the majority came to Carolina.

Here they settled first at Charleston, where they had a church, the rallying post of their several plantations near[3]. Exiles from Picardy established themselves at Strawberry Ferry[4]; others, in 'French Santee' increased their clearings from Wambaw Creek, on the bank of the Santee, till they joined their fellow-refugees at Orange Quarter, and built Jamestown. The swamps that extended far on each side of the river had been drained by the beginning of the eighteenth century, and the country was 'rapidly acquiring the look of the best cultivated parts of France or England[5].' Throughout the state the French planted vines and olive-trees; in Charleston itself they not only built several streets, soon filled with stores and workshops, but they even set up manufactures of silk and wool. Admitted to the privileges of natives[6] they did not forget their corporate spirit; and the influence of *these good, affable, and affectionate people*, as Lawson described them in 1701[7], was not lost upon the austere puritans who had previously reigned in grave isolation in the colony.

1709.

1699.
Mar. 10.

---

[1] Weiss, *Histoire*, 1. 381.
[2] For this we are surely to understand by the 'West Indies' of the *Extract out of the Books of Account* for the year.
[3] Bancroft, 2. 182; Holmes, 1. 433.   [4] Rossier, 232.
[5] Weiss, 1. 395.
[6] Bancroft, 3. 17; or 1696, Holmes, 1. 460; Baird, 165.
[7] *Historical Account of South Carolina and Georgia*, 1. 108, in Weiss, 1. 396.

It was not, however, at once that the huguenots became reconciled to their new homes and new circumstances. After the peace of Rijswijk, some four hundred families declared themselves anxious to join the French colony in Louisiana. The refusal with which they were met [1] did much to fix them in their settlements and to turn their eyes from the now extinguished hope of return.

The last immigration with which we are concerned is that mixed multitude of German and French Calvinists, thrust from the Rhenish Pale, whose need called out for English pity in 1709. A broadside of the day [2] tells how *These poor refugees are the survivers of them who during a short intervall of peace had built up a few cottages, and began to cultivate their country, in hopes of some means of subsistance, but . . . seeing themselves in a manner starving, and destitute of all conveniencies of humane life, have thrown themselves into the arms of Britain's charity.* They were *A very industrious people, used to hard labour,* and the country would not be the loser by a present exercise of help. But the arrival of four thousand people, and *More daily expected,* was a problem not without embarrassment. Nearly seven thousand were, in fact, encamped for a time on Blackheath [3], and the archbishop of Canterbury lodged above three hundred in the barns of Lambeth House. But a permanent relief was not long preparing. In July the queen issued a Brief commanding a subscription [4]. She took two hundred into her

1709. May.

July 6.

---

[1] Sir Charles Lyell, *second Visit to the United States*, 159; 1849.

[2] *Brief Representation of the distressed State of above four thousand poor German Protestants fled out of the fruitful Palatinat by the Rhine and Neckar*: among the Wake papers, vol. 17.

[3] Macpherson, 3. 5 f.

[4] Letter of Archbishop Tenison, July 7. The only obstacle was the presence of some catholics in the crowd. 'I am sorry,' wrote the archbishop to Bishop Wake, July 28, ' to understand by yours of the 25th instant that any of our order should be frighted with the noise of a *lyon in the way.* The Palatines are 10,000; among them are some papists, but their number is inconsiderable. When we had here at Lambeth 329 Palatines in our barns, there were but eleven papists among them': Wake papers, as above.

employ[1], and shipped three thousand to New York. Some stayed in the city; others went on to the banks of the Hudson, and finally established themselves in Pennsylvania[2]. If we add this number to the sum of the earlier immigrations, remembering that, at the beginning of the eighteenth century the entire European population of New England did not exceed two hundred thousand[3], we shall readily conclude the added weight of the French factor and the extent of its influence.

---

[1] Letter of the same, July 16; among the Wake papers, as above.

[2] Macpherson, 3. 6. In June 1710, says Holmes, Colonel Robert Hunter arrived as governor of New York, ' bringing with him 2700 Palatines; many of whom settled in the city of New York; others on a tract of several thousand acres in the manor of Livingston; while others went on to Pennsylvania': 1. 502 f.

[3] Baird, 167 f. In 1681 the number of working hands in Virginia was reckoned at fourteen thousand: Holmes, 1. 401.

CHAPTER IX.

THE FRENCH IN THE ENGLISH REVOLUTION: THE COLONY IN IRELAND.

IN the different counties of England the history of the French settlement suffered no break by the dynastic arrangement which made William of Orange king: the revolution mainly affected it by a great increase to the dispersed population. London however, so bound up was the town-life with that of the court, saw the position of the refugees completely changed. It was now fashionable to support these aliens, who had been received hitherto under protest and with suspicion: and it now befitted the courtier to frequent their churches.

For the share of the French soldiery in the success of the stadhouder was no light one: and his anxiety to secure their services was met by a steady adhesion which justified his confidence in them when enlisted under his command. At the time that they crowded into Holland his first desire was to form them into two regiments [1]. But when such an addition to the forces was proposed to the Estates of Holland, the burgesses demurred before reversing their favourable scheme of retrenchment. By a perfunctory form they promised to send up the matter to the Estates-General; and no action would probably have been taken [2] but for the prince's resolve not to let the opportunity slip. He at once took the officers into his own pay, and the

---

[1] Count d'Avaux, *Negociations*, 5. 203.
[2] What the Estates did was practically to shelve the question: Koenen, *Vluchtelingen in Nederland*, 86. To speak, with Count d'Avaux, of their having 'refused' is to say too much.

1686.
Jan. 16.

Estates were driven to a compliance. They voted a sum of 40,000 gulden[1], ultimately perhaps 180,000[2], to maintain them until vacancies should occur in the regular regiments: but, with the guarded prudence of the nation, they procured the amount from the fund appropriated to the secret charges of the diplomatic establishment. The recollection of 1672 made them stay before courting a new breach with France, and they gladly accepted Fagel's device which saved them from giving a public welcome to those traitors who, in the language of Count d'Avaux, had 'deserted' from the fleur-de-lys[3]. William's point was however gained, and the army was increased, if in number, much more in efficiency[4]. A college of French cadets was established at Utrecht[5]; and the older officers were dispersed among nine fortified towns[6], to give example and excite ambition of their fine and proved discipline.

Indeed, when the stadhouder enrolled afterwards some entirely French regiments in the view of his English enterprise, it is not so much their number as their advanced training that calls for note. At their head stood Schomberg, who had once left France lest he should be found fighting against his faith to support a despotism he abhorred, and who now left a like position of supreme command in Brandenburg[7] to come

---

[1] Count d'Avaux, 5. 228.

[2] Vol. 6. 52: but the precise fact is uncertain; Berg, 1. 26 f. The distribution was to colonels 1800 livres, majors 1100, captains 900, lieutenants 500, ensigns and cadets 400; Count d'Avaux, 5. 219 f.: the last figure nearly as much as that of a married minister; cp. above, p. 51, n. 7.

[3] The oat that bound them to the Estates of Holland was of a peculiar stringency. It may be read in the *Mémoires* of Bostaquet, 340.

[4] Berg describes the pitiful state of the Dutch cavalry before this time: 1. 24 n.

[5] It was at the expense of the Estates-General: vol. 1. 26.

[6] Weiss names Breda, Maastricht, Bergen-op-Zoom, den Bosch, Zutphen, Arnhem, Grave, Utrecht, and the Hague: 2. 45.

[7] Charles Ancillon, *Histoire de l'Établissement des François réfugiéz dans les États de s. a. e. Brandebourg*, 172 f.; Berlin 1690, duodecimo. It may be noticed that the story of Schomberg's presence at the meeting at Cleve of the Great Elector and the prince of Orange in 1686 has its refutation in

to the more present succour of the protestant cause in another country. His regiment of horse in the new armament was officered by 144 of his companions in exile. The two dragoon regiments of the prince of Orange contained fifty-four more [1]; there were besides sixty volunteers attached to other regiments. Of foot there were as many as 556 officers [2] commanding 2250 men [3]. In an army of 15,000 it is hard to overstate the importance of the French contingent, schooled as it had been in the finest discipline of Europe, and experienced in all the campaigns which the vanity of their king had created. Disbanded on William's acceptance of the English crown, it was reconstituted in much greater force for the Irish campaign, and made up four regiments, Lord Galway's horse and the three foot regiments of La Caillemotte, La Melloniere, and Cambon [4]. It was further swelled by numerous recruits, whom sympathy with the protestant revolution and the fame of its success,

---

the fact that the marshal did not leave his first place of exile, Portugal, until the following year: L. von Ranke, *History of England*, 4. 408 n.

[1] *Mémoires de Bostaquet*, 195 & 341 f.

[2] Count d'Avaux, 5. 305; in Berg, 1. 28.

[3] J. Michelet, *Louis XIV et la Révocation*, 309 f.; Paris 1874. Weiss has here fallen into a curious mistake. By adding the 180 officers mentioned by Count d'Avaux to the 556 officers of foot, he gets the total 736; which he recites again as dispersed among the Dutch regiments, thus doubling the real number: 1. 295, cp. 2. 46 f. He seems to have read the account in Berg, 1. 28 carelessly. I do not know where he found the thirty-four officers of William's body-guard, 1. 296; and Count d'Avaux's number 180 must be corrected by the exact list in Bostaquet.

[4] The cavalry numbered 689, and the infantry each 967: T. Trenchard, *short History of standing Armies*, 53; 1698 (reprint, 1731). The death of the younger Ruvigny at the Boyne gave his regiment to Belcastel; and in 1698 Cambon's became Lord Lifford's. Another regiment, that of Miremont, with a roll-call of 898, was at first partly, in the end wholly, French: Agnew, 3. 175-186. The statement of Misson, 362, that in 1698 there were eleven regiments in English pay has been repeated by G. de Félice: it is justly suspected by Mr Smiles, 266 n. Perhaps it arose from adding to the English establishment the seven regiments of foot formed by refugee French in Savoy when Lewis attacked the duchy. But so, the reckoning is too small, and forgets the cavalry regiment there: *Bibliothèque des Sciences et des beaux Arts*, 14. 165; the Hague 1760, duodecimo.

upheld by sedulous solicitation, had drawn from Brandenburg, from the Lower Rhine, and from the cities of Leman.

How nobly this army fought in the ensuing war is a commonplace of history: its 'decisive part[1]' in the defence of protestantism in the island has of late been given its just prominence. The picture of the death of Schomberg, and his appeal to the instinct of revenge[2], when he saw the dragoons of Lauzun come up, at last to be combatted on equal terms, addresses itself so strongly to the imagination, that one is apt to lose sight of the point of view in which the refugee soldiers, unless in the excitement of battle, themselves regarded their duty[3]. But we may know from Baron d'Avyan[4], who commanded a battalion at the Boyne, that their strenuousness in pushing on the re-conquest was owing to a fixed belief not only that it was the cause of God but also that it was *The preamble of their return to France*[5].

It was nothing less than this reason that led them in England, as everywhere, to promote that party which expressed the most vigorous defiance to Lewis the Fourteenth. They looked forward thus to a restoration to their country, purified, they fondly hoped, by opposition and defeat. The chances of rousing the mass of their fellows in France and extorting a revival of the Edict of Nantes were eagerly canvassed: it was rumoured that Lewis's council itself was for the design[6]. In the negotiations for the peace of Rijswijk their interests were prominently

---

[1] Charles Read, intr. to Bostaquet, xxv.

[2] 'Allons, mes amis, rappelez votre courage et vos ressentiments: voilà vos persécuteurs'; cited from Paul de Rapin, who was present, in Read, xxx n.

[3] It is stated in the pref. to *les Plaintes des Protestants*, 22 and 30, that 7000 French perished by the sword or by sickness in the Irish campaign. The figure may be only four times too great.

[4] So, with M Read, I spell the name, comparing the form *d'Avène* or *d'Avesne*, in which it occurs in Mr Agnew's lists, 2. 181. Weiss and Mr Smiles give *d'Avejan*.

[5] Antoine Court, *Histoire des Églises réformées*, MS in Read, xxvi. n.

[6] Gilbert, letter to the earl of Galway, in the *Mémoires envoyés à Londres*, 30 f.

brought forward[1]. The scheme was to erect a protestant church in France on the model of the Anglican, the nomination of bishops being dictated by the king[2]. But in the web of political considerations the huguenots were lost sight of, just as, in a later opportunity, they were disappointed at Gertruidenberg and Utrecht.

Meanwhile their enthusiasm reacted upon the English. 'In the church of England,' says Leopold von Ranke[3], 'a consciousness of its protestant character was awakened most vividly' by the French troubles. 'The exiles stood far nearer to the nonconformists in creed and ritual than to the high-church party, but no regard was paid to this. Henry Compton, bishop of London, devoted to the unhappy strangers an attention which they could ordinarily have expected only from one who was in complete agreement with them.' In fact they helped not a little to formulate the public opinion that offered the kingdom to William of Orange[4]. It is not within the scope of this essay to trace the course of events which produced a revulsion from this warlike protestant spirit[5]. The

---

[1] The movement was a general one. The Swiss refugees applied to Jurieu, those in Brandenburg to the elector: as above.

[2] The *Mémoires* just named speak of an analogous proposal to form a 'despotic government' for the French church in England, subject to the authority of the archbishop of Canterbury, which fell through in consequence of Tillotson's death; 35 ff. With these schemes we may compare that which was discussed between Archbishop Wake and Dupin in 1717 to 1720 relative to a union of the English and the *Gallican* church: *Projet d'Union*; Oxford 1864.   [3] *History of England*, 4. 267 f.

[4] The fact has been commonly ignored or depreciated by the English historians: it has been given its fit place by foreigners, Capefigue and Michelet; cp. F. Ancillon, *Tableau*, 4. 305 ff.; *Life of Rachael, Lady Russell*, xlix, 1819, quarto.

[5] 'We blame the king for he relies too much on strangers, Germans, hugonots, and Dutch,' says the *True-born Englishman*; see Agnew, 1. 36. A sketch of the refugees—' these hot-headed and flippant-tongued gentlemen,'—after contemporary writings, may be found in a clever but desultory article in the *Edinburgh Review*, 99. 479 ff.; April 1854. The internal quarrels of the refuge clergy may be found in miserable detail in such books as Lions, *l'Ex-Jésuite démasqué*, London, 1717; Dubourdieu's *Appeal to the English Nation*; Michael Malard, *Address and Representation of Grievances*, 1720.

huguenots, by the time this new reaction came on, were too firmly established to suffer much by it. We are only concerned to notice how, by the impulse they gave to trade, they served to develop those whiggish principles, unconnected with favour or disfavour to foreigners, that effected or at least consolidated the Hanoverian succession [1].

1689. April 14.

April 24.

Among William's first acts as king of England was to appoint a committee to enquire into the necessities of the French immigrants. Their Report stated *That the French ministers and divers other protestants of France, fled hither for refuge, being summoned, appeared, and expressed a high sense of their gratitude for the generosity and charity of this House in taking their distressed case into consideration; and to shew how ready they were to manifest their fidelity to the Government of this nation, they represented how the youngest and strongest of their body were lately formed into three regiments, who were ready to lay down their lives in defence of the protestant religion and liberties of England; that there are nearly twenty thousand more of them who exercise their trades in divers parts of this kingdom.... but that there still remain above two thousand persons, some of them old, others infants, others sick and impotent, but all unable to provide for themselves; divines, physicians, merchants, gentlemen, common people, many of them heretofore rich and flourishing in their own country, but are now reduced to the utmost misery, and must infallibly perish and starve, unless assisted by this House* [2].

April 25.

The immediate result of this Report was an annual grant of 17,200*l.*; and on the following day there appeared a royal Proclamation for the encouraging French Protestants to transport themselves to this Kingdom [3], in which their majesties promised to do their *Endeavour in all reasonable ways and means so to support, aid, and assist them in their several and respective trades and ways of livelihood, as that their living and being in this country may be comfortable and easy to them.* The invitation

---

[1] See, above all, Lecky, *eighteenth Century*, 1. 187-202.
[2] *Ulster Journal of Archaeology*, 1. 218.
[3] Agnew, 1. 35; N. Tindal, continuation of P. de Rapin, 3. 89.

was successful, and it should seem that fully twice as many immigrants came after the Revolution as had come before. In 1698 one counted twenty-two French churches in London [1] and a hundred ministers enjoying a state salary, besides those that lived at their own charges. *Of this multitude of poor exiles, we are told, barely three thousand are at alms or, as they say, on the Committee* [2]. It is therefore remarkable that every attempt made to naturalise them was unsuccessful until 1709 [3], and that this statute was actually repealed within three years [4].

1709. Mar. 23.
1712. Feb. 9.

The truth is that the English have never taken kindly to foreigners; our corporations, ever jealous of their immunities, would seldom waive their immunities even in favour of exiles suffering for religion. In other countries the good-will of the people or the pervasive authority of the king accorded them a larger measure of comfort. We are not therefore to wonder that not above fifty thousand of them did in fact come to live in England [5].

---

[1] Misson, 119. Malard in 1720 reckoned 'about twenty'; *Address*, 113.
[2] P. 363.
[3] The immediate cause of this Act (7 Anne c. 9), which allowed naturalisation on oath and reception of the Lord's supper in some reformed congregation in the kingdom, was the arrival of the crowd from the Palatinate; see above, pp. 99 f.
[4] The tory government had already in 1711 moved its repeal: they carried it on the second attempt. It seems that at the first bringing forward the refugees were so frightened that more than two thousand took advantage of the act. When it was sought to reinstate it in 1748 and 1751 the motion was twice defeated. At length in 1774 naturalisation was made possible on the condition of seven years' residence (14 George III. c. 84): Macpherson, 3. 5 f., 22, 260 f., 557; Agnew, 1. 57 f.
[5] Macpherson, 3. 617. Bishop Burnet says, 'In all there came over first and last between forty and fifty thousand of that nation'; *History of his own Times*, 1. 664; followed by Hume, *History of England*, 8. 165; ed. 1825. The *Bibliothèque des Sciences*, &c., 14. 163, allows more than seventy thousand. Even in 1687, an unfavourable year, as many as 497 'new converts' were readmitted to the church in Threadneedle Street at one meeting in May: Smiles, 341. Erman and Reclam therefore go beyond their authorities when they assert that owing to the hatred of French manners the Refuge in England was disproportionately small, though it may be admitted that during the troubles that preceded the Revolution many left England for

The distinguishing characteristic of the settlement in England since the Revolution was the gradual concentration of the dispersed manufactories into the outskirts of London. The colony in the Spitalfields grew with amazing rapidity, now fed most of all from the coasts of Normandy. As late as 1863 they had a Société Normande, the first provident club in England[1], besides several similar institutions[2]. But, except in these social or convivial associations, the French by degrees lost their corporate unity. Even in 1725 one of their ministers could speak of the difficulty of filling up a vacancy in his church *By reason of the small and daily diminishing number of French ministers in London*[3]: and in time the colony had to seek its ministers in Holland, Switzerland, and Geneva[4]. The decrease was con-

---

Brandenburg or elsewhere: *Mémoires*, 1. 249. In illustration of this last fact we may cite the case of Suzanne de Robillard who afterwards became the mother of General de la Motte-Fouqué. Her *Récit* in the *Bulletin*, 17, 493 f., 1868, tells how she escaped from La Rochelle in the spring of 1687, and was thrown on the coast of South Devon. She would have stayed at Exeter, 'le pays y étant beau et bon,' had it not been from a fear of persecution, accentuated by the Declaration of Indulgence. So she settled at Voorburg, near the Hague. The preface to *les Plaintes des Protestants* merely does not estimate the refuge in England as greater than those in other countries : 20.

[1] It was founded in 1703. M Waddington enumerates, besides the Société des Réfugiés Normands, the Société de Lintot, and the Club Normand; the last never admitting any but persons of proved Norman extraction: *Protestantisme en Normandie*, 17 f. There was also in Spitalfields a quarter claiming a Picard origin: Rossier, *Picardie*. 251.

[2] Maitland mentions the French Almshouse in Black Eagle-street, and a house of charity called The Soup, the latter as existing about 1715, and both in Spitalfields: 2. 1303. Above all, there was the French Hospital, which a bequest of James Gastigny in 1708, sustained by a grant from the royal bounty eight years later, founded in the parish of S Luke's. It was incorporated by royal charter, July 24 1718. Its motto, *Dominus providebit*, gave it the current name of La Providence: Burn, 181-184; Agnew, 1. 73 f.

[3] Letter of Le Moine, minister of Brown's Lane Chapel, Spitalfields, to Archbishop Wake, September 3 1725, among the Wake papers, vol. 27, nr 116. The inducement, it is true, was not great; Le Moine's income was only 40*l.*, and that of the other ministers in London only 60*l.*

[4] Sayous, *le dix-huitième Siècle à l'Étranger*, 1. 26.

nected with the general acceptance of the Anglican ritual¹, which was but a step to the entire abandonment of huguenot traditions².

The French communities in the counties of England grew smaller, and the society in London became assimilated to the rest of the population: but meanwhile Ireland was made the object of extensive schemes of colonisation³. There was no trouble here about the status of the immigrants, for the rights of natives were obtained by a simple oath before the lord chancellor⁴. The government was in fact only too glad to receive them⁵; and the emigration of the catholics made such an access of industrious people the more to be desired. Had William the Third and Lord Galway been able to carry their point with parliament, Ireland would have received several thousand huguenots whom the Swiss cantons were unable to house⁶. As it was, the settlement assumed sufficient dimensions to call for a detailed notice.

---

¹ This was the case at Brown's Lane, where the change had increased the attendance. Yet Le Moine observes 'Les François de ce quartier ont eu jusques ici tant d'esloignement pour les communes prières,' that the embarrassment had almost neutralised the benefit: as above.

² There is this much truth in the comment of Erman and Reclam, 'So they ceased to be French churches': as above.

³ Besides those mentioned below, there is one of which I have been unable to trace more than the origin, but which I am assured was actually formed on the duke of Ormond's estates. The beginning was a letter to the duke by one Raselle, in which the writer, with profession of strong loyalty on his own part and on that of his fellow-exiles, says, 'Il plaira donc à mgr de voir si lestat souhaitteroit de peupler l'Irlande de bons protestans et de tres fideles suiets, apres quoy on prendroit des mesures iustes pour faire reüssir un si charitable proiet': among the Carte papers in the Bodleian Library, vol. 216, nr 47.   ⁴ Agnew, I. 58.

⁵ As early indeed as September 19 1662 the Irish Parliament had passed an Act for encouraging protestant strangers and others to inhabit Ireland. It expired in seven years, and was renewed for a like term in 1692: *Ulster Journal of Archaeology*, 4. 200 f.

⁶ The request was made to the Estates-General in 1689, that 4000 should be sent to Ireland; Address in the State-Papers chamber at Amsterdam, in Koenen, 53 f. In February 1692 Galway wrote that the king

The French officers whom the close of the war of 1689-1691 left unemployed[1] retired for the most part to Portarlington in Queen's County. The estates which included this village had been granted on a custodian lease to the Earl of Galway in 1692; complete ownership was given in 1696[2]. He formed the project of creating a 'model' French town by the co-operation of the disbanded officers. For this purpose he built about a hundred houses[3], which were inhabited by the end of the century by some hundred and fifty families. Most seem to have come in 1699[4], but Galway had founded the French church as early as 1694[5]. He also built an English church and two schools. It was here that Isaac Dumont de Bostaquet, whose memoirs give the huguenot character in its truest and most genial phase, spent the last years of his life[6]. But it was not only officers, but also private gentlemen, that colonised Portarlington. One reason existed in the excellent schools[7], to which some of the great names of Ireland owed their education. And the aristocratical temper of the place made it a refuge of the noblesse in the days even of the French Revolution.

1696. June 26.

---

approved the plan; *Bulletin*, 9. 269 f.: and another letter of his, dated January [20] 30 169[2]3, shows that William had not forgotten it; but the project was now reduced to 600 households: *Bulletin*, 10. 68 f. This modified colonisation took effect in the following spring: Agnew, 1. 244.

[1] In 1692 there were 121 such officers on pension in Ireland. Dumont de Bostaquet, as captain, was entitled to 114*l*. 1*s*. 3*d*. a year, but seldom received the full amount: *Mémoires*, 348, n. 2.

[2] On the outlawry of Sir Patrick Trant and other circumstances relative to the settlement, see a prolix and pretentious paper by Sir Erasmus D. Borrowes in the *Ulster Journal of Archaeology*, 3. 63 f., 216 f., 1855; 6. 339 f., 1858.

[3] About 1700 there actually were 130 houses, more or less; but Galway did not build them all. For the fact, see the *Ulster Journal*, 3. 216 f.

[4] Vol. 3. 66.

[5] Service began June 3: it remained French until Sept. 20, 1816; Read, intr. to Bostaquet, xli. n. The minister was paid by government; Burn, 250.

[6] The names among the officers living here of Lieutenant de *Hauteville* and of Captain Charles de *Ponthieu* (Read, as above), might suggest that we were reading the history of Normandy in the eleventh, not of Ireland in the seventeenth, century.   [7] Burn, as above; Smiles, 272 f.

The little town soon became a centre of refined learning; and the quiet and industrious life of the people offered a pattern of patient labour, thrift, and orderliness, that could not fail of good influence on their neighbours of the country [1].

A smaller settlement of the same kind was formed at Youghal [2], county Cork, in 1697. The corporation enfranchised them on payment of six-pence; but did not allow them to vote or to serve as churchwardens until they should have resided seven years. They seem to have had no public service.

Other officers and persons of consideration resorted to Dublin, where they had three churches. Those who adopted the Anglican office had been allowed by the archbishop the use of Saint Mary's chapel, in the cathedral, as early as 1664 [3]: nonconformists had churches in Peter-street and Lucas-lane [4]. No French service now exists; but two consistories and a French charitable fund give witness to the colony. Among the immigrants of the lower class were silk-workers and florists; those of the higher ranks have founded some of the best-known families in Ireland, as Trench, La Touche, and Saurin; and one set up the first literary journal in the country [5].

Of an entirely different character was the French settlement at Lisburn. The English government, wishing to protect the woollen manufacture at home, resolved by way of compensation to promote the linen-trade in Ireland. With this view an act was passed in 1687 *For encouraging the linen manufacture of Ireland, and bringing flax and hemp into, and the making of sailcloth in, this kingdom* [6]. 'This law,' says the

---

[1] Smiles, as above; cp. the *Ulster Journal*, 6. 339 f.
[2] See the rev. Samuel Hayman in the *Ulster Journal*, 2. 223 f.; 1854.
[3] The French service ceased in 1816 or 1818; Burn, 247.
[4] These have long ceased. See Burn, and the *Bulletin*, 2. 135 f.; Burn says that the hostility of the government, especially in Ireland, to any form of dissent allowed but small favour to these congregations, and accounts thus for their early disappearance: 250 f.
[5] Lecky, 2. 300.
[6] 7 & 8 William III, c. 39 (*Statutes-at-large*); cp. an Address of the House of Lords in 1698, in Macpherson, 2. 704.

historian of commerce, 'laid the foundation of the great and flourishing manufacture of linen and cambrics in Ireland[1].' William invited from Holland[2] a French exile, Louis Crommelin, to begin the work. He brought with him in the following year a thousand looms and wheels, and a whole colony of weavers and spinners[3]. They established themselves in Antrim, at Lisburn, or, as it was then called, Lisnagarvey; and Crommelin[4] was appointed overseer of the Royal Linen Manufactory of Ireland. In 1705 the Irish House of Commons made the workers here freemen in whatever city or corporate town they chose to reside and exempted them from sundry burthens[5]. The original settlement included many tradespeople and not a few of good birth and breeding. It was a gain to the neighbourhood not only from its example of peaceful industry, but also as adding an energetic element to a population of a temper already intensely protestant[6].

1693. Mar. 27. A similar industrial colony was made at Waterford[7]. As early as 1693 the municipality ordered that houses should be prepared for fifty families of French protestants, *To drive a trade of linen-manufacture, they bringing with them a stock of money and materials for their subsistence until flax can be sown and produced on the lands adjacent, and that the freedom of the city be given them gratis*[8]. It was not likely that these conditions should attract many; but enough came to obtain and to use the abbey-chancel for their public service until 1819[9].

---

[1] Macpherson, 2. 685.

[2] He had emigrated from S Quentin to Amsterdam: *Bulletin*, 8. 462 f.

[3] C. N. de la Cherois Purdon, in the *Ulster Journal*, 1. 212; 1853.

[4] He seems to have been a man of substance, for he sank 10,000*l.* in the concern, the government allowing him eight per cent. upon it: vol. 1. 286.

[5] It is interesting to remark what were considered the burthens of freemanship; the functions of petty constable, sidesman, and churchwarden, and the liability to jury-service: vol. 1. 219.

[6] The French church was closed in 1798; vol. 2. 179: or 1818: Burn, 19.

[7] See the rev. T. Gimlette, in the *Ulster Journal*, 4. 198 ff.

[8] Vol. 4. 201.

[9] Vol. 4. 202 & 219: or 1813; Burn, 244 f.

Others settled at Kilkenny, Carlow [1], and Cork: in this last place there seems to have been formed at one time a considerable community. Jacques Fontaine, whom we have already met in the west of England [2], became their minister in 1695, and he set up a manufactory of flannels. *If*, he says, *the French in Cork have shewn me much goodness it is due to the people of the town at large to remember that they have almost all offered me the same regard*[3]. His energy attracted other refugees from several parts of Ireland [4]: but the blow struck at the wool-trade by the prohibition of its export ruined his manufacture, and he withdrew to the retirement of Bantry Bay, to Bearhaven, and took to fishing [5]. The troubles he suffered from the 'tories' of the neighbourhood made him anxious to fortify himself by a colony of his countrymen. He persuaded thirteen old soldiers to come, and gave them land and money: but nothing could keep them in that wild corner of the earth; in three years' time hardly any remained [6]. The settlement at Cork also languished, until a new colony arrived in 1715, which added to the significance of the imported population, as well as to the trade of the town: but its date and origin deprive it of more than a collateral reference to our subject [7].

---

[1] Lecky, 2. 344.
[2] See above, pp. 89 f.; and cp. pp. 19 & 97, n. 5.
[3] *Mémoires*, 242.
[4] Pp. 239 ff.
[5] Pp. 254 ff.
[6] P. 267.
[7] The sail-cloth industry was brought in by Jean la Trobe in 1715; but in time decayed. The third restoration was the work of Bishop Chenevix and Lord Chesterfield in 1746; but the people now introduced were only in part of French extraction: *Ulster Journal*, 4. 206 ff. The church lasted from April 29 1712 until about 1813; and its record remains in French Church-street: Burn, 249 f. On the high characteristic of the refugees in Ireland generally, see a sermon by Philip Skelton; *Works*, 3. 380 ff.; ed. R. Lynam, 1824.

CHAPTER X.

THE REFUGE IN SWITZERLAND.

In the huguenot dispersion Switzerland is of chief interest as giving a thoroughfare to those who sought shelter in Germany[1]; the actual settlement was of minor consequence. For the immediate influx was greatly swollen on account of the laxity with which the Swiss frontier, as compared with the Flemish or the seacoast, was guarded[2]. Moreover, across the border, the fugitives were met by a people, friendly with the friendship of an intense religious sympathy, who did all in their power to counterwork the vigilance of the patrols. Thus, says the historian of the Genevese church[3], 'among the forests of the French Jura, on the hill of Saint Cergues, by the lake of Joux, the towns of Nyon, Rolle, Morges, Yverdun, set woodmen and shepherds *Under cover of the labours of their estate*, to watch the byways and guide the travellers through.' And other towns on the border, as Rhône, Chancy, Avully, Cartigny, acted with a like forethought and independence.

From this neighbourhood to France, the Pays de Vaud[4] received a great crowd of fugitives. There was a mountain here charged with a fund for the refugees from Gex, which originated in a Dutch subscription of 1670. Its object was diverted from the churches in Gex to their exiles, in 1685; and

---

[1] Even by the end of 1685 two hundred ministers had taken refuge in Switzerland: Erman and Reclam, *Mémoires*, 1. 192.
[2] M de Solomiac, in the *Bulletin*, 9. 143; 1860.
[3] J. Gaberel, *Histoire de l'Église de Genève*, 3. 367; Geneva 1862.
[4] Territorially it was annexed to Bern; but at least at the beginning of the immigration, its refuge has a different character from that of the canton proper.

the Bourse des Réfugiés du Pays de Gex thus established subsisted until 1843 [1]. Between four and five thousand settled there [2], and a vastly greater number were for a time entertained in the country. Lausanne was, above all, a city of refuge. Within a few months of the Recall it counted eighty ministers [3]; in a single day two thousand people are recorded to have come within its walls [4].

But Geneva was the great place of transit, and we have here the advantage, which we do not possess in any other refuge, of knowing the precise number that arrived in the town, from the charity registers. More than half the fugitives were provided with the means of continuing their journey without recourse to the Bourse Française; but with the remainder this institution, which had existed since 1545 [5], was sorely taxed to furnish the sums necessary for their maintenance, some coming *So bare of raiment that they were fain to wait the darkness or ever they would knock at the city-gates* [6].

The influx began in 1682, and lasted for near forty years. During this time the towns of Leman gave shelter to 22,000 persons [7] who needed relief, to 12,000 travelling northward in haste, and to 27,000 travelling at their own charges. The population of Geneva alone was permanently increased by between 3000 and 3600 inhabitants. The hospitality of the people was boundless. *It should seem*, wrote a fugitive [8], *that the walls of their chambers dilated at will, so ready are they to entertain new-comers, come though they may in dense throngs, and*

---

[1] Théodore Claparède, *Histoire des Églises réformées du Pays de Gex*, 236 ff.; Geneva 1856.

[2] The number actually was 4412, in the following distribution: Lausanne 1505, Nyon 775, Morges 716, Vevey 696, Moudon 275, Aigle 231, Yverdun 214: *Bulletin*, 9. 144.

[3] Erman and Reclam, as above.

[4] M de Solomiac contrasts this with the four thousand who came to Zuerich in a month: in the *Bulletin*, 9. 143.

[5] Gaberel, 3. 359 and 362.   [6] Vol. 3. 368.

[7] Gaberel says, 'families or individuals.' 3. 369; but the difference of the supposed equivalents is so great that, in the uncertainty of his meaning, I have adopted the lesser specification.   [8] In Gaberel, 3. 369 f.

though they must be put up twenty in a room. Sickness and the sufferings of the road make sad havoc among us, and the wards of the hospital will not contain all our comrades, few of whom dare hope for recovery.

The activity of the Bourse Française was unceasing. In the earlier part of the century its expenditure had fluctuated between seven and fifteen thousand florins: in 1685 the amount was 88,161; thenceforward to 1720 it ranged from ninety to a hundred and fifty thousand[1]. In forty years it spent 5,143,266 florins, this single city; while Bern with its comparatively immense resources spent at most four million. These figures, also, it must be understood, express only the public charity of Geneva: and the bounty of individuals may have nearly rivalled that of the city.

Nor was it unhampered by external difficulties. When in 1685 *The larger and more respectable part* of the huguenots of Lyons had betaken themselves to Geneva, *carrying with them all the money they had been able to collect for six months back*, Lewis twice ordered his resident to demand their surrender[2]. The magistrates parried the demand by asserting that the fugitives had gone to Avignon. On another instance they actually expelled two thousand, and when night came sent out and took them back. When Lewis was informed he menaced the Genevese with invasion: but, Bern, Zuerich, Basel, and Schaffhausen holding together, he suffered some negotiation and yielded[3]. It was the same reason, the pressure of foreign complications, that prevented his paying regard to the ironical answer of the Genevese council, when he remonstrated against their giving shelter to the fugitives of the Pays de Gex. That baillage of Gex, they said, *Had always given*

<small>1685.
Nov. 20.
1686.
Jan.</small>

---

[1] In 1709 it reached the enormous figure of 234,672 florins: Gaberel, 3. 370.
[2] *Histoire van de Vervolging*, 2. 34, 43, 52, 60; cp. Claparède, 213; and A. Michel, *Louvois*, 266.
[3] Gaberel, 3. 376 ff. The evangelical cantons offered a support of thirty thousand men: J. C. Moerikofer, *Geschichte der evangelischen Flüchtlingen in der Schweiz*, 189; Leipzig 1876.

Geneva its menservants and maids, and it would be hard to fetch them from any other place[1]. The domestic plea was not to be gainsayed.

In spite of all obstacles, the fugitives arrived in constantly increasing numbers. In Jacques Flournoy's diary we read how the rush from the Pays de Gex filled the city, and wellnigh exhausted the French Bourse. *Daily*, he wrote, in 1687, *there comes an amazing multitude.... Scarce a week, it has been remarked, but we have as many as three hundred; and so it has been since the end of the winter. Some days there come as many as* 120 *in sundry throngs; the more part craftsmen, but persons of quality not a few.... They come principally from Dauphiné*[2]. Later in the year he says, *Days have been known when seven or eight hundred fugitives have come in. It is affirmed that in the five weeks ending with the* 1st *of September, nearly eight thousand arrived; so that although they daily take their departure by the lake, there are commonly more than three thousand together present in the city*[3]. The opportunity was seized by the landgrave of Hessen-Cassel to send deputies inviting a part to his dominion; and he gathered a good number[4].

1687.
Nov. 1.

When the fugitives left, on the road to Germany, they were taken charge of by the protestant cantons, who had made an arrangement by which Bern, Zuerich, Basel, Schaffhausen, and Sankt Gallen, should meet a certain proportion of the charges of relief[5]. From Schaffhausen they were supported down the

1686.

---

[1] Claparède, 219. The emigrants from Gex were at least not hindered by their venal governor, Passy, who suffered for it by a life spent in the galleys: p. 218.

[2] MS. at Geneva, in Weiss, 2. 187; also in Arnaud, *Protest. de Dauphiné*, 3. 15.

[3] As above. Bishop Burnet observed two hundred in one day, twelve or thirteen hundred a week; *History of his own Times*, 2. 1169 f.

[4] Kochler, *Réfugiés in Preussen und Kurhessen*, 59.

[5] Weiss gives, 2. 212 f., from a despatch of Tambonneau, January 4 1687, the following percentage: Bern 44, Zuerich 30, Basel 12, Schaffhausen 9, and S Gallen 5: which varies from that of Erman and Reclam, 1. 241 f. But there were several readjustments of the figures: see Moerikofer, 179–186. When Weiss adds that the arrangement was limited to the vaudois

Rhine until they reached Mainz. But here began the great confusion. Who was to pay for the six hours' sail to Frankfurt, which had the effect of thoroughly disorganising all the good arrangements of the previous voyage[1]? The immigrants moreover came in such numbers and in such rapid succession, that it was really impossible to feed them, much less to give them conveyance into Hessen-Cassel, or to Halberstadt, where the elector of Brandenburg began his portion of help. Many are the complaints of Frankfurt, both to the elector and to the Swiss association[2].

Before the end of 1685 the elector had written to all the princes of the Augsburg Confession and to the United Provinces[3], asking their coöperation in support of the exiles in Switzerland; and in 1688 a memorial of thanks was proffered by the grateful people, who notwithstanding found themselves still in need of help and wished to enlarge the settlement in the cantons[4]. Thus, with foreign aid, Switzerland became not only a place of transit, but also a permanent refuge[5].

1688.
Mar. 25.

Geneva benefited by the coming of workers in silk and wool

exiles, we must remember that, whatever the intention, its advantages were accepted by emigrants of all sorts, as we may see from a letter of Claude Rey, minister at Erlangen, November 15 1687, recommending such huguenots as were bound thither to go by way of Schaffhausen for this very object: *Bulletin*, 16. 129.

[1] See a complaint of the French consistory at Frankfurt to the burgomasters of Basel, July 4 1699, in F. C. Schroeder, *troisième Jubilé séculaire de la Fondation de l'Église réformée française de Francfort-sur-le-Mein*, 86 ff.; Frankfurt 1854: a monograph justly praised by M Francis Waddington, in the *Bulletin*, 8. 79 n. They asked to have the detachments limited to seventy or eighty persons, the departure of each divided by six or eight days, and the voyage of their ships extended from Mainz to the end.

[2] See also a letter asking help of the archbishop of Canterbury, August 30 1699; in Schroeder, 89: and cp. below, p. 127.

[3] *Resolutien van Holland*, October 7 1688; in Koenen, *Vluchtelingen in Nederland*, 53 f.

[4] *Bulletin*, 9. 149–153.

[5] It is said that in 1699 there were eight thousand huguenot exiles in Switzerland, besides three thousand vaudois: Koenen, 83 n. This is well below the mark.

from Nîmes, print-manufacturers from Dauphiné[1], goldsmiths from Paris, Dijon, and Macon[2], watchmakers from Blois[3]. A far greater advantage was brought here and to Lausanne[4] by the many families of rank, the artists[5], and the men of science, who raised the social culture and amended the idiom of these cities. The presence of Abauzit, one of the child-refugees,—he was but five years old at the Recall,—soon connected Geneva with the entire intellectual life of the time[6].

For here we are to notice, what has already come into prominence in the society of Rotterdam, the bent, far from solely religious, which the French impressed upon the culture of the cities where they gained free scope for influence. Even in theology, Geneva now seemed to be reverting to the liberal traditions of Saumur[7], where Cappel had extended to the Bible the

---

[1] Arnaud, 3. 23.   [2] Weiss, 2. 218.
[3] Depping, *Correspondance administrative*, 4. intr. lix; 1852. It is said that in the very year of the Recall there were two hundred goldsmiths in Geneva, refugees of the north of France: Moerikofer, 234. — A brief reference may be allowed here to the French community at Constantinople. Perhaps the most grotesque act of faith Lewis can be accused of, was a request he made by his ambassador that the Grand Seignior would procure the conversion of his Calvinistic subjects or else hand them over to him: report of Coljers, resident of the Estates at Paris, in the *Resolutien van Holland*, May 31 1686; cited by Koenen, 45 n. Whether this was enforced seems doubtful: we only know that one M de Girardin was sent over in 1686 to see to it: *Hollandse Mercurius*, 1686, 128. In any case, the Genevese who had settled in the city at the beginning of the century were joined at this time by a number of huguenot fugitives. They were simple workpeople, and, not being able to support a minister of their own, they had recourse in the matter of baptisms, marriages, and burials, to the chaplains attached to the Dutch, Swiss, and English embassies. See some notes found among archbishop Secker's papers and printed by M Waddington, in the *Bulletin*, 4. 384 ff, 1856.
[4] It was from a Dauphinois family planted at Lausanne that Jean Louis Reynier, general in the French Republic and under the First Empire, was descended: Arnaud, 3. 24.
[5] Among these are reckoned the famous Jean Petitot and the brothers Étienne and Michel Liotard, painter and engraver: Moerikofer, 190 ff.
[6] See a good chapter in Sayous, *le dix-huitième Siècle à l'Étranger*, 1. 81 ff.
[7] Cp. the same, *Littérature française*, 1. 180 ff.

laws of historical and exact criticism, where Josué de la Place had held original sin to be but the morbid growth of ages, and where Amyraut had sought between the mysteries of grace and predestination a middle way that should satisfy at once faith and reason[1]. This direction of the intellectual current of Geneva must connect itself with the spread of the philosophy of Descartes, upheld in Geneva since 1669 by one of its most weighty pioneers, Chouet, the master of Bayle and Basnage. Chouet, though not himself a refugee, was the chief of a school that derived its main strength from the huguenot emigration[2]. Gradually pervading the educated among the Genevese, the temper of the community lent itself to the influence; and we are not to wonder that many of the chosen friends and correspondents of Bayle were numbered among the citizens of the Calvinistic capital. The impulse ran from metaphysic to natural science. Scientific experiments became the vogue, as they had been a little earlier in England[3]; and Geneva became renowned for its physicians.

Firmin Abauzit might seem to gather within one body all the attributes of the society which he illustrated and which his personality transfused. Save in the one department from which all this special type of culture had flowed, that of metaphysics, he was the confessed master of every branch of knowledge. Newton declared him fit to arbitrate between himself and Leibnitz[4]. Yet the wishes of the learned world, the invitations of the English court, could not surprise Abauzit out of his simple manners; could not draw him into a public career, or turn the modest scholar to the ambitious writing of books. We know him therefore not from the works which a sedulous after-age has

---

[1] Weiss, 2. 240 f.

[2] Among whom was eminent the professor Burlamachi, an exile from France, though of Italian birth. 'C'est une bibliothèque vivante et le véritable Photius de notre siècle,' says Bayle, who commemorates in him 'la plus prodigieuse mémoire du monde, jointe à un jugement très-délicat et très-profond': *nouvelles Lettres*, 1. 17 ff.; in Sayous, 1. 186 f.: cp. 229, and *le dix-huitième Siècle*, 1. 77 ff.

[3] Bayle, 1. 30; in Sayous, *Littérature française*, 1. 185.   [4] Weiss, 2. 245.

wrested from his unwilling desk, so much as from his letters and his life, from the stamp he left on the society of Geneva and from the homage of Jean Jacques Rousseau[1]. He has been described as 'the true and self-contained exemplar of philosophical Christianity[2]:' but his Christianity was that of the philosophical habit not that which finds its roots in philosophical enquiry. It was the religion of the philosopher, not of philosophy. What it lost in precision, it gained in breadth and charity. Voltaire could see in Abauzit but *The chief of the Arians of Geneva*[3]; but Voltaire's vision was bounded by the intellectual horizon, and the human lay beyond. Yet it is this human value which in history is above price, from its rareness and its force of life and life-giving. The intellectual is common enough; we might pursue its trace in the little world of Geneva, through the books and letters of huguenot thinkers such as Le Sage or Marie Huber. But, with all their printings, their power over the rest comes not into comparison with his who wrote nothing, who made none of his stores public, the plain humble townsman Abauzit.

The refining influence of the exiles told throughout the Pays de Vaud[4]: not less was the material influence. The people knew no other work than husbandry and vinegrowing; both were in rude state. The refugees improved them, and added the culture of orchards and kitchen-gardens[5]. At Yverdun, some Dauphinois set up a cloth-manufactory[6]: everywhere they opened shops, hitherto unknown in the district, and soon rendered the trade of the pedlar, which had been indispensable, useless[7]. A singular project was once started. Vaud was to have a great City of Refuge, to contain a population of thirty

---

[1] Sayous, *le dix-huitième Siècle*, 1. 81 f.; cp. Weiss, 2. 247 f.
[2] Villemain, *Littérature du dix-huitième Siècle*, 2. 107; in Weiss, 2. 246.
[3] Weiss, 2. 245.
[4] D. de Bray, in the *Bulletin*, 3. 17: 'a certain intellectual life.'
[5] Moerikofer, 234; who cites in the next page a statement that 'tout ce qui a fleuri dans le pays de Vaud, dans l'industrie et le commerce, est d'origine française.'   [6] Arnaud, *Dauphiné*, 3. 23.   [7] Weiss, 2. 216.

thousand[1]. Unhappily, the interference of the authorities of Bern prevented the scheme from being carried out. It was their policy of pressing every one to a rigid uniformity[2]—on which indeed their land-system was based,—that here and in other instances hindered the easy settlement in the territory of the canton. They feared that the colonists might justle the rights of the natives[3].

1698. Thus even at Lausanne there was a talk of expelling the huguenots[4], and once they were even recommended to prepare for departure; while at Bern, the order in 1689 that all who lived on charity, save the old and sickly, should be immediately expelled, was only stayed from execution by the urgent representations of the English and Dutch ministers.

The citizens of Bern had never taken kindly to the French immigrants[5]. In 1698 the latter were forced to have recourse to their fellow-exiles at Berlin, who made a large collection for them. A building thus appointed for the receiving of new comers bore its name of the Hôtel de Refuge as late as 1787[6]. We are told that the city-porters had to attend them to the doors of the people they were billeted on, in order to enforce their admission by the inmates. In fact the canton was already sufficiently well peopled[7]. Yet the town profited considerably by those who fixed in it their manufactories of silk and wool, and

---

[1] *Bulletin*, 3. 17.

[2] Which prevented, on the other hand, the immigrants from getting citizenship or being 'incorporés' at Bern: Claparède, 236.

[3] *Bulletin*, 9. 360.

[4] Vol. 9. 268 f. The activity of M de Mirmand on behalf of the refugees is commemorated in the same volume, 142 ff.; and in Moerikofer, 283 ff.—A similar decree of expulsion was once passed by the authorities of Zuerich: *Bulletin*, 3. 621.

[5] In 1696 they numbered 6454, of whom 1824 required support: *Bulletin*, 9. 143 f.

[6] Koehler, 28 f. Comparing the *Bulletin*, 9. 270, it should appear that this resort was called for by a minute of the magistrates that those who lived at alms should set their houses in order before they were driven out.

[7] Koehler, 28; *Historie van de Vervolging*, 3. 113.

who plied embroidery-work[1]. In time, the government and the people came to look well on the strangers who brought them such gain; they helped with a large sum of money the clothworkers who came from Valence in Dauphiné[2] and gave the French leave to purchase citizenship or perpetual denizenship. Of the first one in three availed himself, of the second not one in eighteen[3].

1686.
1700.

Manufactures were also established, and also flourished, at Zuerich[4]; in other cantons, Basel and Schaffhausen[5], the French dispersed themselves over the country and did not form any distinct colonies; in Appenzell the small agricultural settlements do not call for separate notice[6]. In Neuchâtel, the burghers were, at the outset, as generous as any of their brothers: the city was almost exhausted. Collections for the French were made frequently from 1683 onwards[7]; and a considerable settlement was formed in the town[8], while the vine-

---

[1] Weiss, 2. 216. They had been invited by a Resolution of the council dated October 22 1685: Moerikofer, 199. And these early immigrants were commercially the most valuable. Enough had come by the previous March to rouse the hue and cry of Lewis's officers, threatening sundry penalties unless they returned: Claparède, 209 f.

[2] Arnaud, 3. 22; Moerikofer, 199 f.   [3] *Bulletin*, 9. 361 f.

[4] It is said that one manufacturer had attracted 1500 huguenots by the end of 1685: *Historie van de Vervolging*, 3. 55. It was to Zuerich that the son of the renowned Jean Daillé, who presided at the synod of Charenton in 1659, retired. He died in 1690. The records of Zuerich give a transit through the city of 4592 persons between November 1683 and March 15 1684; and from the same date to 1691 a total of 27,081. The expenditure down to 1688 had been nearly 133,000 florins: Moerikofer, 421 & 426 f.; cp. 230.

[5] It is surely an understatement which counts only 15,591 refugees to Schaffhausen from November 1683 to February 1688; *Bulletin*, 9. 143: or 20,095 to a year later; Moerikofer, 427. Even in December 1685 the writer of the *Historie van de Vervolging* declared Schaffhausen to have hardly more room remaining: 3. 113.

[6] Appenzell and Glarus helped the refugees chiefly by the indirect means of contributions to their maintenance in the other cantons. Sankt Gallen was too much out of the way to be otherwise of use. See Moerikofer, 226 f.

[7] *Bulletin*, 9. 487. The refuge numbered three hundred families in 1685: Moerikofer, 228.

[8] Immigrants from Saintonge imitated in their manufactures here the 'painted stuffs' of India; *Bulletin*, 4. 154 f.

growing in the country round was improved by the new cultivators. The chief importance of the colony at Neuchâtel, however, begins at a date beyond my limits[1], when Frederick the First assumed its sovereignty and distinguished himself by his protection of the French and by his giving them the highest offices in the state. It may be remarked that his successor, Frederick William the First, chose for the canton three governors running, from the refugee nobility[2]. The settlement had indeed been effected soberly and without contention. The immigrants blended readily with the people, and formed no 'colonies.' They enjoyed no 'peculiar' jurisdiction as in Brandenburg; and Neuchâtel neither had nor needed a Bourse or a Corporation Française such as had been founded at Geneva or Lausanne[3].

I have noticed the enterprise of building a great City of Refuge in Switzerland. Another plan to find homes for the huguenots, now in a remote island, though like the first resultless, calls for reference from the dignity of its proposer and from its peculiar character, recalling the great huguenot state in America projected but never carried into effect by Coligny[4]. One of the family of the renowned Duquesne had led a colony to the wilderness of the Cape of Good Hope[5]; another, Henry son of the admiral, thought to unite the exiles in Switzerland by making them into a firm commonwealth in the isle of Bourbon. Their fellows were summoned from Germany and the Netherlands; a fleet was made ready. But the French government was beforehand, and despatched some war-ships. Duquesne, bound by honour and the conditions of his banishment, withdrew from the risk of conflict; and the commonwealth lived only in the disappointed memory of its colonists[6].

---

[1] See two interesting notices by M Guillebert in the *Bulletin*, 3. 620-625 and 4. 153-160. A protest is made against Weiss's statement that 'smaller numbers' of the emigrants went to Neuchâtel than to other parts of Switzerland: vol. 3. 623; cp. 9. 465.   [2] *Bulletin*, 3. 622 n.
[3] Vol. 3. 623.   [4] Weiss, 2. 317.   [5] Above, pp. 43 f.
[6] Sayous, 1. 206 f.; Moerikofer, 195; cp. Weiss, 1. 97.

CHAPTER XI.

THE PASSAGE THROUGH SWITZERLAND INTO GERMANY.

THE preceding chapter has shewn how carefully the Swiss provided for the fugitives among the huguenots whose resort was beyond Switzerland. We have now to track them in the various states of middle Germany; and first in the great thoroughfare of Frankfurt on the Main, which is besides a good example of the immense power of charity possessed and used, in face of the intolerance of the mass of the people, by the foreign and reformed residents of the German city. If a generalisation may be allowed here, where each man took the road which led him safest from the terror that invaded his village, we may describe the refugees of Frankfurt as in the main natives of Dauphiné and Languedoc, whose journey had passed through Switzerland[1]: and, happily for them, the energy of the Walloon diaconate was stronger than the grudge of Lutheran authorities.

Frankfurt had once been the principal refuge in the empire for Walloon, Dutch, and English exiles. From the end of the sixteenth century, however, the reformed worship was proscribed; and with this act, closely connected with the general reaction against protestantism in Germany, the congregation in part withdrew to Hanau, partly contented itself with a service in the neighbouring village of Bockenheim. The church here was soon burnt down, and the people had to go as far as Offenbach[2]: it was rebuilt and was their only place of worship until at last

1600.
1608.
1638.

---
[1] Schroeder, *Jubilé de Francfort*, 82.   [2] Pp. 19 ff.

1792.
Sept. 16.

in 1792 one was permitted to exist within the city [1]. It was a happy chance that led the princess of Tarentum to seek here the place of her exile [2]; for, through her rank, her house was allowed during the critical years from 1688 to 1693, when she died, to maintain a ministry for the benefit of a small part of the multitude, which from the spring of 1685 was constantly pouring into the city. For, though the restriction put upon religious liberty prevented as many from settling here as we might otherwise expect, the position of Frankfurt made it the landing-place of considerably more than a hundred thousand fugitives in the twenty years following the Recall [3], besides some thirty thousand more in another twenty years [4].

Like Hamburg in the north, it was one of the chief places where those who sought a refuge in Brandenburg betook themselves. For here they came at once under the charge of the electoral agent Merian, who had orders to furnish everything for their comfort and maintenance in travel. The landgrave of Hessen-Cassel had a similar agency [5]. Most of them came either from the eastern provinces of France immediately, or from the south by way of Geneva and Schaffhausen. Of these latter a great number were persons of consideration and substance [6];

---

[1] The French had been naturalised in 1787: pp. 32 f.

[2] Amalia, princess of Tarentum, was daughter to Wilhelm V, landgrave of Hessen-Cassel: Erman and Reclam, 1. 204 ff. On her charity see Ferdinand Bender, *Geschichte der Waldenser*, 277; Ulm 1850.

[3] See supplementary note viii. It is hard to say how large a proportion of these refugees were vaudois, or again how many huguenots were mixed up with the vaudois.

[4] As late as 1713 and thereabouts the deacons' books contain many notices of men who had been in galleys twenty-six or twenty-seven years, at last freed: Schroeder, 40 f.

[5] *Historie van de Vervolging*, 3. 55.

[6] It should seem that the number of wealthy refugees was very considerable; and this fact may account for the repeated occurrence of catholic abjurations here, as though commerce had dictated also a catholic emigration, which association with the protestants of the Refuge had converted. For the fact, see Schroeder, 30 and 94; and cp. Wenz, *Emden*, 133, and Weyell, *Neu-Isenburg*, 8, 31.

the rest were supported by the Switzers as far as Mainz. Thence as their multitude far exceeded the expectation of the elector of Brandenburg, a preponderant share in the call for relief fell to the French diaconate of Frankfurt. The mere contributions of the Calvinistic societies sufficed for the purpose until 1699; but it was only with much thrift, nor could the dole exceed half-a-florin to each person relieved [1].

1699.

June 17.

In this year however they had to go to their Lutheran fellow-citizens and to the elector of Brandenburg for help: *The French refugees*, they pleaded, *coming from Switzerland in the desire to settle within your highness's territories approach hither daily in crowds, the more part of them in hard case, beggared of all help and lacking the means to perfect their journey; that they had of the Switzers barely sufficing to carry them to Mainz. Finding therefore here no officer nor no money, whereof they had had hope, they know not whither to turn them; whereby many be discouraged and are brought to take their way otherwhere, and the remnant in the diffidence into the which it is like they fall, be moved to desire peradventure to return back to France; howbeit they that have goods go seek a dwellingplace in other lands*, as Holland or England [2]. The Lutheran townsfolk for the first time listened to the appeal [3]; and the elector, encouraged by the promising growth of the colony already planted in his country, set himself at once to arrange for their enlargement. The causes of the new influx are involved in the fortunes of the Palatine refugees. But in this place it is necessary to remark that its character was far from exclusively huguenot. On the other hand, here and elsewhere, it is equally rash to distinguish any particular band of exiles as vaudois [4]. For very many of the banished huguenots took refuge at first among the valleys of

---

[1] From 1685 to 1695 63,698 persons were granted 34,248 fl. 12½ alb.; from 1695 to 1705 34,118 by 17,642 fl. 7 alb.: an albus counting for two kreutzers: Schroeder, 27 and 84.

[2] P. 86.   [3] P. 30.

[4] This is done far too sweepingly by the author of the *Uebersicht der Wanderungen*.

Savoy, and, when the vaudois population was forced to flee, threw in their lot with them. More than this, just as in an earlier proscription the French had at times given themselves out for Walloons [1], so now policy dictated an analogous pretence. We find records of vaudois colonies in Germany coinciding with periods when they are known to have lived undisturbed at home; and these we may accept unhesitatingly as huguenot. The fugitives were aware that in some parts of Germany especially near the French border the prince might colourably entertain vaudois, where he could not risk encountering the hostility of Lewis the Fourteenth by receiving his rebels [2]. Lastly, the confusion might readily arise in the German mind from the identity of language or from the change of the French boundaries; as we constantly find the people of the valley of Pragelas treated as Savoyard, whereas part of it, notably the village of Queyras, had always been French [3], and most of the remainder was incorporated by the treaty of Rijswijk, when the chief emigration began.

But before passing on into the Palatinate it will be well to notice the immigration to the cities of Saxony, connected with Frankfurt alike through commercial interests and the prejudice of sect. Many traders and men of wealth took refuge in Leipzig and Dresden; but their inducement was business, not religious freedom. Of this they had little at the hands of the Lutheran burghers. At Dresden they shared with the reformed Germans a furtive worship, guarded by an oath of secresy, in a private house [4]: at Leipzig the holy communion was only possible by a journey to Halle in the neighbouring electorate of Brandenburg [5]. In the duchy of Sachsen-Hildburg-

1689.

---

[1] For instance at Mannheim; see a sermon preached there in 1821 by Charles Killian, 21; cited by Schroeder, 83 n.

[2] F. Waddington in the *Bulletin*, 8. 79 n. It is to be remarked that it was as a Frenchman and under the influence of Lewis XIV that the strenuous priest-colonel Arnaud was expelled from Piedmont. He sought in vain to prove himself vaudois: Schroeder, 83 n.

[3] Bender, 260. [4] Weiss, I. 227.

[5] They were allowed a room in the Rentey-Gebäude for common worship,

hausen[1] they fared better, and the little community joined the Dutch residents in a church of their own[2].

The year of the Recall was marked by a dynastic change in the Palatinate fraught with significance in its immediate results upon the country. The extinction of the Simmern branch of the house of Wittelsbach gave the succession to Philipp Wilhelm of the younger line of Neuburg, while it admitted of a possible claimant in the person of the late elector's brother-in-law, the duke of Orleans. The new elector, though a catholic[3], received the fugitive with a hospitality doubly commendable, because of his own religion and because of the nearness of his estates to the French border. The exiles came in very large numbers, and were settling everywhere in the electorate, when Lewis the Fourteenth surprised them by taking steps to enforce his brother's claim. It does not fall within my scope to detail this inroad, the most terrible ravage even of this pitiless king[4]: but its effect in scattering once more the unhappy fugitives that lingered there, forms perhaps the hardest feature in the history I have to trace. We know of it not at all from themselves;

---

at a date variously put at 1700, Erman and Reclam, 1. 261, and Waddington, in the *Bulletin*, 8. 313 f.; 1701, Weiss, as above; and 1707, *Uebersicht der Wanderungen*, 80. They did not unite with the German reformed body until 1758.

[1] Or, as it has been since 1826, Sachsen-Altenburg.

[2] The church at Hildburghausen was built in 1721, *Uebersicht der Wanderungen*, as above; by means of a collection made in England and elsewhere, about 1717. The canvass may be found among the Wake papers, vol. 28; where the 'colonie naissante' is described as owing its formation to the surcharge of Wismar (= Weimar?) and Switzerland. The former name apparently relates to a settlement otherwise unrecorded. Similarly of the settlements in Nassau and in Lippe-Detmold we know little beyond their existence: Erman and Reclam, 1. 281. A vaudois settlement in Schaumburg, in 1688, which included a few Dauphinois, is noticed by Bender, 291; who also mentions the immigration, principally huguenot, into the county of Solms-Braunfels-Daubhausen, p. 292: cp. below, p. 142, n. 3.

[3] It would be hardly necessary to support this statement by a reference to Spittler, or to a well-known letter in Macaulay, 2. 100, had not Weiss fallen into the strange blunder of calling him a Calvinist, 1. 234.

[4] See Jobez, *Histoire de Louis XV*, 1. 167 f.

K

only from the compassionate churches that received and sheltered them. Their notices are little more than suggestions of the bitter suffering and misery that fled to them for succour; little more than the bare recital of how many were taken in at Frankfurt or Hanau, in Hesse, Brandenburg, Holland, or England [1].

When the troops of Duras were withdrawn, some of the French thought to return: their friends in other parts of Germany gave them help [2]. But the warning of 1689 was fresh in the elector's mind. He published a Declaration only allowing Switzers, Piedmontese, Lorrainers, and such, to reside within his territories. In spite of his displeasure, the French continued to come; and he had to renew the order, adding that these had wronged his bounty by using a false pretence [3], and that for the future all the French were to be banished [4]. Hence the second dispersion of the palatine settlers, largely increased by newcomers from France and Savoy [5]; and hence the numerous new colonies in middle Germany about this date.

1698.
July 20.

---

[1] Schroeder, 82; J. B. Leclercq, *Histoire de l'Église wallonne de Hanau*, 108 f., Hanau 1868; Koehler, 27 f. Frederick the Third published an edict in their favour, May 11, 1689.

[2] Leclercq, 109.

[3] It seems that the pretext of being Walloon was still used by the huguenots; see Schroeder, 91 f.

[4] Letter of Struve, May 1699, cited in Schroeder, 82 f. 'We are now invited,' said Dr Wake, the future primate, 'to preserve the remains of the same,' the huguenot, 'church and of some of those of the vallies of Piemont with them. A flock little in number, but of great worth: and such as we cannot suffer to perish without fixing an eternal infamy upon our names for our uncharitableness': *the Case of the exiled Vaudois and French Protestants stated*, 28; a fast-day sermon April 5 1699, published in quarto.

[5] The French preachers at Mannheim, Heidelberg, Frankenthal, &c., were thrust out; obliterating an old monument of the duke of Alba's persecution: Schroeder, 83; Koehler, 27; Ancillon, *Établissement des François réfugiez*, 346 f.; who describes their reception in Brandenburg. Besides Heidelberg and Frankenthal, Otterberg, Schoenau, S Lambert, and Anweiler dated from the sixteenth century: Mannheim was founded early in the seventeenth, and Oggersheim and Billigheim before the Recall: Schroeder, 91.

The younger branches of the Hohenzollern had from the first followed their head, the Great Elector, in zealous care for the exiled huguenots. The marquess of Brandenburg-Ansbach encouraged the rise of a French church at Schwabach: where an industrial colony held its distinct vitality until this century[1]. His cousin of Brandenburg-Baireuth early published a Declaration inviting settlers, through which some came to Baireuth and very many to Erlangen. Here they founded the beautiful New Town called after the then-reigning marquess Christian-Erlangen[2]. Their prosperity indeed was in despite of the citizens, whose ill-will would have scattered them over Baiersdorf and the surrounding villages; and in the town they met with little hospitality. Once, in 1687, there was a sad plight. The marquess was away, at Vienna, when three hundred exiles appeared, soon a thousand; the countrymen closed their doors[3]. But the marquess was as good as his word. He arranged for the building of the Neustadt, and commanded the coöperation of the citizens. He was more than repaid for his pains. 'Erlangen owes its industry, its prosperity, the building of its handsomest quarters, to the incoming of the French protestants[4].' They wove and dyed and set up tanyards. Coming at first from Vivarais, Dauphiné, and Languedoc in particular[5], their numbers were immensely increased by the Palatine campaign of 1689. Save in the trade they planted, the only record of their extraction is to be found in their church and in the permanence of French surnames.

1685. Nov. 23.

In turning to Wuerttemberg we have to bear in mind what

---

[1] F. Waddington in the *Bulletin*, 8. 226 f. The French service ended in 1813. On Inguenheim of Metz who presided over the establishment of this colony, see Othon Cuvier, pref. to Jean Olry, *la Persécution de l'Église de Metz*, 47; ed. 2, Paris 1859.

[2] *Uebersicht der Wanderungen*, 81; *Bulletin*, 8. 220.

[3] See a letter of the minister Claude Rey, November 15, in the *Bulletin*, 16. 129.

[4] *Bulletin*, 8. 219. The French church, also intended for reformed Germans, was founded July 14 1686 and opened 1693. The French service ceased in 1818.

[5] *Bulletin*, 8. 220.

was said above with regard to the doubtful mixture of the immigration. Claude Brousson went into the duchy in the winter of 1685 to entreat the reception of huguenot fugitives. The regent replied to his solicitations that he dared not admit them to an open country so close to Strassburg, the governor of this fortress having already signified the displeasure of the French king that any should harbour his 'rebels and deserters[1].' Accordingly the first settlers in the duchy are described as vaudois. Doubtless, coming chiefly from Languedoc, and passing through Savoy, they impressed the religious panic upon the villagers and carried many with them. They had hardly established themselves in Wuerttemberg when the French invasion made all again uncertain; and most of the vaudois, with five hundred huguenots, responded to the invitation which the duke of Savoy had been induced by the pressure of the Estates-General to offer, and returned once more to their native valleys[2].

The first colony was practically wiped out. The second was an effect of the peace of Rijswijk, which, by transferring some parts of Savoy to France, drove three thousand protestants into the districts laid waste by recent war, to the east of the Black Forest. There they camped, until they saw return to be impossible, and became reconciled to the formation of a little society by themselves, where name and conversation and faith should keep alive the memory of their former homes[3]. Until 1822 they had their own synods[4] and own church-organisa-

---

[1] Léopold Nègre, *Vie et ministère de C. Brousson*, 147 ff.; Paris 1878: from the Court MSS. at Geneva. Cp. Moerikofer, *Flüchtlinge in der Schweiz*, 197.

[2] The date is given as July 1689, by Baur, *Kirchengeschichte der neueren Zeit*, 243. It is placed a year later by Koehler, *Preussen und Kurhessen*, 29. The nomad body gathered strength as it passed through Switzerland, so that when it reached Savoy it numbered several thousand; Baur, as above.

[3] Weiss considers these settlers as vaudois; 1. 232: the accurate Schroeder however remarks that they were partly huguenots who had tarried while they could in Piedmont, p. 93.

[4] Between 1701 and 1822, they held fourteen synods. They were more independent than most of the communities in this part of Germany, and had small relations with Frankfurt: Schroeder, 93.

tion[1]: only in 1828 did they finally abandon the French language in their public worship. Even now, we are told, they retain in their social life the manners and characteristic of their fathers [2].

A portion of the same immigration was diverted northwards into the margraviate of Baden-Durlach. They received kindness at the hands of the marquess Friedrich Magnus, who assigned them lands near Carlsruhe. Here they built the 'French' Neureuth [3], which was a separate French parish until 1821 [4]. Six other villages long preserved the impress of this settlement. The rest journeyed on into Hesse, and into the county of Isenburg-Buedingen, where some established themselves at Waldensberg [5] and Neu-Isenburg: the latter, a creation of the immigrants, may be treated in some detail; for it is a type of their colonisation under favourable conditions, and has besides some features of peculiar interest in the fortunes of the exiles.

---

[1] The old organisation was abolished by the synod of Stuttgardt, 1822; as above.

[2] A picturesque description of these villages, some twenty in number, may be found in M Victor Tissot's *Voyage au Pays des Milliards*, 32 ff. ed. 20. Paris 1875. 'La physiognomie ouverte, le regard vif et franc, l'œil généralement noir, ainsi que les cheveux, le teint coloré, révélans une population qui boit du vin et a peu de goût pour la bière; enfin, notre langue encore parlée par les viellards octogénaires, avec un gentil accent méridional et des expressions du temps : tels sont les traits qui caractérisent encore aujourd'hui ces bons gens' : p. 33. Schroeder enumerates Gros Villar, Petit Villar, Perouse, Pinache-et-Serres, La Balme, Lucerna, Sinac-et-Koerres, Le Queyras (or Duennenz), Les Mûriers (or Schoenenberg), Le Bourset (or Neu-Hengstett), Gochsheim, Diefenbach, Lomersheim, Muetschelbach-und-Gruenwettersbach, and Nordhausen: pp. 42 f. and 90 n. I cannot determine whether Mentoule specified by Weiss is identical with any of these. The vaudois origin of several of the names is evident. Schroeder distinguishes as purely French the remaining colonies in Wuerttemberg, at Kanstadt, Ludwigsburg, and Stuttgardt.

[3] Welsch-Neureuth. The others were Pforzheim, Friedrichsthal, Reihen, Hilsbach, Friedrichsfeld, and Reilingen: pp. 44 & 93 n. These are all that Schroeder enumerates, though in the text he speaks of eight or nine.

[4] Weiss, 1. 232.

[5] The date 1699 is fortified by the casual mention of Koehler, 104, who calls it (wrongly) vaudois.

CHAPTER XII.

THE REFUGE IN AND ABOUT HESSE.

1699
Sept 20.

THE founders of New-Isenburg were greeted on their first arrival by a Privilegium, or charter, from count Johann Philipp[1], which provided for the erection of a town with a mayor and four aldermen[2], a minister, schoolmaster, and organist (artt. v., ii). The municipal court was to do justice in civil suits and matters of police, to a ten-florin fine; above this the count's court alone had jurisdiction[3]. Each settler was to have land allotted him for house and garden, seed-ground and pasture[4]; he was allowed the common rights of fuel, water, and the waste, and given wood to build homestead and barn (vi.). Save in the newly-annexed meadows of Sprendlingen, no taxes were to be paid for ten years; and after this term they were only to come due on a reduced scale[5] (viii.). The people were declared free of conscription: the tithes they should pay were to be devoted to the support of their own minister and schoolmaster; and their

---

[1] A monograph of Philipp Weyell illustrates the memory of the good count of Isenburg and Buedingen, who died in 1718; *die französische Kolonie Neu-Isenburg bei Frankfurt*; Neu Isenburg 1861.

[2] The schultheiss and schöpfen were to be annually elected.

[3] Weyell, 5 f. & 30 f.

[4] In a proportion of 5 to 1; the unit being four morgen or $2\frac{1}{2}$ to 3 acres; art. viii.

[5] House-tax 5 florins; and for the croft, 10 albus the morgen of arable (say a florin for $2-2\frac{1}{3}$ acres); 15 albus the morgen of pasture (a florin for $1\frac{1}{4}-1\frac{1}{2}$ acre).

comfort and convenience met by the establishment of two inns and a half-yearly fair.

Under such provisions was Neu-Isenburg founded by a mixed multitude of French and vaudois. The former came from Dauphiné, Burgundy, Champagne, the Sédanais, and the Pays Messin, from Guienne, even from the duchy of Foix [1]; and, while their prosperity attracted many who had first sought refuge elsewhere in Germany [2], a protective clause in the Privilegium long saved the colony from being overrun by the Lutherans of the neighbourhood [3].

Service was first held, in 1700, on a plot of ground where, we are told, 'a year earlier there was nothing but a horrible, dense, wood.' The roots of a great oak gave the clergyman [4] a pulpit, from which he spoke to a throng formed by his future flock and by many strangers from Frankfurt and Offenbach as well. And the commonplace, *It is good for us to be here*, seemed to gain a new import from the hope of the time and the fitness of the scene [5]. The exiles, however, though the count supplied materials, could not afford to finish the church for some years [6]. At length they were enabled by their fellows in Holland to complete it. The count built them a hall, a twelve-sided tower, which as their fortunes throve they purchased from him, and which is the Rathhaus to this day [7]. But their prosperity was very fluctuating [8]. At one time an epidemic sickness thinned the growing population, and drove many on to Copenhagen and other settlements, or even back to France. At another, thanks

1700.
May 20.

1702.

---

[1] See the lists in Weyell, 7-9.   [2] P. 9.

[3] Art. xiii. forbad the sale of land in the municipality to any except persons of the count's, that is of the reformed, religion : p. 31.

[4] Isaac Bermond of S Fortunat in Vivarais : p. 13.

[5] 'What lacked in outer pomp,' is the comment of the local historian, ' was redeemed in inward strength ': p 16.

[6] It was founded May 25 1702 : even in January 1706 it was still incomplete. The wooden structure was ruinous in fifty years, and a new one of stone had to be opened in 1775 ; pp. 16-19.

[7] Bought for 600 fl. in 1710; p. 3.

[8] Even in 1740 the United Provinces helped to pay their minister ; p. 15.

to rich presents from their friends in Holland, they are seen flourishing in their workshops, weaving stockings and serges, making wigs and hats, cobbling and brewing, or minding gardens and husbandry [1]. They had their surveyors and surgeons: every one was employed. The women were busy in dairy or laundry, the children in netting or leather-sewing. Thus they succeeded in tiding over the troublesome beginning; and, though gradually reduced to a minority by the influx of German residents, so tenacious are they of national life that even now some hundred families claim for themselves a French descent [2].

Some of the same emigration that founded Neu-Isenburg went on into the county of Hanau. The colony in the town dates from the suppression of the protestant worship at Frankfurt; when the count invited the reformed population to build a new town beside his old one. They came in crowds, and built a great church [3]. But the date of their chief increase was at the Recall, when many wealthy people settled at Hanau, and very many more made it their thoroughfare. Between 1685 and 1714, we are told, there was scarcely a week, or a day even, in which the diaconate had not to succour some new waifs [4]. And the means at the disposal of the Walloon church were not large; it was put to great straits in harbouring the throngs of ministers and people [5]. Yet the friendly diaconate gave help, not only to those who came to Hanau, but also to the churches of [a]Mannheim, [b]Friedrichsdorf, [c]Dornholzhausen, and [d]Wuerttemberg [6]. Of those who remained inmates of the town the

margin:
1596.
1600. April 9.
[a] 1687. Feb.
[b] April 20.
[c] 1690. Oct. 15.
[d] 1698.

---

[1] But the soil was sandy, and little fertile; Weyell, 15.

[2] Weyell gives the entire population as 2682, the citizens as 430; 9 & 31. The author of the *Uebersicht der Wanderungen* speaks of there being a doubt as to the French or vaudois origin of the colony. The names in Weyell shew the considerable French element, which the anonymous compiler, pp. 40–42, 88 f., describes as only 'afterwards' decidedly preponderant.

[3] Schroeder, 19 f.   [4] Leclercq, 256.

[5] Among the former was David Ancillon, the father of the historian of the Refuge in Brandenburg: pp. 110 f., 232.   [6] pp. 108 f.

only lasting record was preserved in the craft of jewellery which they brought in with them and which long retained its fame in Germany[1].

The establishment of most of the colonies in this part of the country was in a great measure due to the activity of Pieter Valkenier[2], Dutch envoy to the empire first at Augsburg and afterwards at Ratisbon[3]. It was he also who promoted the settlement of some half-dozen villages in Hessen-Darmstadt[4].

1686.
1688.
1699.
April.

The refuge in Hessen-Homburg was of older standing. In the winter of 1685 the landgrave Friedrich the Second welcomed a number of exiles from Picardy and the isle of France[5], who almost immediately set about building the new part of Homburg called Louisenstrasse. Next year, a league apart, huguenots from Champagne, Dauphiné, and Languedoc[6] founded the village of Friedrichsdorf. The settlers were allowed the privileges of natives and immunity from taxation for ten years; and they prospered and set up a thriving manufacture of flannels[7]. It has been observed that to this day Friedrichsdorf preserves better than any other colony the language of its fathers and

1687.
Mar. 13.

---

[1] Erman and Reclam, 5. 273; 1788. Goethe mentions it in 1815: Koehler, 103.

[2] Often known, by a widespread mistake, as Walckenaer: see Koenen, *Vluchtelingen in Nederland*, 201 n. On his activity cp. Weyell, 5; Schroeder, 94.

[3] Ultimately he was minister to the Helvetic confederation. He acted also, on one occasion, as almoner to the Elector of Brandenburg: Schroeder, 89.

[4] Schroeder, 93 f. These are commonly believed to be vaudois. Yet in one of them certainly the inhabitants recall their Languedoc origin, 83 n. The vaudois entry in the autumn of 1688 (partly from the Palatinate) may be read in Bender.

[5] F. Waddington adds 'vaudois' and places their arrival a little later: *Bulletin*, 8. 80. A few came from Languedoc and Dauphiné and perhaps from the French part of Savoy: Schroeder, 92.

[6] Also from Pragelas. The author of the *Uebersicht der Wanderungen* is clearly rash when he states the settlers here and at Dornholzhausen to be mainly vaudois. A misstatement of his about the minister at Friedrichsdorf (see the *Bulletin*, 1. 83) may warrant a suspicion of his accuracy with regard to the congregation. Cp. a note of Schroeder's, 83.

[7] See an account in the *Bulletin*, 1. 81 f.

'the old refugee-traditions of faith, order, despatch, integrity¹.' Contemporary perhaps with this settlement was that at Dornholzhausen, the interest of which was purely agricultural. Here, as at Friedrichsdorf, the people have succeeded in maintaining their French service to the present time².

The landgrave of Hessen-Cassel, Karl the First, issued as early as April 18, 1685, a Freiheits-Concession allowing French immigrants to build churches and appoint their own ministers and teachers³. Various privileges were detailed, and certain places recommended by reason of the fruitfulness of their soil or their advantages for commerce. Of these only Cassel, Gudensberg, and Hofgeismar were actually chosen⁴. The landgrave's wish was to attract the manufacturing and trading classes; and enough had come by the month after the Revocation to form a congregation at Cassel⁵, enough by the end of November to need and to gain the use of the Carmelite church, to the indignation of the Lutheran ministers⁶.

Nov. 29.

The immigration divides itself into three epochs⁷. The first includes the three years following the Recall. During this period, the number of the French in Cassel⁸, and in the

---

¹ Schroeder, 92: cp. the vigorous language of M Waddington, *Bulletin*, 8. 79.

² It has been observed that the churches of Hessen-Homburg and Hessen-Darmstadt stood in a peculiarly close relation to Frankfurt; which fact may explain their vitality. In several the French service was maintained as late as 1829: Schroeder, 94.

³ Chr. von Rommel, *zur Geschichte der französischen Colonien in Hessen-Cassel*, 9; Cassel, 1857.

⁴ The others were Homberg, Felsberg, Grebenstein, and Melsungen: Koehler, 58.

⁵ They met, we are told, at seven in the morning of the 28th of October [November 7] in the house of one Grandidier a tradesman: *Bulletin*, 1. 347 ff.: cp. C. von Rommel, 89.

⁶ The *Brüderkirche*; see C. von Rommel, 19. A collection was ordered December 1: one of the administrators being Lenfant, the historian of the Council of Constance. Help was thus given to Frankfurt, Heidelberg, Mannheim, and Maastricht: Koehler, 58.

⁷ See a catalogue of the settlements in supplementary note ix.

⁸ To speak however of three thousand in the spring of 1686 is to say too much: *Bulletin*, 1. 348.

villages of Immenhausen and Hofgeismar, so increased that a huguenot architect Paul du Ry[1] was summoned from Holland to build two new villages, Karlsdorf and Mariendorf, and ultimately the fine suburb of the capital long known as the Franzoesische Oberneustadt[2]. The influx was vaudois, but of the vaudois chiefly within French dominion. Immenhausen was filled from Embrunois and Pragelas, and its overflow went to Mariendorf[3]. The population of Hofgeismar had a similar origin, from Pragelas and Queyras[4]: and as it became surcharged, it gave many colonists to Brandenburg and formed the main foundation of Karlsdorf[5].

1687.
1688.

Cassel was now busy with workpeople. They made carpets and cloths, hats and gloves, jewellery and all sorts of ornamental wares: the townsmen complained that they were undersold[6], There were two French congregations, with three ministers; each had its reader and six elders[7]. For their civil concerns there had been since 1686 a French Commission[8], whose jurisdiction held even over the German burghers of the Oberneustadt,

---

[1] His son and grandson followed him as court-architects in Hesse: Koehler, 65 n.
[2] It was enlarged and improved by Landgrave Friedrich II. The church was founded August 3 1698, and opened in 1710: a French service is still occasionally held. The overflow of the Oberneustadt went in 1694 to Hertingshausen and elsewhere: pp. 60 & 64. Germans were admitted by an ordinance of February 11 1697: p. 62.
[3] The landgrave gave the new colony its support for a year; and distributed lands. Its church was built between 1701 & 1705: p. 78.
[4] A hundred and fifty households came in 1685: p. 72.
[5] P. 74.
[6] The French set up manufactories of tobacco and looking-glasses, but these did not succeed: C. von Rommel, 19; cp. the *Bulletin*, 1. 348.
[7] The entire number of elders had been raised to eight in June 1686: *Bulletin*, as above. The consistory at Cassel had supreme jurisdiction over all the churches in the landgraviate, and from 1724 the senior member was inspector-general. But ordinary business was transacted, according to the situation of the churches, by the consistories of Cassel and Marburg respectively: Koehler, 67 f.
[8] The *Commissaires de la régence pour les affaires des français*: C. von Rommel, 14; who as kurfürstlicher hessische Staats-Rath is careful about these things.

as well as in suits where both parties were French in the Altstadt. They had also a separate Court of Appeal, with its Ober-Appellationsgerichts-Rath, a Kanzleirath, assessor, clerk, and remembrancer [1]. The distinct French society was completed by a hospital given by the landgrave [2], and by the benevolent fund which he set on foot wherever the French came to settle [3].

1687.

Karlsdorf and Mariendorf soon filled [4]; and new colonies were planted in the province of Upper Hesse. To the university of Marburg came Denis Papin, whose digester had been astonishing the Royal Society of London, and who nearly gave the world the appliance of steam to locomotion [5]. He was professor of mathematics; Gautier of theology. The latter bequeathed to his fellow-exiles some land at Frauenberg hard

1687-8.

by; and the colonisation of Frauenberg and Louisendorf went together. Louisendorf represents Hammonshausen, a village ruined and without inhabitants; when now revived, it was named afresh after a princess of Hesse. But it did not flourish at once. The French [6] could not be happy in the rough huts which were all they had for dwelling; they resolved to seek a new home in some other country. The landgrave however forestalled them,

1691.

and built them houses [7].

The colonies grew quietly for some years, and the villages, as they became too crowded, sent out offshoots to waste-lands near. The only hindrance they had to contend with was the countrymen's tenacity of their mark-rights; and this in many

---

[1] Koehler, 66 f.   [2] *Bulletin*, 4. 541 f.   [3] Koehler, 69.

[4] The overflow went to Frankenberg (336 families), to Schwabendorf (30 families), and to other places, as Geismar and Ellershausen: p. 59.

[5] Schroeder, 92; Smiles, *Huguenots*, 289 ff.

[6] They came principally from Die in Dauphiné: *Uebersicht der Wanderungen*, 85.

[7] A similar case occurred at Schwabendorf near by. The stocking-weavers were discontented; and some in fact dispersed in 1690. But the rest reasonably concluded that the cost of travelling might equal the expense of building good houses; which they carried into effect. The colony had been founded, June 30 1687; its church was opened in 1711: Koehler, 96 f.

instances drove them to found new villages in the open country[1]. The settlers reclaimed moors; they improved the meadows and the art of gardening[2]. They bred cattle and opened mines of coal[3].

A second period of immigration followed the peace of Rijswijk, by which some thirteen thousand protestants, a mixed throng of huguenots and vaudois, were thrown upon Germany. The landgrave of Hessen-Cassel was at his wits' end at the approach of perhaps half this multitude[4]. He hurriedly sent messengers to the duke of Brunswick, to the duke of Sachsen-Gotha, to the diaconate of Frankfurt, already exhausted by its work of charity. England, Holland, and Switzerland sent their help[5]; and the rush of immigrants was met by the making ready of a number of villages for their reception[6]. Before the autumn of 1699 a thousand had invaded the landgraviate. Some were given Treysa[7] and Wolfhagen, a place which had been ruined in the tumult of the Thirty Years' War, to rouse into a new prosperity. Eight villages were founded for them; the chief, Syburg, or as it came to be called Carlshafen[8], a beautiful town hidden in a rocky circle of steep cliffs[9].

1699.
Aug. 14.

---

[1] C. von Rommel, 18 f. Of such an origin was Kelse: Koehler, 73. At Schwabendorf they had to fell a thousand oaks before they could begin building: pp. 96 f.

[2] On the agriculture, see Arnaud, *Protestants de Dauphiné*, 3. 22; who shews how much of this progress was due to Dauphinois immigrants. Before this time, asparagus, cauliflower, and artichokes, were known only to the landgrave; the refugees made them common everywhere: C. von Rommel, 20, n. 2. They are said also to have introduced turkeys, and possibly potatoes: *Bulletin*, 1. 349.   [3] *Bulletin*, as above.

[4] It is stated that six thousand of them actually settled in the landgraviate: *Bulletin*, as above.   [5] Koehler, 60 f.

[6] A thousand came from Dauphiné alone: p. 79. The Dauphinois element is distinguished at Kelse and Wiesenfeld.

[7] It was peopled by a hundred households of an industrial interest, from Dauphiné. They were allowed their worship in the hospital church, until a French church was built near by at Frankenhain. The colony was soon dispersed among the other settlements: pp. 84 f.

[8] It received the name in 1717: p. 61.

[9] P. 71. Schoeneberg belongs to the same colonisation. It had its

Isolated in the province of Fulda was the French village of Gethsemane or Goettsemanns. The Dauphinois farmers who peopled it had long been straying about in search of a settled dwelling. From their first stopping-stage, at Vach and Hersfeld, they had posted themselves on the top of a hill by Friedewald. But still they had to depend for their religious service on the willing help of the minister at Vach. This failing, they came to attend the German church of the neighbourhood, until at last in 1742 they were able to engage a minister of their own[1]. The friendly union with the German community all this time had not however blunted their national instinct. To this day their striving to continue French in speech and habit is remarked as more intense and vivid than that of any other of the Hessian colonies[2].

The last period in the immigration was in the year 1720, when the exiles,—some vaudois[3],—who had long been wandering in Wuerttemberg and Baden, some forlornly hoping for the means of getting to Brunswick, came and found rest in four villages of Hesse. The names of the two latest,—Gottestreu and Gewissensruhe,—are a fit commentary on the history of these longsuffering people[4].

The accounts of the refuge in Hessen-Cassel give the impression of an industrial and agricultural settlement[5]: but all were

---

church in 1706; but at the end of the century it numbered no more than twenty-two families, equally distributed in French and German nationalities: p. 73.

[1] The case of S Ottilie was similar. The German minister at Helsa supplied the need of weekly services. Printed sermons were preached by a reader who came for the purpose from Cassel, and the inspector-general at intervals administered the Lord's supper: p. 81.

[2] Koehler, 86 ff.

[3] A mixture existed at Todenhausen and Wiesenfeld. The former made up two several villages, parted by the little river Wettschaft, Deutsch- and Franzoesisch-Todenhausen. The church subsisted from 1744 to 1755: p. 90 ff. Wiesenfeld was colonised by some who had at first settled in the district of Solms-Braunfels: pp. 94 f.

[4] C. von Rommel, 10 f.; Koehler, 62, 82.

[5] At Treysa and Frankenhain lands were assigned to the immigrants, and

not such. The second immigration brought in, it is said, some hundred and fifty noble, or at the least gentle, families [1]. Without an element of this kind it would be hard to understand how the French were able so long to hold their ground, especially in Cassel, against the national prejudices. We have noticed a few cases in which their interests clashed [2]; but the French were unpopular for other reasons. Their lively, lighthearted, behaviour in common life seemed frivolous to the staid German: their talkativeness in church, where they would hand round their snuff-boxes, and where the minister would mount the pulpit with his hat on; their strange dress with short cloaks, *like apothecaries;*—all these things could but separate them from the people of the place [3]. The one point of contact was in the German reformed community, whose good offices were often useful to the poorer of the huguenots. As the latter lost the language they had brought with them, they in almost all cases united themselves to the kindred body. 'The French communities,' says Koehler, 'have now become part of the people. Only here and there we meet a few of elder age who use the French tongue by preference, while a certain French type or a French name gives new witness to their origin [4].'

---

much hemp was cultivated. In Frankenhain, where the church dates from 1754, the huguenot factor hardly survives; but their legacy in sundry industries of wool-combing, stocking-weaving, and hat-making, remains a permanent benefit to the place: pp. 84 f.

[1] *Bulletin*, I. 348.

[2] The Germans cannot have been well pleased at the regulation which placed their own parochial business in the hands of the French presbytery, in places where no other existed: Koehler, 68.

[3] C. von Rommel, 18.

[4] P. 68.

CHAPTER XIII.

THE PLANTATION IN BRANDENBURG.

THE establishment of the huguenots in the electorate of Brandenburg is a subject which from its immense extent it is hard more than to touch in the two short chapters now following. The literature runs from the small volume, yet much longer than its contents should allow[1], of Charles Ancillon, published in 1690[2], to the profuse collections of a Société de Savants known after their editors by the names of Erman and Reclam[3], and

---

[1] 'Ce styl diffus des réfugiés' said Capefigue, *Louis XIV*, 6. 36, of Basnage unfairly. Ancillon might better illustrate what is doubtless a true characterisation of common refugee writing.

[2] *Histoire de l'Établissement des François réfugiez dans les États de s. A. electorale de Brandebourg.* Caveirac's sneer that 'il écrivoit pour la gloire du dieu des réfugiés et pour celle du prince qui leur servoit de refuge,' *Apologie de Louis XIV*, 87, s. l. 1758, may find its vindication in such noisy fulsomeness as this from the dedication : ' Il est impossible de faire voir que les siècles passez ayent jamais vû d'actions aussi génèreuses que celles que votre altesse electorale a faites en faveur des réfugiez, et par consèquent les siècles à venir n'en auront point de plus glorieuses à admirer dans l'histoire qui leur sera laissée'; or again, 'votre a. e. a mesme parû ce qu'on disoit autrefois qu'étoit l'empereur Trajan, un dieu mortel'; pp. 8 f. Friedrich Wilhelm has not only 'done infinitely more' than Fabius Maximus or Busa or Hiero of Syracuse; he is not only a greater lawgiver than Philip Augustus (p. 277), a greater benefactor than S William of Nevers or Cosmo dei Medici (p. 287), but even, in the language of the apostle, 'nous disons que son a. e. est enfant de Dieu, et que ce qu'il sera n'est point encore apparû, (p. 291); and Brandenburg is the Valley of Blessings of the Book of Chronicles (p. 23).

[3] *Mémoires pour servir à l'Histoire des Réfugiés dans les États du Roi*; Berlin 1782-1792. The names of the editors first appear in the second volume; and M Reclam died before the series was completed.

filling eleven years and nine volumes in their issue[1]. The importance of the settlement may warrant this exhaustive handling: but happily for me most of the literary apparatus belongs to a date beyond the scope of this history. My object can only be to describe the immigration and the way the immigrants settled down: it would be foreign to the purpose to enquire into their state beyond the limit of the seventeenth century, or to diverge into the engaging study of their influence on life, thought, and manners, when the electorate became a kingdom.

All states that are liberal of naturalisation towards strangers are fit for empire[2]*;* and it is no curious nor inconsiderate judgement which will find in the establishment of the French in Brandenburg a presage of the dignity of the kingdom of Prussia. *If a man be gracious and courteous to strangers it shews that he is a citizen of the world and that his heart is no island cut off from other lands, but a continent that joins to them*[3]. Friedrich Wilhelm, the Great Elector of Brandenburg, may shew also a signal picture of this other saying. Himself a Calvinist, he had been from the treaty of Nijmegen the friend and ally of Lewis the Fourteenth[4]. But the French joint action with the catholic aims of the English king, and the growing oppression of the huguenots in church and home, urged a recoil from former friendship the more violent since its appeal lay equally to the elector's instincts of faith and of public policy. The final proscription of his own religion in France attached him loyally to the league of Augsburg. In little more than a fortnight from the issue of the Edict of Recall, his counterblast in the Edict of Potsdam declared that he had not only definitely ranged himself on the 1685. [Oct. 29.] Nov. 8.

---

[1] Handbooks have also appeared more recently by C. Reyer, *Geschichte der französischen Kolonie in Preussen*, Berlin 1852; and K. F. Koehler, *die Réfugiés und ihre Kolonien in Preussen und Kurhessen*, Gotha 1867. The latter work has been of special service in the history of Hesse-Cassel. Poorly written as it is, it is crowded with a mass of facts elsewhere for the most part inaccessible.

[2] Bacon, *Essay of the true Greatness of Kingdoms*.

[3] *Essay of Goodness*.

[4] Burnet, *History of his own Times*, I. 747.

side adverse to Lewis, but also that it was his purpose to do all he could to befriend as many huguenots as he could gather in his dominions. The ground had already been prepared by his envoy at Versailles, Ezechiel Spanheim, whose father Frédéric had left the Palatinate to settle as minister and professor at Geneva and finally at Leyden. The son was as much a scholar and divine by training as he was by profession a diplomatist[1]; and he made use of the means which his position afforded him to spread among the huguenots of the French capital a knowledge of the advantages they might hope for in Brandenburg, and of the kindness and warmth with which they would be received[2]. Spanheim's successor, Count d'Espence, followed in the same lines, and it was through his choice that the renowned preacher Jacques Abbadie came to the elector's chapel in 1680. The Edict of Potsdam appeared the fulfilment of these silent anticipations[3].

It began by stating that the elector had appointed a commissioner at Amsterdam to take charge of the fugitives and supply them with provisions and a passage as far as Hamburg, where they would come into the care of the Brandenburg resident (art. i). Those who came from the south of France or were otherwise prevented from travelling by way of Holland, might go to Cologne or to Frankfurt, where the electoral agents would furnish them with passports, money, and boats, whereby they might betake themselves into the duchy of Cleve (ii). The Edict went on to suggest certain places for settlement. They might stay in Cleve or Mark, or they might proceed to places

---

[1] In 1702 he became ambassador at the court of S James's. He died 1710.

[2] Sayous, *la Littérature française à l'Étranger*, 2. 132 f. Erman and Reclam mention a short-lived colony at Landsberg, a league from Berlin, founded before 1661 by some huguenots won over by the address of the Brandenburg envoy von Schwerin: 1. 57 f.; cp. Weiss, 1. 126.

[3] I have used the original copy as circulated at the time in Dutch: *Edict van sijne ceurvoorstelijcke Doorluchtigheyt, &c.*, printed at the Hague. It may be read in all the special histories, as Erman and Reclam, 1. 129-141; Reyer, 85-89.

like Stendal, Brandenburg, and Frankfurt in the electoral March[1], to Halle, Magdeburg, and Calbe in Magdeburg, or to Koenigsberg in Prussia. Wherever they went they should meet with every commercial encouragement (ii, iii). Goods, furniture, merchandise, or wares, that they should bring with them, were declared free of all charges and impositions[2] (iv).

Some of the provisions of the edict shew how advantageous it was to repair the desolation which war had inflicted on the country by the bringing in of these huguenots. Thus, *In case that in the towns, boroughs, or villages, where the said persons of religion shall go to inhabit, there be found houses dilapidated, void, or quitted by their tenants, the which the owners are not able to restore to good condition, these we hereby assign and grant in full ownership to the said immigrants ;* who were also given building materials, and a variety of privileges (v). Another clause tells how all the magistrates were ordered to make lists of houses to let, and how wherever an immigrant found the space for building a house, he might have also the garden and meadow free, and no taxes for ten years[3] (vi).

---

[1] Werben and Rathenow were also designated, but I do not hear that they received any colonies.

[2] This liberality towards the huguenots was seconded, according to the ideas of the time, by two protective enactments, one prohibiting the export of horses to France, the other all import of French commodities: *Historie van de Vervolging*, 3. 37. The same spirit is expressed by the note of Ancillon as to the freedom of the immigrants' goods: 'Ils les ont affranchies en disant qu'ils les avoient sauvées de France'; pp. 262 f. It should seem that the prohibition of French imports was only temporary. But it was soon found desirable to fix a duty of ten per cent. upon such commodities: Declaration of February 22 1689. The manufacturers in France had been forced to meet the constant diminution of their trade by a corresponding abatement of price. German merchants in Brandenburg were therefore enabled to undersell the refugees. To encourage the latter it was provided that when they were capable of supplying all the country needed, the duty on French imports should be enhanced to 25 per cent.: pp. 236-246; Koehler, 25.

[3] At the expiration of this term it was found necessary to extend the privilege for another five years, after which the usual taxes were to be commuted for a fixed charge: pp. 26 f.

In towns, they were to have immunities and privileges and maintenance of the kind we have already seen accorded by the goodwill of the Dutch nation or by the authority of the duke of Brunswick[1]. Every town where the refugees made their settlement was to have a church and minister supported by the state[2] (xi); and their private contentions were to be arranged by a judicature of their own (x). The working of these two articles illustrates well the special character of the French settlement in the electorate. The latter provision created the elaborate 'peculiar' of French jurisdiction which subsisted from 1686 to 1812[3]; the other indeed promised the continuance of that church-discipline which had been the centre of huguenot life in France[4], but the republican synod was very soon replaced by a High Consistory which was nothing less than a committee of council, as we should call it, for the affairs of the French church[5]. This is the instinct of the system of the Hohenzollern. Everything must be directly under the hand of the minister: no space can be given for free development[6].

---

[1] See above, pp. 36 f., 71.

[2] Such ministers as could find no place in the colonies, or were disabled by age, the elector supported from his privy purse: Ancillon, 60 f.

[3] *Bulletin*, 19. 178 f.; Ancillon, 76-111. In 1699 the provisional Prozess-Ordnung was replaced by the Ordonnance Française, closely modelled on the Code Louis: Koehler, 23.

[4] One clause provided 'that the French do have the exercise of their religion, according to the customs, and with the same ceremonies, that were used among them in France': Ancillon, 63 f.; cp. 353 f. In concession however to the custom of German worship, the French ministers uncovered their heads when officiating, and abandoned the use of gowns: pp. 71 f.

[5] An Ordinance of December 7 1689 created a Kirchen-Commission, which came into existence May 4 1694. A Patent of July 26 following gave it all the powers of the German Ober-Consistorium; but its action was limited by an Ordinance, regarding the internal constitution of the church, of March 8 1698: Koehler, 24.

[6] Cp. the notice of Ancillon that a despotism was required for those who received support from the state. They did not know the ways of the country, and therefore were obliged 'à avoir une grande soûmission et à se laisser conduire.' It was impossible to allow them to live 'une vie cyclopique': pp. 215 ff.

The appeal of the elector, upheld by the open-handed bounty of his people[1], did not fail to attract a multitude of fugitives to the country: the poorest but the most industrious of the emigration, is their character given by Frederick the Great[2]. From Metz came the minister David Ancillon, founder of a distinguished Prussian family[3]; and with him two or three thousand people of the Pays Messin[4], who are said to have brought into Berlin the culture of gardens and orchards[5]. Ancillon shared with four French gentlemen, who had settled some years earlier in the electorate, the work of organising the new colony. He undertook the establishment of his own friends and neighbours from Metz. The Count de Beauveau, the father of the French Church in Berlin[6], and its first almoner, took care for the emigrants from the isle of France, his native district; Henry de Briquemault, governor of Lippstadt[7], for those from Champagne; Gaultier de Saint Blancard, Languedoc; Claude du Bellay, Poitou: while Abbadie saw to the comfort of the exiles of Béarn[8]. Everything was done on the most orderly

---

[1] The *Historie van de Vervolging* names '100,000 rijkxdaalders,' or thalers, as having been collected by December 1685; 3. 109: cp. Koenen, *Vluchtelingen in Nederland*, 53.

[2] *Mémoires pour servir à l'Histoire de la Maison de Brandebourg*, 2. 298; Berlin, 1751.

[3] His son Charles is the historian of the Refuge; he was judge of the French court: Haag, *la France protestante*, under the name. His descendant Frédéric was honourably known as a statesman, and the author of the *Tableau des Révolutions*, to which I have occasionally referred.

[4] Weiss, 1. 136. Peyrat says decidedly 3600: *Histoire des Pasteurs du Désert*, 1. 83; and so Wenz, *Emden*, 178.

[5] The colony at Berlin seems to date from 1661; the church from 1672: Erman and Reclam, 1. 58 ff.; cp. Kochler, 57.

[6] Cuvier, pref. to Olry, *la Persécution de l'Église de Metz*, 52.

[7] Ancillon says that the large number of persons of rank pensioned by the elector resorted to Lippstadt in preference to any other place, on account of the generous society of the governor and his wife: pp. 53 f.

[8] Weiss, 1. 133-137. Abbadie's services were also valuable in maintaining a close connexion with the stronghold of Calvinism. His visits to Holland in 1684, 1686, and 1688 acquainted the refugees there with their prospects in Brandenburg, and increased the colony.

system; and thus it is with small exaggeration that Charles Ancillon says, *The refugees of each province at home are almost all established in one place together*[1]. The general supervision of the settlement was entrusted to the minister of state Grumkow, whose exercise of his function, while it may not merit the overcharged flattery of Ancillon[2], will support equally little the 'vulpine' character, shewing 'the depths of his own greed, of his own astucities, and stealthy audacities,' which Mr Carlyle attributes to him[3]. And the elector, by his personal watch over all details of the arrangement, was able to complete the task of distributing the French among his provinces, without giving any of that disturbance in the domestic balance of the people, which so great an influx might seem almost inevitably to involve. His deep interest in the prosperity of the Refuge made him supply from his privy purse the unaccustomed charges which else had drained his Exchequer; without ostentation, he saved the need of imposing a single new tax[4].

Bearing in mind what has been said as to the essentially despotic character of the Brandenburg colony[5] it falls now to review the colony in detail: and such a review will allow a free division between the towns and the country, or between the trade and the husbandry of the refugees. The higher ranks may be treated apart, as their interests were several, in connexion with the society of Berlin. Westphalia, as the first part

---

[1] P. 84. 'The colonies,' he adds, 'are all naturally placed, so that it may be hoped that they will last as long as if they that compose them had been born in the country, or as if they yet lived in the land of their birth': p. 85.

[2] Ancillon, 25 ff.

[3] *History of Friedrich II of Prussia*, I. 392: 'Grumkow, a cunning, greedy-hearted, long-headed fellow, of the old Pomeranian nobility by birth, has a kind of superficial polish put upon his hyperboreanisms: he has been in foreign countries, doing legations, diplomacies, for which, at least for the vulpine parts of which, he has a turn. He writes and speaks articulate grammatical French; but neither in that nor in his native Pommerish Platt-Deutsch, does he show us much, except the depth of his own greed, of his own astucities and stealthy audacities.'

[4] Koenen, 55; Reyer, 104 f.   [5] Cp. above, p. 148 & n. 6.

of the electorate to which the French came, received a mixed company, which from its number and from the rapidity of its inflow barely admitted a regular distribution. Its towns, Cleve, Wesel, Emmerich, and at a later stage in the settlement Duisburg, were well fitted for the purpose of serving as a refuge to the exiles. Their neighbourhood to France made the journey the less difficult, and their close relations with the United Provinces prevented those who stayed in them from that isolation which might be feared from a deeper penetration into the country[1].

Magdeburg and the electoral March had a more permanent advantage from the ingress, repeated in the vaudois exodus of 1687[2], and in the arrival of fugitives from France, Piedmont, and the Palatinate in the following years[3]. The rage of the Thirty Years' War had spent itself in the ruin of this country. Magdeburg since its sack in 1631 had lain a wreck: but its position on the Elbe gave assurance of its prosperity, could only the moving power be found. The French,—in number, says Ancillon, beyond count,—supplied the needed energy, and Magdeburg became *one of the strongest and most flourishing colonies in the state*[4]. Its trade with Hamburg was restored, and industries of many sorts, and of wool particularly, were established. Halle was the scene of a like transformation. It was now *filled with so many manufacturers* of stuffs and lace, *and resorted to by so many merchants of experience and means*, that it soon became a rival to the commercial eminence of Leipzig[5].

The refugees scattered over the Uckermark found the tract a vast desolation; but knowing the rare richness of the soil they were not discouraged from the attempt to give effect to the

---

[1] Ancillon, 55.

[2] This settlement mainly affected Stendal, Spandau, and Burg-an-der-Ihle, *Uebersicht der Wanderungen*, 18. It was in fact in this year that the elector gained possession of the last-named place, by exchange from the duke of Sachsen-Weissenfels; Bender, *Geschichte der Waldenser*, 278.

[3] They came to Magdeburg in 1689: Koehler, 28.

[4] Ancillon, 51. [5] Pp. 48 f.

systematised scheme of settlement laid down by the elector. They made their own separate colonies in groups, Battin, Bergholz, and Gramzow, each comprising six or more villages; and they built anew the deserted town of Prenzlau[1]. Hemp and flax were grown; and the tobacco-plant, until now scarcely heard of in the country[2], was cultivated with such success that it not only met the demand at home but added to the revenue of the state by its export to Bohemia and Silesia, and to the markets of Poland, Sweden, and Denmark[3]. The French, by their natural taste for making gardens about their cottages, gave to the entire March a fresh look of comfort; and their kitchen-gardening yielded them a profit the greater as the art was almost their sole property. The common society of the colonists, united in religion and speech, was finally and firmly welded together in the closing years of the century by the new exiles of Savoy,—the same horde we have already seen in Hessen-Cassel,—and a few years later by the remnant from the town of Orange[4]. It is said that many of the present landowners occupy the same holdings that were given them at this time.

If the agricultural classes made the most rapid change in the face of the country they settled in, in the duchy of Magdeburg, in the Marches, and in electoral Pomerania, the progress effected in all the crafts and manufactures in which France had been supreme, and for which Brandenburg had been almost entirely

---

[1] See on the whole, supplementary note x. Gramzow-in-Uckermark must not be confounded, as it often has been confounded through a fluctuation in spelling, with Gransee-in-Mittelmark.

[2] See Reyer, 191 f., who illustrates the fact by an anecdote. The cultivation of tobacco extended to Burg in the Mittelmark and Stendal in the Altmark.

[3] Weiss, I. 173.

[4] To the places referred to above, p. 42, n. 2, may be added the *short History of the Revolution in Orange*, 1703, quarto. At the first warning of this new emigration, Geneva sent messengers to help her in making ready for the refugees, not only to the protestant cantons, but also to Holland, England, and Brandenburg: p. 29. Their memorial in the last country remains in the town Oranienburg.

dependent upon her, was no less decisive[1]. The French moreover nearly succeeded in creating for the elector a maritime trade, of which Koenigsberg was the only centre in his European dominions, but which existed in a considerable prosperity in his trading stations in the West Indies, at Saint Eustace and Saint Thomas, on the Guinea Coast and at the mouth of the Senegal[2].

The manufacture will be most conveniently studied in connexion with its centre, Berlin; and the following chapter may well embrace, besides, the settlement and condition of the educated and idle classes, the ministers, soldiers, and nobility, whose life elsewhere appears but as a reflexion of their state in the capital. In conformity with the Prussian system, Berlin is the type of everything in the smaller towns: there is no art or culture outside which is unrepresented there.

---

[1] Ancillon, 221.
[2] Weiss, 145 f. These depôts were ceded to Holland in 1720; their original intention had been naval.

CHAPTER XIV.

THE FRENCH COLONY IN BERLIN.

FRIEDRICH WILHELM, the Great Elector, died in 1688: but his death implied no change in the administration of the French state he had embodied in his people. Friedrich the Third, King Frederick the First of Prussia as he became in the first year of the eighteenth century, followed the lines his father had drawn for him in an identical spirit[1]. He had not his father's genius of creation, but he had the same earnest perseverance of aim and the same thorough business-like activity. His failing was that, in his ambitious seeking after the royal title, he imported a luxury into his court, which became a vogue of extravagance, and caused his subjects more than it was worth in an enhanced taxation[2]. It was a vice however that hardly touched the huguenots, and they grew up in their new busy world as though the Great Elector was still among them. A class of their number even were the gainers. For his death gave a wider field to the intellectual power of the electress Sophia Charlotte, sister of our George the First, and wife to King Frederick[3]; and among the lettered men she gathered about her at Berlin and Charlottenburg, her influence consolidated the severed fragments, which might else have run into antagonism, and built up from them the intellectual society of Berlin, which increased in force with the rise of the Academy

---

[1] 'Ce n'est qu'un même esprit,' says Ancillon: *Établissemen'*, 32.
[2] Koehler, *Réfugiés*, 20.   [3] Cp. the *Bulletin*, 2. 670.

and attained a real and just prominence under Frederick the Great.

For the present it is the trade and craft of the colony that strikes the eye. To the old towns of Berlin and Coeln, Friedrich Wilhelm had joined Neu-Coeln and Friedrichswerder: his son finished Friedrichstadt and Dorotheenstadt. Excepting the last, the aristocratical part, all these quarters were swollen by the working men of the immigration [1], who introduced a multitude of arts as yet unknown in the rougher civilisation of the north, and who throve by the end of the century to the tale of ten thousand souls, weavers of stockings, serges, and all sorts of woollen stuff; silk-workers; makers of hats and gloves; busy in tanyards and oilworks [2]: locksmiths, ironmongers, cutlers, goldsmiths; not an industry but claimed its place among the labours of the French [3], very few but were their special or their exclusive possession [4]. As in England, paper and glass were before this time only made in the commonest and coarsest kinds. Paper was now manufactured in its finer qualities at Berlin, and also in several of the remoter settlements [5]. The looking-glasses of Neustadt-an-der-Dosse were said to excel the ware of Venice [6]. These are types in the domain of material

---

[1] Weiss, 1. 170.

[2] Rossier notices the preparation of colza-oil as introduced into Brandenburg from Amiens and Abbeville; *Protestants de Picardie*, 252.

[3] The Dauphinois element in this creation of trade has been discriminated by Arnaud, *Protestants de Dauphiné*, 3. 22 f. Dyeing and watchmaking were among their importations; and they formed a major part of the hatters and glovers of Berlin, Frankfurt, and Magdeburg, and of the glovers of Halle and Halberstadt: cp. the *Uebersicht der Wanderungen*, 73. Cuvier, on his side, traces the work of the exiles of Metz in cutlery and jewellery, in chandlers' ware, wig-making, distilling, and sundry other things, besides the common industries of silk, gloves, and hats: pref. to Olry, *Metz*, 51 f. See, on the whole subject, the *Mémoires de la Maison de Brandebourg*, 2. 299 ff.

[4] The engravers, jewellers, goldsmiths, and clockmakers of Berlin were long solely French: Koehler, 32.

[5] There was for instance a paper-mill set up by one from Grenoble at Burg-an-der-Ihle: Arnaud, as above.

[6] *Mémoires de Brandebourg*, 2. 305.

progress: and they might find a thousand parallels ranging from great manufactures to the smallest, but not therefore the least important, gains to thrift and daily comfort [1].

Besides the manufactures and the shops of the French, the colony included a large mercantile element. Berlin, Frankfurt-am-Oder [2], and Magdeburg held a correspondence not only with the inner parts of the country, but also through their rivers, with the maritime towns and abroad. The river Spree extended further the prosperity and industry of Berlin. At Koepenik trade grew up round the elector's country-house. Brandenburg for awhile seemed to see its old fame revive, when at the moment of the first immigration the elector threw open *the old monastery near the cathedral* to the penniless crowd [3], fed them some time, and helped them for several years [4].

The French achieved a commercial supremacy; and the native population, first jealous as of competitors and strangers, were lessoned by their excellence to put themselves and their children under their guidance [5]. The trade of Brandenburg

---

[1] Ancillon commemorates the introduction of sedan-chairs and of cookshops. 'The establishment of cookshops has cost the elector infinitely more pains than that of the hand-chairs: at the same time we must admit that it is of greater value to the public': pp. 266 f.

[2] The favourable position of Frankfurt, and the existence soon of a university there, attracted, we are told, 'not only workpeople and tradesfolk, but even manufacturers of sundry sorts, and persons of all ranks, making a goodly company': Ancillon, 47 f Its first industry was specially of wigs and wool-carding: in the following century it was occupied with tobacco-planting until 1770, when silk became the prevailing interest: *Bulletin*, 19. 132.

[3] *Historie van de Vervolging*, 3. 41. Ancillon gives an additional inducement in the cheapness of living; pp. 52 f.

[4] They made a large cloth-manufacture, and also drove a trade in carpets and stockings: *Uebersicht der Wanderungen*, 72.

[5] Ancillon tells how this example benefited the Germans. 'Many who erewhile sought for bread now find it in their houses. Their work is taken home; they do it in the midst of their families; and they are paid to the time and to the price: in such wise that they who formerly knew not where to look for food for themselves or for their children, have now sure wages to sustain their household withal': pp. 224 f.

became for a time French, and it was governed in the minute protective spirit of the system of Colbert[1]. In the larger enterprises of mines and metal-founding the refugees opened a field almost unworked. A rude tin-trade Germany had always known but hardly developed. This, with the imported arts of iron and steel smelting, furnished the houses with ironmongery of home-workmanship. The refugees diverted to their workshops the copper which Sweden had hitherto sent to the markets of France, and they were able in their turn to supply an export of the metal to Holland and Poland[2]. The iron-trade had another importance, in connexion with the step of Brandenburg into the rank of kingdoms, since the new furnaces gave it the arms for which she had previously depended on foreign countries.

As in England and Holland, a large part of the immigrant gentry, whose profession had been in the army of Lewis the Fourteenth, freely transferred their services to that of their new country; and the historians of the French colony exhaust themselves in telling of the achievements of their heroes at Neuss, and Kaiserswerth, and Bonn[3]. But here as elsewhere the significance of the French soldiery was in their moral sway, which multiplied many times their real efficiency[4]. Their numbers also were far from contemptible[5]. Two splendid companies of Grands Mousquetaires were formed of officers only, under Marshal Schomberg and his son[6]; another was of horse-grenadiers[7]. Their sons were distributed into corps

---

[1] Weiss, I. 158. There was a Factory Board, of which the president had a seat in the electoral council. Every quarter an inspection was made, not only of the manufactures of the French, but also of the manufacturers themselves: Ancillon, 225-231.

[2] Weiss, I. 164 f.

[3] Ancillon, 198 ff.; Weiss, I. 183; Smiles, *Huguenots in England*, 275 f.

[4] Cp. above, pp. 101 ff.

[5] The officers alone must have numbered six hundred: Weiss, I. 139.

[6] They were conspicuous in the bravery of their equipment: Ancillon, 181.

[7] There were also corps of engineers and miners: pp. 184 ff.; cp. Erman and Reclam, I. 255 n.

of gentlemen-cadets: and the liberal justice of the elector gave pensions to those who from any cause did not choose to resume the military office; or they were attached to the service of the civil administration. Every officer who entered Brandenburg received a promotion of rank[1]. The private soldiers were enrolled in new companies to the German regiments; and the regiments of the marquess de Varennes and of Henry de Briquemault were mainly formed or recruited from the body of the refugees[2]. General de Briquemault was also governor of the important garrison-town of Lippstadt, which, like Prenzlau, was the resort of an unusual number of officers and noble families.

These noble families, whether in the Friedrichstadt of the capital or dispersed about the electorate, were welcomed with a marked courtesy. They took at once the place in the social order which they had occupied in France[3], and, whether by places or pensions, a fitting maintenance was furnished them. In common with others of the German princes, it was the aim of Friedrich Wilhelm to impress upon the unpolished surface of the manner of his court something of the refinement and the grace of France. The desire was perhaps premature; but the influence of the strange noblesse, so far as it went, was solid and civilising. To be brought through the French language into communication with the rest of Europe was by itself no small gain: but this larger and more enduring intercourse was founded less by the magnates of the court than by the preachers of the French churches and the masters of the French schools.

The church was as precisely organised as the rest of the arrangements of the colony; and it was fortunate that the ability, for the most part, of its officers extended their scope of action and kept that close alliance with the humanities and

---

[1] See, on the whole, Ancillon, 163–209.
[2] Weiss, 1. 140 f.
[3] According to art. xii. of the Edict of Potsdam.

their exponents which must always be essential to the healthy progress of a religious establishment [1]. When Ancillon wrote, in 1690, Berlin had its two churches and a service of nine ministers [2]: a tenth was attached to the hospital which the electors had built, and which he maintained at his own charges, for the behoof of the French [3]. To Halle, Magdeburg, and Frankfurt-am-Oder, were each assigned three ministers: other towns had two or one as the case might require; no colony was without the means of public worship. Ancillon is constantly appreciative of the social or mental excellences of these clergymen [4]; their spiritual qualifications being taken for granted. And his applause, or the homage of his silence, was worthily bestowed. Jacques Abbadie stands out for us as the representative of this union of culture and religion, the author of the *Treatise of the Verity of the Christian Faith*, which Madame de Sévigny judged *The divinest of all books*, who, coming to England in the friendship of Schomberg, was dignified, though he knew no English, with the deanery of Killaloe. The tendencies which he promoted were carried into a wider field by the band of scholar-divines and philosophers who gave their stamp to the schools founded for the French at the outset of the immigration: and these schools in their turn preserved

---

[1] Erman and Reclam assert that there were thirty ministers in Brandenburg at the end of 1686: vol. 1. 192.

[2] Ancillon, 41 ff. This fact must be repeated with stress; in spite, or because, of the insolent commentary of Mirabeau. 'Quant aux connoissances proprement dites, elles ne gagnèrent point au refuge. Mm Reclam et Erman parlent avec emphase des gens de lettres qu'il amena; mais ceux qui portoient ce nom parmi les réfugiés, n'étoient que des théologiens, et tout au plus des demi-savants. On ne citera pas un seul ouvrage d'un très-grand mérite, écrit par un réfugié d'Allemagne': *de la Monarchie prussienne*, 1. 38; London 1788. And this, pace Gibbon; see below, 162 n. 2.

[3] Pp. 341 ff. There was also a French almshouse governed under minute and stringent regulations: pp. 325-336.

[4] See his notice of 'the ministers of quality' of Berlin; p. 42: or of those of Halle, 'très-habiles et fort gens de bien,' p. 49. The ministers of Magdeburg 'are an honour to their flock, even as the flock is an honour and a gain to the town'; p. 51.

the tradition in the colony and spread it at large among the German people.

In the original scheme of plantation the French college of Berlin and the university of Frankfurt-am-Oder held an important place [1]. The former, the Königliche Französische Gymnasium, as it came to be called, was open to all Frenchmen free [2]. It supplied them, by means of five masters, with the elements of education in the branches of theology, letters, and philosophy [3]. The students were intended, as the completion of the course at the school, to proceed to the university of Frankfurt [4], the foundation of which, for their especial benefit, was completed in 1694 [5]. Here they were not only admitted free, but allowed an exhibition of fifty crowns each towards their support [6].

Learning and professional acquirements everywhere took their own rank. Physicians, surgeons [7], apothecaries, could exercise their calling without the need of a new diploma; and places were found for them in the court and hospitals. The apothecaries were given lodgings and supplied with drugs;

---

[1] At the same time, the gymnasium of Frankfurt, which had been founded for the benefit of needy subjects of the electorate, was made accessible to the French: pp. 45 f.

[2] Ancillon, 146 ff.

[3] There was a régent for the rudiments, a second for religion, and three besides for the humanities: pp. 151 f.

[4] See a monograph of M Tollin, noticed in the *Bulletin*, 19. 177.

[5] The foundation was assisted by a gift of a hundred florins from Hanau; Leclercq, *Hanau*, 108; as well as by contributions from other quarters.

[6] This allowance was 'to provide for their fare and to buy such books as are constantly necessary to them.' For the rest, they had 'the entry of the public library, which is very fine, and whence they might at pleasure carry the books they wanted to their chambers, there to keep as long as they would': Ancillon, 46 f.

[7] Ancillon notices the success of the kindred mystery of the barbers. Heedless of the implied suspicion, he adds that, as Dionysius of Syracuse had his daughters taught to shave for fear of the malice of any subject, so also the electors employed a French barber,—but as a mark of confidence: pp. 136 f.

money was advanced; and no colony was without its doctor[1]. At Berlin the more eminent of the faculty became the fashionable practitioners of the Dorotheenstadt. But men like Jacques de Gautier and Samuel Duclos were more than this. They and their fellows helped to reform the old-fashioned practice of the country and to establish the higher medical college[2]. Their work in the furtherance of science, on a smaller scale, ran parallel with the general impulse which was given towards exact research by the scholars of the immigration, and of which Étienne Chauvain[3] was the most prominent exemplar.

Chauvain's chosen study was physical science, but he is known to us almost entirely as the apostle of Cartesianism in Berlin. A native of Nîmes, he had lived and worked with Bayle at Rotterdam before he came to preside over the French college[4]. Holland had before now acquainted Germany with the teachings of Descartes: but the school of thought was first organised by the activity of the huguenots[5]. Some of them doubtless misliked it from its possible affinity to catholicism[6]: but no feature of the emigration is more remarkable than the spirit with which the refugees, generally, pursued and propagated a creed with the ultimate issues of which they could have little sympathy, and which perhaps they hardly suspected[7].

1695.

---

[1] Ancillon, 125 ff.   [2] Weiss, I. 154.
[3] His name is commonly spelt *Chauvin*; I follow Windelband, *Geschichte der neueren Philosophie*, I. 432. Chauvain was born in 1640, and died April 6 1725.
[4] See his title in the *nouvelle Biographie universelle*. Chauvain's chief work was the *Lexicon rationale, sive Thesaurus philosophicus Ordine alphabetico digestus*, published at Rotterdam in folio, 1692, and reissued in its best form at Leeuwarden, 1713.   [5] Windelband, as above.
[6] This we may see from the temper in which Jurieu applies to Cartesianism and Gassendism the touchstone of the 'real presence' in the eucharistal offering: *Politique du Clergé de France*, 79. But the charge of hostility must not be pressed so as to include the huguenot thinkers as a class. This is done however by Capefigue, *Louis XIV*, 3. 13 f.
[7] The French academies had been leaning towards Cartesianism: see Jean Rou's account of his conversion to it; *Mémoires*, I. 16-25.

At the French college Chauvain was followed by Isaac de Beausobre, worthily distinguished as Le Grand Beausobre, who like his predecessor had spent the first year of his exile at Rotterdam[1], and who added to the minute scholarly enquiry inaugurated at Berlin by Chauvain, that historical genius which gave birth to the *Critical History of Manichaeism*—'a treasure,' Gibbon calls it, 'of ancient philosophy and theology[2].' He was the one Frenchman who could soothe the unreasoning prejudice against all things French, of the modern Vandal of the Baltic[3], Frederick William the First. In teaching and in society Beausobre ruled the opinion of Berlin, and his long life carried on his influence to a date when the rest of his comrades of the dispersion had quite died out. As a historian his authority has survived, while that of his friend Isaac de Larrey has vanished: as a theologian he was not only prominent in the defence of his own faith against the disputations of Toland, but he became also the arbiter of biblical exegesis in the colony, through the translation of the New Testament which,

---

[1] He was born at Niort in 1659 and became minister at Châtillon-sur-Indre two years before the Recall. His death took place June 6 1738: *nouvelle Biographie universelle*, under the name.

[2] *Decline and Fall*, ch. xlvii. n. 1: 'the learned historian spins with incomparable art the systematic thread of opinion, and transforms himself by turns into the person of a saint, a sage, or an heretic. Yet,' he adds, 'his refinement is sometimes excessive: he betrays an amiable partiality in favour of the weaker side, and, while he guards himself against calumny, he does not allow sufficient scope for superstition and fanaticism.' The book was published in two volumes, quarto, at Amsterdam, 1734 and 1739.

[3] The title, with that of 'the sergeant of Brandenburg,' he owed to ' his huge scorn for social culture, as much as his grotesque passion for soldiers of gigantic size'; Christian Bartholmèss in the *Bulletin*, 2. 671 f. The king's dislike of the French had caused a gradual secession from his colonies to Denmark and elsewhere, when at last in 1719 an enquiry was made into their grievances, and the Declaration of February 29 1720 was issued. This Order continued all preceding edicts and added to the privileges of the refugees: it may be read in a *Lettre à un Ami de Genève, sur la Constitution et la Prospérité des Colonies françaises dans les États du Roi*, 32 ff.; Berlin 1778: cp. Koehler, 35.

with its commentary, he made in company with Jacques Lenfant, still honourably known as the historian of the Council of Constance [1].

Such are a few of the great names among the scholars of the Refuge. The list might be enlarged by Alphonse des Vignoles the biblical chronologist, by Jacquelot the champion of orthodox Christianity, by Formey the disciple of Beausobre and a man of broad erudition beyond the rest: I have only named the leaders of the new fellowship [2]. It remains to say in brief how they obtained the means of literary preparation, what were the appliances by which they pursued their laborious research, and by which so much of their completed toil was given to the world.

From the beginning of the immigration, the elector had thrown open his private library to the refugees. Under the direction of its keeper, Ezechiel Spanheim, better known as a statesman than as a man of letters, though to either quality he had, as I have said, a warrantable title, the library became a place of meeting, a centre of intercourse, for the dispersed scholars. But, besides this, that they might not lose sight of the progressive literature of the day, a bookseller was maintained, in ordinary to the elector, to keep and vend new books, and to publish the special French literature which the colony must produce. This bookseller, Roger, it was, who put forth the work of Ancillon, in a form worthy of the presses of his native country. Independently of the peculiar convenience, a periodical literature grew up in French, beginning with the Nouveau Journal des Savants in 1696.

In these various ways and degrees the imported colony exerted the influence, which France always brings with it, upon the society into the midst of which they were thrown. The society of Berlin was in fact the creation of the exile; and it

---

[1] Two years the junior of Beausobre, he was his fellow-student at Saumur, whence he proceeded to Geneva. The French invasion drove him from his ministry at Heidelberg to Berlin in 1688.

[2] Cp. the *Mémoires de Brandebourg*, 2. 307 f.

was the refugees who gave it that mobile course of thought, that finer culture, that tact in matters of art, that instinct of conversation, which had before been the unique possession of France. They diffused their own spirit, quick, fine, lucid; the spirit of French vivacity and precision [1].

---

[1] *Bulletin*, 2. 667-682. Cp. generally Koehler, 32; Sugenheim, *Aufsätze*, 42-52. 'As policy and religion,' said a statesman of later times, 'alike recommended the elector's action, his generosity may readily bear the show of self-interested calculation; but his mind, by nature large, was not made to hide egoïsm with the mask of religion, and he needed not to have recourse to so petty artifices: he saw at once honour and profit in this great measure; he was as sensible of the one as of the other. What is certain, is that in the administration of empires we find few instances of progress in civilisation that have borne such good fruit as that which the elector reaped from the French immigrants': Frédéric Ancillon, *Tableau*, 4. 303.

CHAPTER XV.

FRANCE AFTER THE EXODUS.

To return from the wide survey we have been called upon to make in accompanying the huguenots in their exile, and to gather up briefly its mixed result so as to illustrate its reflexion upon the country which banished them, is a task embarrassed by several considerations as well of history as of partisanship. The classical base for such a review is a memoir drawn up by Marshal de Vauban with the object of gaining a reversal of the Edict of Recall[1]. At the outset it is well to note that Vauban was himself a partisan, a declared foe of Lewis the Fourteenth's centralising policy. Voltaire's comment that *His conduct proved that a citizen could exist under an absolute government*[2], points the limitation that one must set to his criticism of such a government. And this particular memoir is also a piece of special pleading. He was bound to make out a case for the restoration of the huguenot church. But I quote these considerations with no aim of withdrawing from the trustworthiness of what he affirms; on the contrary to prepare the paradox that, in spite of his presumed defects as an equal judge, he has understated his position.

His first fact, the emigration of eighty or a hundred thousand souls, is indefinitely below the truth. Caveirac indeed places

---

[1] It may be read in Rulhière, *Éclaircissements historiques*, 1. 380 f.; its conclusion in A. Michel, *Louvois*, 314.

[2] *Écrivains du Siècle de Louis XIV*, under the name.

fifty-five thousand against the two millions of his opponent[1]. But he was writing in controversy, and in controversy he was notoriously dishonest. In the *Apologie de Louis Quatorze*, with a forced symmetry, he reduced to one-tenth all the figures of his previous *Mémoire politique-critique*[2]: and his latter estimate is probably six times too small, just as his antagonist's is six times too great. But in the statistical question it is impossible to arrive at a certain result; and the range which calculation or conjecture has allowed to successive historians may make one pause before attempting a dogmatic solution. Basnage, a year after the Recall, reckoned the emigrants above 150,000[3]: next year Juricu raised the total above 200,000[4]. Writing later Basnage found between three and four hundred thousand[5]; and the estimate has been accepted by Sismondi[6]. Lastly Voltaire, followed in our own day by Hase, counted 500,000[7]. These are a few of the sober calculations, and their mean will perhaps supply the ultimate figure. I need only mention, among impossible guesses, that of Limiers[8], which raises the account to 800,000, because it has been taken up by the Prussian statesman von Dohm[9].

---

[1] *Apologie de Louis XIV*, 78; Paris, 1758: as against the *Lettre d'un Protestant*, 12.

[2] Cp. the *Apologie*, 87, with the *Mémoire*, 88.

[3] Pref. to *les Plaintes des Protestants*, 7.

[4] *Lettres pastorales*, 1. 450; 1687: cited in the *Uebersicht der Wanderungen*, 93. The number occurs also in Benoît, 5. 1014, and in Isaac de Larrey, *Histoire de l'Angleterre*, 4. 655. In the present century it has been repeated by F. Ancillon, *Tableau*, 4. 301.

[5] *L'Unité de l'Église*, 120, Amsterdam 1716; according to Caveirac, 78: but the place is not to be verified.

[6] *Histoire des Français*, 25. 522. So also La Martinière, *Histoire de Louis XIV*, 4. 339; the Hague, 1742. Similarly Lacretelle gives 80,000 families: *Histoire de France*, 59; ed. 4, Paris, 1819.

[7] *Kirchengeschichte*, 503, ed. 8, Leipzig, 1858; in the *Uebersicht der Wanderungen*, as before. Similarly Hume says 'above half-a-million,' *History of England*, 8. 165.

[8] *Histoire de Louis XIV*, 4. 289; cited by Caveirac, as above.

[9] Noticed by Koenen, *Vluchtelingen in Nederland*, 70. Menzel gives

Some of these estimates are almost certainly the rough inference from the total of refugees computed in one country: the difference in number or relative proportion of the single Refuge has been taken as a fair basis for generalisation. In others it is hard to discriminate the influence of mere conjecture. The only historian who professes to have pursued the enquiry in exact detail is Capefigue; and from his minute scrutiny of the *cartons des généralités* as prepared in the closing years of the seventeenth century he obtains a computation of two hundred and twenty-five or thirty thousand [1]. Such a result must be accepted as the absolute minimum; for it was the plain interest of the intendants who drew up the returns, to put all the facts which revealed the folly of the king's action at the lowest cipher. And, allowing the accuracy of Capefigue's work, there are other reasons for increasing his total. A few examples will explain this.

If we take the reports of Bouchu, Le Bret, and Bâville, for Dauphiné, Provence, and Languedoc, drawn up in the closing years of the seventeenth century, we shall find the protestant population before the proscription to have been respectively 60,000, 72,000, and 240,000; and the loss through the exodus 15,300, 14,400, and 42,000 [2]. The percentage is thus 25·5, 20, and 17·5, of the whole; and we may allow an indefinite depreciation in the latter numbers, probably an indefinite exaggeration in the former [3]. Hence we are prepared to meet on the other hand a considerably higher proportion in places where more adequate details are furnished. Bégon's returns

---

700,000; *Staatsgeschichte*, 197; ed. 5: cited in the *Uebersicht der Wanderungen*, as above.

[1] *Louis XIV*, 1. 260; ed. 1844.

[2] Rulhière, 1. 318 & 327. The report for Languedoc goes on to say that 6000 returned: Michel, *Louvois*, 145 f.

[3] Michel would greatly diminish the sum of the previous protestant population of Languedoc, which is that given by the duke of Noailles in October 1685: p. 185. Arnaud, on the other hand, from his special study, amends the numbers for Dauphiné to 65,000 and 15,000: *Protestants de Dauphiné*, 3. 17 f.

for Picardy are instructive in this connexion. In the gouvernement of Calais and Ardres there had been 3000 huguenots; the emigration was 2700. The élections of Doullens, Abbeville, and Amiens, out of a protestant population of 2260, had lost 1740: out of forty families the Boulonnais lost twenty-eight [1]. The proportion in these places is thus 90, 77, and 70 per cent. Other singularly high figures may be quoted. The town of Châtaigneraie in Poitou suffered a loss of 730 out of an industrial population of 800 [2]. From La Rochelle the emigrants numbered between 3300 and 4000 [3]: an intendant at the close of the century said one-third of the people of the généralité, and observed with anxiety the depopulation of Saintonge and Aunis even then going on [4]. Legendre computed that two-thirds of his congregation at Rouen followed him into exile [5]. The three élections of Montdidier, Péronne, and Saint Quentin, in Picardy, had a remnant of only 310 [6]; and the Pays Messin of but 3197 [7], while we hear of 3600 of its people in the single Refuge of Berlin [8].

In the face of these statistics, even if they bear, as some obviously bear, an exceptional character, we cannot set the emigration at a lower fraction than one-fifth of the total huguenot society. If the body numbered two millions, the outflow will be 400,000. If this appear an extreme estimate, it must be remembered that one-fifth is also extreme on the other side. Reducing the former aggregate to 1,500,000, it will be clearly within the bounds of moderation to leave the total exodus a range between 300,000 and 350,000.

How are we to distribute this immense aggregation? Holland

---

[1] Rossier, *Picardie*, 246. A suggestive record concerns the gouvernement of Montreuil. There had been three protestant households; of which one had died out, one had emigrated, and one remained.

[2] Lièvre, *Poitou*, 2. 224 f. The population of Thouars, numbering 7000, was reduced by one-third: vol. 3. 361.

[3] Delmas, *la Rochelle*, 287.
[4] P. 280.
[5] Waddington, *Normandie*, 16.
[6] Rossier, as above.
[7] Cuvier, pref. to Olry, *Metz*, 44 f.
[8] See above, p. 149, n. 3.

certainly claims near 100,000[1]; England, with Ireland and America, probably 80,000[2]. Switzerland must have received 25,000; and Germany, including Brandenburg[3], thrice that number[4]. The remainder will be made up from the north of Europe, and from the exiles whom commerce or other causes carried in isolated households elsewhere, and of whom no record is preserved to us. Even should the number allowed for these smaller settlements be thought excessive, it is to be borne in mind that the appropriation of the fragments is far more conjectural than the assessment of the grand total, and that, excepting in a few single instances, no attempt was ever made towards a census of the refugee communities[5].

The tale then of the emigrants was above 300,000. It follows to ask what was the material loss involved in their exodus. Caveirac is again the lowest in his estimate: he will not grant the export of more than 250,000 livres[6]. He might have learnt from Count d'Avaux himself, that those least likely to magnify the sum confessed that by the very year of the Recall

---

[1] According to a despatch of Tillières, the agent of Count d'Avaux, dated May 24 1686, the Refuge in Holland was already reckoned at 75,000: Weiss, 2. 25. We may fairly add a quarter to the sum from the early date of the estimate and from its suspicious source.

[2] Dubourdieu speaks in 1718 of near 100,000 in England and Ireland: *Appeal to the English Nation*, 219.

[3] Frederick II's estimate of 20,000 in Brandenburg is far short of the truth; *Mémoires*, 2. 298: and Mirabeau's allowance of 100,000 to all Germany may not be excessive; *de la Monarchie prussienne*, 1. 33.

[4] We might increase the figure by an inference from the local divisions of the emigrants. Erman and Reclam notice the almost exclusive direction of the huguenots of Languedoc, Provence, and Dauphiné, to Switzerland and Germany: *Mémoires*, 1. 239. And on any showing the religion was more powerful in the south and east than in the other quarters of France.

[5] Thus the register of the French colony in Brandenburg, which counted 12,297 in 1697, did not extend beyond towns where there were churches, nor did it include the soldiers of the refuge: Erman and Reclam, 2. 36; 1783. The return of December 31 1700 was alike imperfect; it amounted to 14,844. The registers were not established until about 1703: F. de Schickler, in the *Bulletin*, 28. 39.

[6] *Apologie*, 81.

twenty million livres had gone out of the country[1]; and it is certain that the wealthier merchants deferred their departure in order to carry as much as they could with them. Two hundred and fifty traders are said to have quitted Rouen in 1687 and 1688[2]. Probably the actual amount was very far in excess of these twenty millions: and a calculation is cited by Macpherson which even affirms that every individual refugee in England brought with him on the average money or effects to the value of sixty pounds sterling[3]. A more telling exhibition of the financial damage to France is shown by the history of the Amsterdam Exchange, where the rate of interest was reduced in 1684 from $3\frac{1}{2}$ to 3 per cent., and where in 1687 it was difficult to obtain more than 2 per cent[4]. There was a glut of specie abroad; while the French exchequer had to make up for the prevailing depression by the universal use of a paper-currency[5].

1688. June.

Jurieu said truly *The protestants have carried commerce with them into exile*[6]. But they did not merely carry away the material wealth of the country, but also the credit on which it subsisted. The emigrants of La Rochelle are allowed by the intendant Tessereau to have been *Of the principal inhabitants as touching birth, substance, and reputation*[7]. The catholic

---

[1] Weiss, 2. 19.

[2] Émile Lesens, pref. to Philippe Legendre, *Histoire de la Persécution faite à l'Église de Rouen*, xx; Rouen, 1874. The intendant of Alençon notices the emigration of most of the 4000 huguenots in the élection (the 3000 in the town, he says, 'drove a great trade' in linen); they had gone to Holland or England taking with them their effects, their savings, and the sums resultant on sale of their merchandize: Waddington, 36 n.

[3] *History of Commerce*, 3. 617.   [4] Weiss, 2. 22.

[5] *Mémoires de Fontaine*, 149; and Castel's note.

[6] *Lettres pastorales*, xix; in Lièvre, 2. 224.

[7] Delmas, 287. Ménard instances the fugitives of Nîmes, 'who carried away great riches: whence commerce has had extreme detriment, and likewise the arts and trades': *Histoire de Nismes*, 6. 291. Turgot reported of Metz in 1699, 'the number of protestants which was infinite is now reduced to 1700 souls, very zealous but self-restrained, who make not a tenth of the population. Nevertheless it is they who hold the commerce en depôt and

merchants of Metz complained that it was impossible to recover the connexion with foreign markets which the flight of the most considerable traders of the town had broken[1]. Trade stood still or went backward. It was well if it could meet the home-demand; export was out of the question. The same tale is repeated at Rouen, Caen[2], La Rochelle[3], Nîmes. Everywhere commerce was crippled with the loss of its masters and with the lessening of production.

After what has been said, in the different scenes of the emigration, of the strong impulse given by the refugees to manufacture, it will be needless to add many statistics of the injury caused by their withdrawal from France. Two great instances are typical of the rest. Lyons which had employed 18,000 silk-looms had but 4000 remaining by the end of the century[4]. Tours with the same interest had had 800 mills, 80,000 looms, and 40,000 workpeople[5]: in 1727 there were only 70 mills, 1200 looms, and perhaps 4000 workpeople[6]. Of its 3000 ribbon-factories only sixty remained.

1698.

Equally significant was the ruin of the woollen trade of Poitou. Little was left of the drugget-manufacture of Coulonges

---

are the richest of the people': MS. in the Metz library, nr 248, pp. 100 f.; in Cuvier, 44 f.

[1] MS. in the town-library, nr 249, p. 278; cited by Cuvier, 45 f.

[2] The merchants who remained at Caen found it hopeless to repair the injury caused by the secession of a great part of their body: Waddington, 36 n.

[3] The shipping-trade fell with the ruin of the outward commerce: Delmas, 287.

[4] Burn, *foreign protestant Refugees*, 255.

[5] The industry was worth ten million livres to the town: Count de Boulainvilliers, *État de la France*, 2. 155; London 1727, folio.

[6] The exportation of this industry assisted a tendency of English taste. 'For a long time,' we are told, 'foreign silk-goods continued to be preferred in this country, and in the year 1668 the tide of fashion set entirely in favour of French fabrics; so that it became a complaint that *The women's hats were turned into hoods made of French silk, whereby every maidservant became a standing rebuke to the French king of one half of her wages*'; cited from *the Danger of the Church and Kingdom from Foreigners*, a pamphlet of 1722, in Burn, 13 n.

and Châtaigneraie¹, or of the industry in serges and bombazines at Thouars²; and the export traffic between Châtaigneraie and Canada, by way of La Rochelle, was in the last year of the century absolutely extinct³. At Metz in 1688 not a fourth part of the accustomed supply of cloth was manufactured: this is certain from the lament of the revenue-officer. The price of cloth had fallen and, as a result, little wool was on sale⁴. M de Vaubourg, intendant of the généralité of Rouen, stated that whereas ten or twelve years since there had been a great export of the hat-manufacture of the town to Holland, England, and the north, so many of the manufacturers had lately emigrated that the productive power of Rouen, Caudebec, and the neighbourhood, was now only equal to the wants of the country itself⁵. Nîmes, says the local historian in the middle of the eighteenth century, 'was now deprived of much of its prosperity: nor has it even yet recovered from all its losses⁶.'

Such are a few of the material results of the emigration, selected from different parts of the country, and taken mainly from the official returns⁷. They are facts which the intendants could disparage but could not ignore: and they are almost always recited with a mark of regret⁸. Only one intendant seeks to hide the dishonour of the cause of decay. Bouchu declares, in delight at the economic discovery, *If the manufacturers and craftsmen of Dauphiné have quitted the province and gone out of the kingdom, they are only the 'new converts'; so that this emigration is purely accidental, and religion not commerce is responsible for it*⁹. To Bouchu, probably, all statistics appeared

---

¹ Lièvre. 2. 224.   ² Vol. 3. 361.   ³ Vol. 2. 225.
⁴ The tanners and cap-makers were equally badly off: Cuvier, 47.
⁵ MS. in the Rouen library in Waddington, 36 n.: cp. Macpherson. 2. 650.
⁶ Ménard, 6. 291. But decadence was sometimes succeeded by vigorous revival; as, after a time, the velvets of Utrecht were imitated with better profit at Amiens the original seat of the industry: Rossier, 251.
⁷ A mass of statistic is collected in Weiss, 1. 106-117, l. 2.
⁸ Lièvre, 2. 223 f.   ⁹ Michel, *Louvois*, 165.

in 'accidental' isolation, and incapable of forming the elements of a cumulative inference.

To obtain this combined view of the general issues to the material prosperity of France, we have the added complication of the effects of the war about the Spanish succession. The results to the outside world may be stated at once in the words of the learned editor of the *Correspondance administrative* of the reign. 'Lewis the Fourteenth did not render France *all catholic*. Unwittingly he made foreign countries better workmen, to the great detriment of French industry[1].' 'The habits of order and work,' says Blanqui, 'with which' the huguenots 'were informed spread themselves through all Europe: and so the powerful reform effected by Colbert ceased to bear the narrow stamp of nationality which it would perhaps have otherwise preserved[2].'

In the twenty years following 1683 France lost a revenue of 3,582,000 pounds sterling, by the decrease of her exports to Holland and England alone[3]: in fifty years the revenue fell from 215,566,633 to 140,278,473 livres. When it is urged that this ruin was due solely to the pressure of war[4], it is open to reply that the war touched other countries as nearly, without involving the same collapse. Only of France could it be said, 'The war had drained her resources; credit was exhausted; the public debt had risen to 3,000,000,000 livres. . .

'The cruel winter of 1709 set the climax to the general misery. . . The people in many parts died of famine. Revolts broke out: taxes were resisted. Smuggling was carried on by force of arms and by the soldiery themselves. Bands of

---

[1] G. B. Depping, *Correspondance administrative*, 3. intr. lviii. f.

[2] *Histoire de l'Économie politique*, 2. 9 f.; ed. 4, Paris 1860.

[3] Macpherson's figures, 2. 609 f., give this gross total. The only item which must certainly be struck out, as unconnected with the emigration, is the 280,000*l.* of wines and brandies. Of the remainder near two millions are made up of the loss in manufactured silks and linen, which left France only about 200,000*l.* in the export of cambric to England.

[4] Thus Mirabeau, 1. 32; cp. Macpherson, 2. 650.

countrymen took by assault the town of Cahors: and a great company of the people of Quercy and Périgord, breaking all bond with the government, which taxed even the acts of marriage and baptism, fell into a condition of nature, marrying themselves without rite, and themselves giving baptism to their children[1].' *Touchés de tant de merveilles*, to echo with perverse emphasis Bossuet's paean for the Recall, *épanchons nos cœurs sur la piété de Louis*.

---

[1] É. Boisnormand de Bonnechose, *Histoire de France*, 2. 130 f.; ed. 13, Paris 1864: cp. Lacretelle, 1. 60.

CHAPTER XVI.

THE POWER OF THE REFUGEES AND ITS REFLEXION UPON FRANCE.

THERE is a story in Plutarch which tells of the banishment of Themistocles, how he came a suppliant to the court of Persia, and in what fashion Xerxes welcomed him; how the king made prayer to Ahriman, *That it might please him to put such a counsel in the hearts of his enemies, as that they might thrust forth all their worthiest citizens.* Thrice in the night he was heard to mutter in his broken sleep, *Themistocles is mine,* Ἔχω Θεμιστοκλέα τὸν Ἀθηναῖον. Such, notes Ancillon, was the spirit in which the huguenots were received in Brandenburg[1]. The truth applies generally. Every protestant government was confident that in giving shelter to the exiles of Lewis the Fourteenth, they were going the surest way to undermine the fortress of his arrogance and power[2]. Ancillon here looks chiefly at the military aspect of the dispersion, and Marshal de Vauban insists on the eight or nine thousand men *of the best of the realm*[3], the 600 officers, the 12,000 soldiers *better seasoned than the catholics*, whom the Edict of Recall scattered among Lewis's foes. The emphasis is just, and the numbers err only on the side of

---

[1] *Établissement des François réfugiez,* 168 f.
[2] This was given prominence by Innocent XI in his letter to the emperor; I quote from the Dutch version: 'Daer zijn 200,000 ketters, die uyt zijn rijck sullen gaen, om haer te voegen by de vyantlijcke party, en die gewapender-hant in haer vaderland weder sullen komen, indien 'er eergens eenigen oorlog opstaet'; in the *Hollandse Mercurius,* 1688, 39 f. Cp. above, pp. 15 f., 19 f.
[3] Cp. above, p. 18 and n. 3.

incompleteness. The fury of Almanza is a sufficient proof, even in defeat, of the force added to the ranks of the enemies of France [1].

But the moral force was greater than these numbers express; and the military influence of the refugees is insignificant by comparison with their power over political opinion, over knowledge and literature [2]. Their influence, save in creating or restoring Calvinistic churches, was seldom distinctively religious: it was protestant, but in a sense truly political. On the other hand, their departure from France reacted with violence upon the spiritual condition of the country; and this reaction, as will appear in its place, was, to look at it from the wide standing-ground of the historian, the most permanently disastrous feature of the emigration.

The first conspicuous energy of the refugees was directed to the writing of pamphlets [3]. They furthered tendencies which were growing in men's minds, but had not yet ripened into action. Every impulse which opposed catholicism or the policy of Bourbon, everything that hinted suspicion of absolutism in church or state, was pushed by their ardour to its avowal [4]. They formulated the articulate phrasing of liberal opinion. The revival of the Dutch allegiance to William of Orange, the resistance to James the Second, the European union against Lewis the Fourteenth, all these political motions are traceable in their public expression, to the strenuous labour of the French exiles against their mother-country [5]. The Recall of the Edict of Nantes is the prelude to the league of Augsburg.

---

[1] See Smiles, *Huguenots in England*, 275.

[2] 'More,' says J. G. von Herder, 'than Lewis's political enterprises and his wars, more than the letters of flattery he sent now and then, seasoned with presents, to scholars abroad, did that oppression of the huguenots conspire to build up a French polity in Europe, but a polity far different to that the king dreamt of': *Adrastea*, i. i. viii.; *sämmtliche Werke*, 9. 82.

[3] Among the journalists of Holland, François Michel Janiçon gained a deserved eminence.

[4] Cp. Capefigue, *Louis XIV*, 3. 11.

[5] F. Ancillon, *Tableau des Révolutions*, 4. 307.

Pamphleteering was the application to an immediat want of a general literary enthusiasm. If political newspapers grew up under refugee auspices, so also did journals devoted to science and letters. We have seen how the example of Bayle created a class of this literature, alone in its multifarious interest and wide popularity. Berlin, London, and afterwards even Dublin, followed with publications on the same lines. The huguenots founded not only a school of literature, but also a language of their own, a strange congeriës of all the dialects and provincialisms of their homes. Their effect upon France depended upon a preliminary translation. And it was by this channel that the intellectual work of the exiles became reflected in the temper of the eighteenth century in France. 'La science de Voltaire,' says Capefigue, 'n'est qu'un spirituel développement des doctrines de Bayle. C'est la même école, plus française, plus appropriée à nos goûts et à l'esprit du peuple [1].' The philosophy which the huguenots spread, Cartesianism in Brandenburg [2], and still more the free thought of Bayle, gave the praeparatio evangelica, the real origin of the intellectual current which passed into full tide in the middle of the succeeding century.

This philosophy is the note of the dispersion; but it is only a symptom of a diversely varied genius. In Geneva, as we have seen, it went hand in hand with a careful study of natural

---

[1] Vol. 6. 36 f.; cp. 3. 10 f. The contrast he points between this petty 'dissertatory spirit' and the dynasty of Christian, or catholic, orators, may appeal more vividly to the subjects of the historian's church than to those whose view is not abridged by the skreen of an ecclesiastical system.

[2] See above, pp. 159 f. Instances among the refugees in Holland are Jacques Gousset, professor at Groningen, 1691–1704, and Michel Rossal, student at the same university from 1688, and professor 1706-1744. Gousset appears in Rou's correspondence: for Rossal, see W. B. S. Boeles, app. to W. J. A. Jonckbloet's *Gedenkboek der Hoogeschool te Groningen*, 60; Groningen, 1864. Cp. J. P. N. Land, *Philosophy in the Dutch Universities*, in *Mind*, 1877. England was peculiar in refusing for the most part the infection. 'Ils ne sont ni Cartésiens, ni Calvinistes,' said Georges le Sage of the English, *Remarques sur l'Angleterre*, 75; 'à peine trouve-t-on un Anglois qui parle bien de Calvin et de Descartes.'

science[1]: and Papin[2], Desaguliers, and Abraham de Moivre are the forerunners of an illustrious company of scientific workers claiming descent from the exiles of the Recall[3]. But history was even more their special field of labour[4]. Histories of England were made by Isaac de Larrey and Paul de Rapin; histories of Lewis the Fourteenth by Larrey and Limiers. Benoît wrote the monumental *History of the Edict of Nantes;* Basnage, the *History of the Reformed Churches* and the *Annals of the United Provinces*. Beausobre and Lenfant have already come before us in their laborious masterpieces of religious history[5]. No subject was too recondite or barren for the indefatigable research of the refugees[6]. The industry of the scholars of the exile is another side to the industry of its crafts-

---

[1] See above, p. 120.

[2] See above, p. 140. In 1698, says Burn, one Captain Thomas Savery, a refugee, obtained a patent for a steam-engine: p. 261.

[3] Of these was John Dollond, brought up as a silk-weaver in Spitalfields; p. 253: and the series is continued in a multiform variety of ingenious research, through Lewis Paul, the anticipator of Arkwright, to Roget, Daubeny, Rigaud, Delarue, Bosanquet, in the present century.—A curious example of the anticatholic temper with which at first science was clouded by the refugees may be found in the autobiography of Samuel de Chaufepié, of which a copy exists in MS. in the Walloon Library at Leyden. Recording the correction of the kalendar, under the year 1701, he adds, 'Il faut rémarquer que cette réformation . . n'a nullement prétendu suivre le calendrier Grégorien, mais faire une réformation là-dessus plus exacte que celle du pape Grégoire 13°'; p. 24. The note recalls Voltaire's story of how the Calvinists reproached Bayle with saying a good word for certain popes,—' gens de bien,'—because ' Ils ne sont pas de notre église'; *Écrivains du Siècle de Louis XIV*, under *Bayle*.

[4] See Sayous, *le dix-huitième Siècle, à l'Étranger*, 1. 46.

[5] See above, pp. 162 f.

[6] M. V. de la Croze, the Coptic lexicographer, was a peculiar product of the Calvinistic refuge, for which he exchanged the Benedictine rule. He became librarian to the king of Prussia, and died May 21 1739. Cp. *Mémoires de la Maison de Brandebourg*, 2. 307. The librarians of the Refuge might form a class by themselves; and seem to have had a long succession at Lambeth-palace: see Smiles's biographical index under *Jérome Colomiès, Hans de Veille, H. C. du Carel;* and cp. *H. Justel* and *M. Mathy*.

men. The dispersion carried with it the habit and the tradition of patient work[1].

It is the laborious vigour of the huguenot personality which colours most strongly the literature of the refugees, and the insistence of the religious historians may serve to obscure another aspect of it no less real than the first. From the furnace of distress and peril the bright generous characteristic of the race came out with quickened exhilaration. They had no longer suspicion to encounter; they were held in honour, if not always in love. The light heart of the Celt was in them purified from its vices, frivolity and love of change; but Calvin himself could not destroy its verve. When we read the memoirs of Bostaquet, and see him, with his household left in the terror of prison or dragoons, travelling across the frontier, wounded and sick, we cannot choose but marvel at the elasticity of mind which can spend the moments of change and rest at the stages of the journey, not in aimless regret, but in a ready and cheerful notice of whatever the place might offer of interest or renown. This is no puritan spirit. Some, indeed, that have resented the social influence of the refugees, have charged them with unworthy tastes and profligate manners[2]; and though the reproach be a calumny, it could not have been imagined had the huguenot's air and bearing revealed the acrid rigour of the covenanter. Secure in his own uprightness, he did not disdain the pleasantness of life and sense.

---

[1] If, says M Read, we except the pamphleteers and writers in gazettes, the historians of the exile are 'remarkable for their sagacity, their penetration, their accuracy, almost always supported in the present day by the exact perusal of original documents': pref. to Rou's *Mémoires*, xxxiii. f.

[2] The extract given above, pp. 61 f., contains perhaps the least serious of these aspersions. The *Mémoires de la Maison de Brandebourg* are fuller and more questionable: vol. 2. 303. Koenen deprecates the influence of the huguenot officers upon Holland, and insists on the diverse character of the immigration at large, since mainly formed of townsmen, as injuring the simplicity of Dutch life, 94; cp. the *Nederlandsche Spectator*, 150, 1750. F. Ancillon is fair and appreciative, *Tableau*, 4. 303: cp. above, pp. 72, 98, 111 f.; also pp. 68, 113 n. 7.

This prodigality of living impulse diffused itself into the religious societies into which the exiles were thrown. Abroad, Calvinism had come to mark a communion that took a perverse pride in its contempt of the world, that held itself aloof in a narrow and insolent insularity. The human was shut out from the range of spiritual toleration. To such a sect the new accession proved, after many rebuffs, a sure help to restoration: for a sect that is cut off from the world without is fast by its death. Calvinism awoke into fresh activity, but outside Calvinism the religious influence of the refugees was, as I have said, slight or transient.

Some of the commentaries and books of devotion they produced are respectable, and have been useful. But the esteem accorded to them was the tribute of a sect[1], and their value rested on other bases than the religious. Scholarship and historical learning are their credentials to the applause of later generations. The controversial accumulation is of a different and fugitive merit; and the category of theology or literature will equally disdain to own this mass of polemic as its possession. In any case its interest was limited to the community that gave it birth; and even so it was not their peculiar vogue, but the vice of their age. Should we seek in the Refuge for a spiritual master, we must travel to our own day to find in the honoured name of Edward Bouverie Pusey the union of the solid judgement of the Englishmen, the quick and genial temper of the French, and that profound scholarship and that spiritual force which we connect and connect rightly with the confessors of the huguenot church[2].

It has been said, I believe by Coleridge, that the long war against the protestant faith in France succeeded in eliminating

---

[1] David Martin merits commemoration for his translation and commentary of the Bible. He died at Utrecht, 1721.

[2] The first of his name in England, Laurence des Bouveries, came over in 1568; but the affection of a pupil may excuse the momentary anachronism.

the entire Teutonic factor from the nation; which means, I suppose, that all that strenuous and much-enduring element of religion, proper to the German genius [1], in this way ceased to have any existence there. And so it is to be accepted, and with more fulness to be conceded. Not alone did serious Christianity in the form of Calvinism disappear, but through the means taken for its overthrow, and in the ensuing revulsion the catholic church itself suffered a damage not to be repaired.

The forced conversions, says Vauban, *have kindled an universal horror of the part therein enacted by the churchmen, a conclusion that they hold no belief in the sacraments they take pleasure in profaning. Wherefore if this policy is to be perfected, we must needs put forth them that call themselves 'new converts,' as rebels, we must banish them with the relapsed or imprison them with the insane. One course only remains, a course full of charity, prudent, proper, politic: we are to conciliate them.*

But Vauban's reasoning fell on deaf ears. The huguenots gained no indulgence: and the fanaticism which tracked their departure, slowly changed into a dull heedlessness in matters spiritual, an indifference which hardly required the genius of Voltaire to crystallise into a speculative indifferentism. This is the saddest picture of France after the emigration. 'Thought without reverence is barren, perhaps poisonous; at best dies like cookery with the day that called it forth; does not live, like sowing, in successive tilths and harvests, bringing food and plenteous increase to all time [2].' And France was now living without belief in the creed it professed, without reverence for whatever is high or holy in man or in society [3].

---

[1] Cp. E. Michel, as cited above, p. 16 n. 1.

[2] *Sartor resartus*, I. ch. x.

[3] In this connexion the verses of La Fontaine might be read as the expression of a cruel satire:

'Il veut vaincre l'erreur; cette ouvrage s'avance,
Il est fait, et le fruit de ces succès divers
Est que la vérité règne en toute la France
Et la France en tout l'univers.'

Similarly one might understand of Lewis's whole religious policy, in its

Every worthy impulse was numbed. The victorious church saw Bossuet, Bourdaloue, Fénélon, die without leaving a single successor; and it seemed as though the exile of the most genuine religious society of the country drew the life-blood of all that remained. The Gallican church, now secure in its liberties and its supremacy, came to realise the worst attributes of a state-church. The age of Lewis the Fourteenth may have created the national school of poetry and literary criticism: more certainly it witnessed its dissolution. To whatever side we look, we see the tombs which called forth the pregnant sentence of Michelet, 'Louis enterre un monde.'

The first energy of the huguenots abroad was directed to political action, hardened and aculeate by hatred; the one class trained to a talent for affairs was removed from the nation whose king stood in fear of such distributed capacity. Centralisation was complete; but the stream of national life was dried up. *When any of the four pillars of government are mainly shaken, or weakened (which are religion, justice, counsel, and treasure), men had need pray for fair weather* [1]. But when the storm burst upon the French monarchy a century later, all these props were taken from it. The educated middle society which should have tempered the shock had long ceased to exist; and it is no perverse judgement which will find in this effacement an augury and an apology for the unreasoning excess with which the national liberation was accompanied. Ignorant that a people cannot rise from serfage to best sovereignty in a day, that the training of generations cannot be cast fire-new at will, men set about creating a perfect commonwealth, when they had not the materials for its foundation. The centralising policy of Lewis the Fourteenth had worked its end, and broken the sinews of the people. Europe may have to thank him for good which she

---

unreason and its heedlessness of the future, that saying which has been spoken in his praise, that he would have been a crusader in the days of Lewis IX.

[1] Bacon, *Essay of Seditions*.

cannot count; France owed him but the debt repaid in the massacres of September and in the emigration of La Vendée.

1792.

When the Great King assailed the Dutch confederation and pushed his arms within view of Amsterdam, the peril was met by the flooding of the country. The jubilation of the people was earnest but not extravagant. It was told however to Lewis, that the Dutch in their arrogant rejoicing had devised a medal displaying Holland in the guise of Joshua bidding the sun stand still. The legend SOL STETIT[1] may more truly typify the decadence which followed the protestant exile. The Age of Lewis the Fourteenth is arrested at the moment of his supreme achievement.

1672.

---

[1] This, I may be allowed to mention, was the motto which concealed the authorship of this essay in its original form, when submitted to the election of Lord Lothian's trustees.

SUPPLEMENTARY NOTES.

I. DRAGONNADES (p. 26, n. 7).

1685.
Oct. 20.

WHEN the news of the Recall was published at Rouen in the Chambre des Vacations, the courageous Rapporteur prefaced the announcement with the following criticism. *This Declaration which annuls the privileges of them of the religion calling itself reformed would yet not have prevailed to restore them to the fold of the church, except the king had used the self-same mean, wherewith in time past the emperour Honorius overcame the Donatists, committing their reduction into the hands of his troops* [1].

Setting aside this ancient precedent it will not be impertinent to examine the common story which traces James the Second's employment of the soldiery to force the obedience of the Scottish covenanters to the instance of Lewis the Fourteenth. The particular application was doubtless invented by the ready genius of Louvois; but James might find in the traditions of his own house examples enough to warrant the expedient without need to look abroad. For the service of soldiers as an engine of extortion was so customary under Charles the First as to inspire one of the four capital provisions of the Petition of Right [2]. On the return from the abortive expedition to Cadiz, 'the soldiers were billeted upon private houses, contrary to custom, which required that, in all ordinary cases, they should be quartered in inns and public houses. Those who had refused or delayed the loan, were sure to be loaded with a great

---

[1] Waddington, *Protestantisme en Normandie*, 98 n.

[2] In precisely the same way the argument *Compelle eos intrare*, notable from the satire of Bayle, was urged by the royalist doctor Daniel Featley against the anabaptists: see his book, *the Dippers di t or the Anabaptists duck'd and plung'd over Head and Ears at a Disputation in Southwark*, 4 f.; ed. 4, 1646, quarto.

number of these dangerous and disorderly guests¹.' *The soldiers*, says Rushworth, *brake out into great disorders. They mastered the people, disturbed the peace of families, and the civil government of the land; there were frequent robberies, burglaries, rapes, rapines, murthers, and barbarous cruelties: Unto some places they were sent for a punishment; and where ever they came, there was a general outcry. The highways were dangerous and the markets unoccupied; they were a terror to all and an undoing to many²*. Sir Robert Philips declared before

1627. Mar. 22.

the Commons, *We are almost grown like the Turks, who send their janizaries, who place the halberd at the door, and then he is master of the house. We have soldiers billetted, and warrants to collect money, which if they do not, the soldiers must come and rifle³.*

1681. Mar. 18.

1685. Nov. 19.

This procedure displays the identical spirit of Louvois' instructions to Marillac; *If by a fair allotment ten should be billeted upon the religionists you may enjoin them to receive twenty*⁴: or later, to M de Beaupré, in the exasperation of failure; *Le roi a appris par votre lettre du 17 de ce moi la continuation de l'opiniâtreté des habitants de la R.P.P. de Dieppe ; comme ces gens-là sous les seuls dans tout le royaulme qui se sont distingués à ne se vouloir pas soumettre à ce que le roi désire d'eux, vous ne devez garder à leur égard aucune des mésures qui vous ont été préscrites, et vous ne sauriez rendre trop rude et trop onéreuse la subsistence des troupes chez eux*⁵.

---

¹ Hume, 6. 170.
² *Historical Collections*, 1. 420; 1659, folio.
³ In the same, 1. 503 f.; cp. the petition concerning billeting of soldiers, 1. 542.
⁴ Rulhière, *Éclaircissements historiques*, 1. 200 ff.
⁵ MS. cited in Waddington, *Normandie*, 2 n. 1. The character of a *dragonnade* should not seem to allow much scope for social courtesies, far less for humorous incident. The story of Samuel Bernard may therefore owe to its uniqueness a record which its importance might not otherwise merit. Seemingly with a view to save his orchard at Chénevière-sur-Marne from destruction, this prudent banker made his peace with the catholic church. His surprise was natural and excusable when, after thus sacrificing his conscience for the good of his fruit-trees, he received a letter from M d'Artaignan, who is commemorated as 'the politest of dragoons,' giving him information of the speedy occupation of his country-house by the major's troop. The civil message was not received in the spirit of good-nature that prompted it, and M Bernard appears to have proclaimed his grievance with no idle insistence. We have a letter soon from Master Robin, the king's gardener, pleading to the king for the injured convert : if this may not be, at all events he desires ' vous prier en mesme temps de donner ordre que son

II. Walloon Churches in the Netherlands (p. 40 n. 4).

The subjoined list is taken from a memorandum of the rev. F. H. Gagnebin of Amsterdam, drawn up for the guidance of the Walloon Commission, of which he is president, and kindly communicated to me by Dr W. N. du Rieu. For the sake of uniformity I have adopted his numbers throughout; where they differ from the incomplete list in Dr J. T. Bergman's *Catalogue de la Bibliothèque wallonne déposée à Leide* [1], the variant has been added within brackets. Often, as notably in the instance of Haarlem, the latter is right; on the other hand he is in error with regard to the date of the church at Groningen. If we would follow Jonkheer Berg the series must be supplemented by the names of Dalem, Olne, Blaigny, Zeist, and others [2]. But his note about Zeist suggests a like explanation in the other cases, namely, the residence there of a nobleman's chaplain, whose services might doubtless be available to the French of the neighbourhood, but who was often in the first instance engaged merely as secretary or tutor, and always probably on a temporary footing.

The dates prefixed to some names of churches below represent the time when, according to M Gagnebin, *On a commencé de s'occuper de leur érection*; the churches printed in spaced type are still existent.

Friesland—

			Date of Extinction.
1657	L e e u w a r d e n	1659	
1683	Balk	1684	1721–1732
	Sneek	1686	1693
	Harlingen	,,	1719 (1699)
	Franeker	,,	1796–1808
	Bolsward	1688	1715

Groningen—

G r o n i n g e n   1619 (1608)

---

jardin soit ménagé. Il y a de beaux arbres fruitiers, et moy qui suis jardinier, je suis plus sensible qu'un autre à la perte d'un bel arbre dont on espère beaucoup de fruit.' The appeal of the orchard was more powerful than that of humanity, and M Bernard hurried home with a reprieve, to find the object of his care utterly desolated by the eager 'courtesy' of M d'Artaignan and his dragoons. See the *Bulletin*, 5. 49 ff.

[1] Pp. 46–57; Leyden 1875.
[2] *Réfugiés in de Nederlanden*. 1. 43.

			Date of Extinction.
Overijssel—			
	Campen	1596 (1598)	1818
1636	Deventer	1686	1822
1683	Zwolle	"	
[Drenthe]	Dwingelo	"	1711
Gelderland—			
	Dalem	1633	1803
	Nijmegen	1644[1]	
	Arnhem	1684	
	Hattem	1686	1693–1714
	Zalt-Bommel	"	1705
	Tiel	"	" (1714)
	Zutphen	"	1821
	Harderwijk	1687	1813–1816
	Doesburg	1688	1714
Utrecht—			
	Utrecht	1583	
	Amersfoort	1687	1710
	Montfoort	1688	1744 (1734)
Zeeland—			
	Middelburg	1574	
1572	Vlissingen	1584	1823
	Zierikzee	1587 (1588)	1827
1587	Arnemuiden	1615	1617[2]
	Goes	1661	1814–1818
1586	Bergen op Zoom	1686	1828
1685	Veere	1686	1810–1818
	Tholen	1688[3]	1814 (1818)
Dutch Flanders—			
	Sluis	1584	1806
1618	Groede	1622	1801–1818 (1808)
	Axel	1638	?

[1] Berg gives the date as 1621: I. 5.

[2] According to pp. 46 and 52 above, the church must apparently have overlived the Recall.

[3] Berg says 1658: I. 5 n. 2.

			Date of Extinction.
	Ijsendijke	1638	1641
	Philippine	,,	1782
	Hulst	1649	?
	Sas van Gent	1654 (1655)	1793 (1794)
1612	Aardenburg	1686 (1687)	1807 (1809)
1685	Kadsand	,,	1797–1818
	Oostburg	,,	1796–1818 [1]

Dutch Brabant, &c.—

	Breda	1590	
	's Hertogen-bosch	1631	
	Maastricht	1633	
	Heusden	1638 (1637)	1807–1808
	Vaals	1663	1797
	Grave	,,	1731
	Eysden	1790	1805

Holland—

	Amsterdam	1578	
	Haarlem	1583 [2]	
1581	Leyden	1584	
	Delft	1585	
1577	Dordrecht	1586	
	's Gravenhage	1589	
1585	Rotterdam	1590	
	Gouda	1624	1818
1651	Naarden	1652	,,
,,	den Brielle	1654	1827
	Hoorn	1685	1718
	Gorinchem	1686	1825 (1824)
	Schiedam	,,	1827 (1828)
	Enkhuisen	1687 (1686)	1722 (1721)
	Voorburg [3]	1688	

[1] Dresselhuis gives also the names of Vaals and Meenen; *waalsche Gemeenten in Zeeland*, 70: I am ignorant whether the former is the same as that I have included under Dutch Brabant.

[2] In this single example I have deserted M Gagnebin's date, 1686, as a plain clerical error.

[3] Voorburg has had no minister since 1813; but a French service is supplied seven or eight times in the summer: Gagnebin.

		Date of Extinction.
Weesp	1689	1699
Noordwijk	1690	1692
Leerdam	1700	1714
Vianen	1725	1814–1818

A list like this might form a commentary on a remark which Schroeder makes in reference to the French communities on the Rhine: 'The churches which are older than the Recall have almost always overlived those which were created by it, as though the religious and ecclesiastical bases of the sixteenth were more solid than those of the seventeenth and eighteenth centuries[1].'

III. Some Reports of Count d'Avaux (p. 49 n. 6).

The French ambassador, in his constant policy of exciting the home-government against whatever was the pleasure or the interest of the prince of Orange, did not hesitate to fabricate stories which might tell for this purpose. Among these figments I am inclined to place the despatch which relates the reprisals taken by the Dutch against Roman catholics resident in the Netherlands. A counter-persecution, according to him[2], actually began. The priests were thrust out from Zeeland, not without violence. Rotterdam, he allows, opened her gates to them; and Amsterdam offered to take them in. But so ill had been their treatment that, when the estates of Zeeland made overtures to recall them, they refused to go back.

The story has no support from other sources; and our rejection of it may be confirmed if we set it beside some other statements of a like character and of equal suspicion[3]. On Fagel's speech of September 20 1685 Count d'Avaux reported[4], *On prit dans ce tems-là une résolution dans les États de Hollande, de chasser tous les jésuites de cette province: on tient jusqu'à present cette résolution fort secret, Mm d'Amsterdam n'ayant pas encore donné les mains, &c.* On the 15th of January following, he transferred his tale of Zeeland to another quarter,—may we not suppose, in pique at the Orange reaction in

---

[1] *Jubilé de Francfort*, 91.

[2] *Negociations*, 5. 202 f.

[3] Dresselhuis also, and on the same grounds, discards the whole account: p. 44.

[4] *Negociations*, 5. 147.

these provinces?—*Les provinces de Gueldres, de Frise, et de Groningue,*
he related [1], *traitèrent fort mal les catholiques, les mettant en prison,
dont ils ne se rachetoient que par des grosses sommes d'argent.*

IV. THE HUGUENOTS AND THE CHURCH OF ENGLAND
(p. 79 n. 8).

With the title of 'the Huguenots ill-treated by James,' Lord Macaulay lays peculiar stress upon the restrictions that limited the distribution of the Royal Bounty. 'James,' he says, 'gave orders that none should receive a crust of bread or a basket of coals who did not first take the sacrament according to the Anglican ritual[2].' The fact is true but the inference is misleading.

According to our latest authority[3], 'The only proviso expressed in 1681 was in these terms, *Provided that they live and continue with their families (such as have any) in this our kingdom of England or elsewhere within our dominions.* Yet a certificate *That they have received the holy communion* crept into the warrants of denization[4], and at a later date a command *To take the oaths of allegiance and supremacy at some quarter-sessions within a year from the date hereof.* James the Second not only specified *The holy communion* but used a more stringent definition *The sacrament of the Lord's supper according to the usage of the church of England.* But after his Declaration for Liberty of Conscience, he withdrew the clauses both as to oaths and as to the sacrament.' We may notice by the way that Lord Macaulay here, after describing the one fact with a positive and detailed insistence, leaves its later contradiction to be gathered from the vague phrasing of a general statement[5].

But history cannot be built up out of acts of parliament or royal orders, and to the view here suggested of the hardships of the refugees we have to place three limitations. First, the service of the

---

[1] Vol. 5. 227.
[2] *History of England*, 2. 79.
[3] Agnew, *protestant Exiles*, 1. 36–58 and 3. 27.
[4] In Mr Cooper's lists the condition appears as early as July 28 1681; *foreign Residents in England*, 30: but the contrary statement of Mr Agnew suggests the explanation that the italics by which the words are distinguished indicate a gloss for the purpose of symmetry.
[5] Vol. 2. 209 f.

state-church had been used under the previous formula, necessarily where no French congregation existed, and commonly, as in pursuance of a state-injunction[1]. Secondly, the huguenots had no antipathy against such a ritual: they only resented its prostitution to the purposes of routine[2]. And thirdly, they were far from grateful at the privilege which the Declaration assured them in company with Roman catholics; if some availed themselves of it, their leaders were prompt in dissuading them from the dishonourable compromise[3].

The relations in fact of the huguenots towards the established church had always been of the friendliest character; and the regard paid them by successive sovereigns gave no scope for action to any of those tendencies subversive of monarchy, which presbyterianism implies. Their loyalty to church and king remained steady and sincere, until their ministry was outraged by Laud; it was the attitude of Laud and Wren to the sectaries of Canterbury and Norwich which forced them to the parliamentary allegiance[4]. Even then some held their attachment to the royalist party[5]; and most united with these conservative few in welcoming the restored monarchy. From 1660 there is nowhere a hint of disaffection until at the close of the century the popular mind confounded the huguenots in its undiscriminating recoil against all things foreign[6].

A letter of Amyraut's to Charles the Second may fairly mark their attitude towards the English ceremonial: *Veterem illam uestram liturgiam legi attentissime: est autem illa sane talis, meo iudicio, ut in multis zelum uere christianum incendere et fidem efficacissime fouere apta nata est. In aliis, omni ueneno caret; uniuerse, illibata religione, et non*

---

[1] Cp. the characteristically-coloured language of Richard Baxter, under date of December 1684: 'Many French ministers, sentenced to death and banishment fly hither for refuge. And the churchmen relieve them not because they are not for English diocesans and conformity. And others have many of their own distressed ministers and acquaintances to relieve, that few are able:' *Reliquiae Baxterianae*, in Agnew, 3. 72.

[2] See especially Fontaine, *Mémoires*, 192.

[3] Cp. above, p. 78 n. 4; and on the other hand, p. 82 n. 2.

[4] Agnew, 1. 12 f. They then became 'declared enemies to the king': Clarendon, *History of the Rebellion*, 1. 447 ff.; Oxford 1849.

[5] Burn quotes the instance of Louis Herault, minister in Threadneedle-street, whose exile for safety's sake was recompensed in 1660 by a stall at Canterbury: *foreign protestant Refugees*, 24.

[6] Cp. above, p. 105.

modo sine conscientiae ullo uulnere, sed etiam cum admodum memorabili pietatis fructu, celebrari et usurpari possit [1].

V. The Royal Bounty (p. 81, n. 6).

The history of the Royal Bounty, as the fund raised by the collections which the king's letters-patent enjoined in 1681 [2], is obscure and partly discreditable to the national financiers. I shall give a summary from the minute research of Mr Agnew [3], adding a few particulars from other sources. It appears that when the collection of 1685 was ordered, 17,950*l*. 13*s*. 0¼*d*. remained over from that of 168[1]2. This sum was lent to the city of London, in whose keeping it lay at interest; its very existence being concealed, lest the amount should deter future subscribers. The surplus of the second collection, from April 22 1686 to December 16 1688, increased the fund by 42,889*l*. 8*s*. 10¾*d*.; and the donations of seven years more added 63,713*l*. 2*s*. 3*d*. The total, 124,553*l*. 4*s*. 2*d*., nearly doubled by parliamentary grants and other benefactions, was borrowed again from the chamber of London by the government, who obtained, as interest thereon at six per cent., an annual vote of 12000*l*. for the refugee laity and 3000*l*. for the clergy [4]; but the value of these figures was reduced by perhaps one-half since payment was in the form of exchequer-bills. In the year of King William's death the estimates are said to have been mislaid, and no grant was made until in 1711 a letter addressed by the church of the Savoy to the heir-presumptive procured, through gratitude, its renewal on his accession in 1714.

1695. Dec. 23.

So far the facts are Mr Agnew's. I must notice however that, according to the papers relative to the trust, preserved among Archbishop Wake's MSS. at Christ Church, the gap between 1703 and

---

[1] Cited by Dubourdieu, *Appeal to the English Nation*, 105 n. Dubourdieu's purpose in the text of his book, when out of polemic, is conciliatory, and his judgement is representative.

[2] Thus the warrant under the royal sign manual, June 24 1718, speaks of *Our Bounty*: Wake papers, 27. nr 129.

[3] Vol. 1. 58-64 and 244.

[4] The relief given by the fund extended to all ministers excepting that of the episcopal church at Canterbury, possibly because this was an unauthorised secession from the Walloon church of the undercroft. See a letter of Le Sueur, July 1717, in the Wake papers, vol. 28.

O

1711 was filled up certainly in 1709 and 1710; one report mentioning the relief of 4843 persons in the former year[1], and the other stating that in 1710 but half the accustomed grant was paid at the time and the rest deferred for four years, so that 35,000*l*. was due July 31 1714[2]. The precedent of putting off payment being thus established, it seems that on November 19 of this year the allowance was only the ordinary sum for the laity and even half the quota for the clergy (1500*l*.)[3]. Arrears were not forgotten but equally not considered; and the abridged subsidy is magnanimously described as the king's *gift*. Coincident with this decrease was the growth of the number relieved. There had been 2412 in 1696[4], 5194 in 1716, and above 7000 in 1721[5]. From Michaelmas 1718[6] to Christmas 1821[7], and from Michaelmas 1722 to Christmas 1725[8], there were again lapses of payment; nor does it appear that this new debt was ever actually redeemed.

These additional data, while they correct one statement of Mr Agnew's, remarkably support his general deduction. Ministers, in fact, were pleased to confound the administration of a trust with the appropriation of a voluntary grant; and in course of time the subsidy was still further cut down. Meanwhile, of course, the French were defrauded of their capital of a quarter of a million pounds sterling.

VI. French Churches in London (p. 82, n. 5).

The migrations of the French churches in London, and the imperfect range of their registers, are by themselves enough to baffle

---

[1] See the report for 1725 in vol. 27. nr 131.
[2] Memoir of September 17 1716, in vol. 28.
[3] As above.
[4] So also Dubourdieu, 118.
[5] Vol. 27. nr 131.
[6] The favourable statement of the work of the French committee, given by Dubourdieu, 113-120, is just anterior to this lapse.
[7] The *Preface prefixed to the Account of the Distribution of the royal Bounty*, bearing this date, mentions that 'the number of the poor refugees is also considerably increased by many of their brethren who daily come from France, especially since the last Edict concerning religion'; p. iii: in vol. 27. nr 128. This must be 'the horrible law of 1715,' noticed by Rulhière, 2. 343.
[8] Vol. 27. nr 131. Cp. the complaint of Le Moine, minister of Brown's Lane Chapel, September 3 1725; in nr 116.

the most industrious antiquary. But there is another difficulty caused by the laxness by which the word *church* is often used to designate a mere temporary service in a private house. I am convinced moreover that in several instances a lacuna in the register implies more than the carelessness of its clerk, and that two distinct congregations meeting in the same or a neighbouring street have been merged together with the simple object of saving the expense of a new book. The old one was passed on to the new congregation[1]. It is probably impossible now to discriminate such amalgams. It is almost as hard to unravel the complications involved by the common service of ministers, the union of presbyteries, and similar arrangements. Perhaps results so indefinite as those contained in the following scheme will scarcely be thought to repay the labour it has cost.

The basis of this scheme is a list drawn up for Mr Smiles's *Huguenots in England* by Mr Frederick Martin[2]. Being a catalogue of the contents of the registers, the table is necessarily incomplete. Burn's statistics add something in this way[3]; and the notices in Dubourdieu's *Appeal to the English Nation*, 1718, and in Jacob Bourdillon's *Jubilee Sermon*, 1782, furnish three dates 1718, 1732, and 1782, by which to extend the life of some of the congregations. These are added within brackets. What little other evidence I have been able to collect is chiefly of a negative character. The 'into (1)' 'into (5)' &c. indicates the church, according to the numbers of this series, *into* which that to which it is appended was merged.

A. In the City of London and in the East.

1. *The London Walloon Church* in *Threadneedle-street*[4]   Since 1550.
2. *Martin's Lane Chapel*, Saint Martin-Ongar[5]
   1686 to 1762 [1782]; into (1).

---

[1] This is known to have been the case when Le Tabernacle (nr 22) was united with Leicester Fields Chapel (nr 19): see Burn, *foreign protestant Refugees*, 147 ff.

[2] P. 467. It is to be regretted that this memoir has disappeared from the book since the second edition.

[3] Pp. 24 ff., 108-115, 134-181.

[4] For this and the three following see above, notes to p. 81. The church was removed in 1840 into Aldersgate-street.

[5] From 1720 its ministers were consolidated with those of the Savoy: Burn, 155.

3. *L'Église de l'Hôpital*, Church-street, Spitalfields [1]
   1687 ; Register 1753 to 1809 or later ; into (1).
4. *L'Église de Saint Jean*, Swanfields Register 1687 to 1823 ; into (1).
5. *La Patente en Spitalfields*, in Brown's Lane [2]
   Register 1689 to 1785 ; into (1) 1786.
6. *L'Église de l'Artillerie* [3]   1691 closed 1786 ; into (1).
7. *L'Église de Crispin-street* [4]
   1693 ; Register 1694 to 1716 ; into (5) 1717 [yet 1732].
8. *Perle-street Chapel* 1697 ; Register 1700 to 1701 ; into (7) 1710.

---

[1] It was afterwards known as L'Église Neuve ; Burn, 178 f.

[2] It had been removed to Brown's-lane certainly by 1725 ; above, p. 108, n. 3 : not, as Burn gives the date, in 1740, p. 169.

[3] The congregation was formed about May 30, 1691 ; but where it met is doubtful. A possible solution may be obtained by combining with it two churches which appear in the lists separately. There are, (*a*) one in Boar's Head-yard, Petticoat-lane, Spitalfields, which emerges first in 1691 and which is noticed three years later as having a consistory in common with the churches of S Jean (nr 4) and of *Leicester Fields* (nr 19), the ministers officiating for the three ; and (*b*) one in Wapping, placed by Mr Burn conjecturally in *Long Hedge-lane*, of which the register runs from 1700 (or 1711 ?) to 1747 and of which the distinct existence is warranted by the mention of Dubourdieu in 1718, p. 56. The separate and local identification of the Artillerie is in 1763, when a new church was built in Parliament-court, Artillery-street, Bishopsgate. This church was opened in 1766 ; but the note that it was partially united with *Leicester Fields* (nr 19) and Ryder's Court (nr 25) must place its formation in the last stage prior to the year 1750 when Ryder's Court was dissolved. The statistics of the three registers are collected in Burn, 159 and 180 : but two additional facts he relates incidentally, may still further embarrass the problem. For it seems that some time before 1697 one Jacques Laborier had a meeting-place in *Artillery-ground*, p. 173 ; and that the Hospital-church (nr 3) held its first services 'on a piece of ground in *Long Hedge Field* leased by the French church of the district,' p. 179.

[4] The affinity of Crispin-street was with the churches in Perle-street (nr 8) and West-street (nr 27). In 1716 it might be said to have swallowed up La Patente, for the building of the former still served ; above, p. 82, n. 1 : but the name and the staff of La Patente supplanted it. When Dubourdieu, p. 53, refers to Crispin-street in 1718 he may mean La Patente ; but in view of the notice of Bourdillon in 1732, and comparing note 2, above, I am inclined to think that La Patente removed to Brown's-lane shortly after 1716, and that the old Crispin-street congregation was reconstituted.

9. *Wheeler-street* episcopal *Chapel*
   Register May 16 1703 to 1742 March 14; into (5).
10. *Pesthouse Chapel*, in the East   Notice 1706.
11. *Blackfriars Chapel*   1710 to 1716 [1718 [1]].
12. *Bell-lane Chapel*, Spitalfields [2]   Register 1711 to 1716 [1718].
13. *L'Église de Swanfields*, in Slaughter-street, Spitalfields
                                                        1721 to 1735.

B. In Westminster and the West.

14. *Somerset-house Chapel* [3]   1653 closed 1777.
15. *La Grand Savoie* [4]   1661 to 1737; into (26).
16. *Castle-street Chapel*, Leicester-square
                                          1672; Register 1725 to 1754.
17. *La Petite Savoie*, in Spring Garden   1675 to 1755; into (26).
18. *L'Église de Hungerford* [5], in Hungerford Market
                                1687; Register 1688 to 1727; into (16).

---

[1] Dubourdieu, 54 f.

[2] Bell-lane and Swanfields chapels are severally distinguished as small and poor congregations: Burn, 175 f.

[3] For this church and the three next in order see above, notes to pp. 83 f.

[4] It should appear from a curious extract in Kennett (whose name by the way I spell with a double *t* against the common manner, relying on his autograph in the Wake collection), *complete History of England*, 2. 472 f., that the ministers were nearly persuaded to hand over their privilege at the Savoy to the jesuit priests, for a handsome douceur and the promise of a new building somewhere between Whitehall and Temple Bar. Dubourdieu however took the preliminary step of consulting Lords Halifax, Danby, Nottingham, and some few others, and their advice was unanimous and decisive: 'Never hearken to any terms with the jesuits; let them pursue their violent measures: suffer not yourselves to be thrust out of your church; for by that means you'll do your own business and the nation's.'

[5] In 1717 Hungerford Chapel is said to have been absorbed by that in Castle-street: the register shows that some sort of independence subsisted for ten years more, but in what way I am unable to guess. In 1718 Dubourdieu speaks of 'the church which used to meet in Hungerford Market' as still existent, p. 55; and a possible prolongation may be conjectured if we understand it to be indicated by the obscure Église de Marche (q. d. *Marché*) of Mr Martin's list under the date of 1719.

19. *Leicester Fields Chapel*[1]
    Register 1688 to 1783; into (7) about 1776.
20. *La Patente* or *Le Temple de Soho*[2]
    Register 1689 to 1782; into (26).
21. *Swallow-street* episcopal *Chapel*[3]
    Register 1690 to 1709; closed 1710.
22. *Le Tabernacle*   1690; Register 1696 to 1710; into (19).
23. *Le Carré*, in Little Dean-street, Soho[4] (episcopal)
    Register 169[0]1 to 1763; [1782].
24. *Friary Chapel*, Pall Mall[5]   Register 1700 to 1754; [1782].
25. *Ryder's Court Chapel*, Soho   Register 1700 to 1750.
26. *Les Grecs*, in Dudley-court, Hog-lane[6]   Since 1700.
27. *La Pyramide*, in West Street, Saint Giles's[7]
    Register 1701 to 1704, 1706 to 1743.
28. *Berwick-street Chapel*   Register 1720 to 1788.

To this list may be added from the colonies in the neighbourhood of London, churches at

Wandsworth   1575 to 1831 and later.

Marylebone, in or near Marylebone-lane
    Noticed about 1656 and 1720[8] [1732] closed before 1782.

---

[1] Above, p. 82, n. 3. Its building is now Orange-street Chapel: Burn, 134 ff.

[2] Above, p. 82, n. 2; Smiles, 342. It stood in Little Chapel-street.

[3] The lease was sold in 1710 and the congregation dissolved: Burn, 139 ff.

[4] Perhaps otherwise known as L'Ancienne Patente. The register is double and overlapping. The first part, 169[0]1 to 1718, is entitled Sohon-square; the second, 1714 to 1763, Berwick-street: Burn, 145 ff. As the church is said to have held intimate relations with Berwick-street Chapel (nr 28) an additional confusion may be suspected.

[5] This was the French service in the chapel royal, S James's; and I am inclined to seek its instauration in the appointment of a new French chaplain-in-ordinary, Philippe Ménard, in 1699: see above, p. 66, n. 2.

[6] See above, p. 85, n. 4, where reasons are given for an earlier beginning. After a removal to Edward-street, a new church was founded in Bloomsbury-street by the bishop of London, January 2 1845.

[7] For its connexion with La Charenton, and its origin not later than 1696, see above, p. 85, n. 2. Of its various names La Pyramide became the usual one: see a letter of October 15 1717 among the Wake papers, vol. 28.

[8] Malard, *Address and Representation of Grievances*, 9.

Greenwich	1686 [1718¹].
Hammersmith	Noticed in 1701 and 1706.
Chelsea (two congregations; register of one) 1714 to 1718 [1729²].	
Little Chelsea	Noticed in 1718.
*Islington*³	Noticed in 1718.
Hoxton	Register 1748 to 1783.

When Jacob Bourdillon began his ministry in 1732, London had twenty French churches 'all vigorous': at his jubilee nine of these were closed, and of the rest some were 'drawing near their end⁴.' This list includes the chapel at Marylebone, but excludes that in Somerset-house, apparently as a private chapel. His omission of the late congregation at Berwick-street may suggest that it has been wrongly separated from some other of the Soho churches, as Le Carré or Les Grecs⁵. I do not know whether the French of Southwark and Fulham had independent churches, or whether they were content with the services at Blackfriars and Chelsea and Hammersmith.

VII. SUPPLEMENT OF FRENCH SETTLEMENTS IN ENGLAND
(p. 94, n. 7).

I have postponed certain settlements to this place because of the doubt that hangs over their relation to the emigrants of the Recall. Those at *Thorney Abbey* and *Whittlesey* I have mentioned in the text; but the foreign population is of an earlier origin, and at first Dutch. They were brought over to drain Whittlesey Mere in the isle of Ely, and a French church was formed at Thorney Abbey in 1652, which subsisted at least till 1727⁶. The colony at Whittlesey itself, four miles distant, dates from 1662, but there is no record of a separate French congregation⁷.

---

¹ Dubourdieu, 55 & 66; Smiles, 346 f.
² See above, p. 93, n. 3.
³ Dubourdieu, 54.
⁴ Burn, 162 ff. Mr Lecky speaks of thirty-five churches at the beginning of the eighteenth century. But this is without warrant: cp. above, p. 107, n. 1.
⁵ I have alluded to the possible confusion, above p. 198, n. 4: La Patente also met at first in Berwick-street, above p. 82, n. 2.
⁶ Burn, 99 ff. ⁷ Pp. 98 f.

Sandtoft Chapel, in the isle of Axholme, was settled under like conditions. A Dutchman, engaged in 1626 to drain Hatfield Chase, fetched with him a number of workmen, who from 1634 supported a service alternately French and Dutch [1]. Their labour finished, they resolved themselves into an industrial community. The district, which had known no occupation apart from agriculture, now became busy with linen-spinning and weaving, dyeing and tanning; and it is to these immigrants that Lincolnshire owes the woad-growing for which it is now famous [2]. But quiet and continued progress was rendered impossible by the wild raids of the isle-men, whose lawless violence drove part of the community back to Holland. Long razed, their church was at length repaired and opened in 1681; but it soon fell into decay, its materials were disposed of, 'and cattle grazed upon its site [3].' This date of restoration has suggested a connexion with the first *dragonnades*; but the subsidiary data given convinces that it is nothing more than a coincidence.

First among settlements of older foundation is *Glastonbury*, where Valerandus Pollanus gathered a congregation of French and Walloons about 1550. Its existence is attested for above a century; but it gradually ceased to form a separate society in the town [4]. A few huguenots appear in the lists as living there after the Recall, but their number cannot merit the distinction of a colony.

Other Walloon churches existed at Maidstone, Thetford, and Stamford: but there is no evidence to connect them with the emigrants of the Recall. Whether it shall be by the help of these or of the colonies mentioned above (page 92), that we must fill up the list of twelve churches organised by the French committee in 1687 [5], refers its decision to the local antiquary; for I have met with no published materials to warrant any opinion.

---

[1] Burn, 101-108.

[2] See a pretentious account by M Collisson, in the *Bulletin*, 8. 344-352.

[3] Burn, as above, adds that ample reliques survive in names and such witnesses of French extraction.

[4] Pp. 90-94.

[5] Above, p. 82.

VIII. Statistics of the Diaconate of Frankfurt
(p. 126, n. 3).

Schroeder gives the following numbers of the refugees to whom relief was furnished by the diaconate of Frankfurt[1]. In 1689 the list divides, and shows a great increase from the Palatinate; the two columns unite again in 1700.

For the year ending May 16,	· 1686	2822			
,,	,,	1687	2656		
,,	,,	1688	5330[2]		
,,	,,	1689	3660		
,,	,,	1690	1661	*Palatines*	2946
,,	,,	1691	1089	,,	6449
,,	,,	1692	1917	,,	6693
,,	,,	1693	2046	,,	8640
,,	,,	1694	1318	,,	8326
,,	,,	1695	444	,,	7751
For the ten years ending May 16, 1705			14,213[3]	,,	19,905
,,	,,	1715	15,306		
,,	,.	1725	12,576		

IX. French Colonies in Hesse (p. 138, n. 7).

From the data supplied by Schroeder[4], C. von Rommel, F. Waddington[5], Koehler, and the author of the *Uebersicht der Wanderungen und Niederlassungen der Religionsflüchtlinge*, I have drawn up the following chronology of the Hessian Refuge[6].

Hessen-Homburg—

1685	Homburg.
1687	Dornholzhausen, Friedrichsdorf.

Hessen-Darmstadt (arranged alphabetically)—
   Arheilingen, Darmstadt, Hahn, Kelsterbach, Moerfelden, Rohrbach, Waldorf, Wembach.

---

[1] *Jubilé de Francfort*, 84.
[2] With the figures for 1687-8, as contrasted with the years before and after, compare above p. 29, and n. 2.
[3] In 1698-9 the huguenot total reaches 2946.
[4] Appendix, and also p. 45.   [5] *Bulletin*, 8. 79 ff.
[6] I know not where to find Holzappel and Haselborn, huguenot colonies.

Hessen-Cassel—

        Lower Hesse.
- 1685 — Cassel.
- 1685–6 — Hofgeismar.
- 1686 — Karlsdorf.
- 1686–7 — Immenhausen and Mariendorf.
- 1688 — The Oberneustadt of Cassel.
- 1691 or earlier — Geismar and Ellershausen.
- 1698–9 — Schoeneberg and Carlshafen.
- 1699 — Wolfhagen and Ippinghausen, Treysa, Leckeringshausen.
- 1700 — Kelse and S Ottilie.
- 1701 — Frankenhain.
- 1722–3 — Gottestreu and Gewissensruhe [1].

        Fulda.
- 1699 — Goettsemanns.

        Upper Hesse.
- 1687 — Frankenberg and Schwabendorf.
- 1687–8 — Marburg and Frauenberg.
- 1688 — Louisendorf.
- 1694 — Hertingshausen [2].
- 1699 — Wolfskaute.
- 1720 — Todenhausen and Wiesenfeld.

X. FRENCH COLONIES IN BRANDENBURG (p. 152, n. 1).

In the following list, the names in s p a c e d type are those mentioned by Ancillon in 1690 [3]. Names in ordinary type comprise the official visitation-list of December 31, 1700 [4]. Neither purports to be complete: on the other hand, where a later date is given to any of these it is to be assumed that the colony was practically refounded by the vaudois exiles of the peace of Rijswijk. Other places, in

---

[1] To these must be added without the chronological series Hombressen, Huemme-an-der-Lempe, and Sielen.

[2] I suspect the date is 1699; in 1694 there was no pressure of influx to push out new colonies.

[3] *Établissement der François réfugiez*, 44-59.

[4] Edited by M F. de Schickler in the *Bulletin*, 28. 39: cp. above, p. 169, n. 5.

italics, are from Erman[1] and other sources[2]. The number added to some names indicates the staff of preachers, and an obelus that the French service was disused in the time that Erman wrote.

1672	Berlin (5).
1685	Magdeburg (3).
1685–1693	*Battin*[8].
1686	Emmerich, Wesel (2), Halle (2), Brandenburg, Koepenick[4], Frankfurt-am-Oder (2), Reinsberg[5], Schwedt and Wiradin, Gramzow-in-Uckermark[6], *Ziethen* (*Gross* and *Klein*), *Ruppin*, Koenigsberg (2).
1686–7	Bergholz[7].
1687	Prenzlow[8] (2), Stargard, Buchholz.
1688	*Braunsberg*[9].
1689	Burg-an-der-Ihle, Spandau.
1690 or earlier	Lippstadt.
1690	Cleve.
1690–1	Angermuende.
1691	Soest, Strassburg-in-Uckermark.
1693	Stendal.
1696	Duisburg †.
1697	Muencheberg, *Neulindow*.
1698	*Colberg, Minden*.
1699	Halberstadt, Bernau, Neustadt-an-der-Dosse †, Neuhaldensleben, *Parstein*.
1700 or earlier	Mannheim-bei-Magdeburg, Chorin.

---

[1] *Mémoires*, 9. 321-331.

[2] *Lettre à un Ami de Genève*, 32 ff.; *Uebersicht der Wanderungen*, 72 ff.; Reyer, *Geschichte der französischen Kolonie*, 188; Kochler, 18, 28, &c.

[3] Including the French villages of Bagemuehl, Woddow, Schmoellen, Wallmow, Graenz, and Eichstadt, and the small town of Brussow.

[4] Erman gives the date as 1693: but the French colony at Koepenick is traced to 1686, only it had service through the chaplain of the French guards, in conjunction with the reformed Germans, until 1690: *Bulletin*, 28. 40 f., Ancillon 56 f.

[5] Afterwards incorporated with Braunsberg.

[6] Including Briest, Fredersdorf, Grunow, Meckow, and Metzow.

[7] This was the bailiwick of Loeckenitz and comprised the French villages of Rossow, Zerreuthen, Grimm, and Fahrenwalde.

[8] The ministry was afterwards reduced to one: Erman.

[9] Then called Cagar. Its union with Reinsberg must account for its omission from the official list.

1701	*Potzlow, Hamm* †, *Lammspring* [1] †, *Cottbus* [2].
1703	Oranienburg †, *Calbe.*
1721	*Stettin.*
1723	*Potsdam.*

To this list must be added *Zechlin* and *Muelenbeck* from Koehler, 18.

---

[1] Or Hammelspring.

[2] Cottbus was not exclusively French. A similar but preponderant German element disguises the colonies at Crossen, Peitz, Soldin, and Zuellichen: Reyer, 188 f.

INDEX.

Abauzit, F., 119, 120 f.
Abbadie, J., 146, 149, 159.
Agriculture of the refugees—in America 95, Appenzell 123, Brandenburg 151 f., Breda 42, Cape Colony 43, Denmark 67, England 94 f., Friesland 38, Hesse 141, Vaud 121. Cp. *Tobacco,Vines*.
Amyraut, M., 7, 120, 192 f.
Ancillon, C., 149 n. 3, 144 n. 2; D., 149; F., 149 n. 3.
Anglican Church and the refugees 105, 191 ff.
Arnaud 128 n. 2.
Avaux, Count d', 28, 29 f., 190 f.
Avyan, Baron d', 104.

Banc des Catholiques 13 n. 2.
Basnage de Beauval, H., 56.
Basnage, J., 53 f., 178.
Baxter, R., on the exodus 192 n. 1.
Bayle, P., 48 f., 54 ff., 120, 170.
Beausobre, I. de, 162, 52 n. 1.
Beauveau, Count de, 149.
Bellay, C. du, 149.
Benoît, E., author of the *Retraite des Pasteurs*, 26 n. 8; *Histoire de l'Édit de Nantes*, 5 n. 3, 178; cp. 35 n. 1, 51.
Berlin, enlarged 155; the French church 149.
Bernard, S., 186 n. 5.
Blancard, S., G. de, 149.
Bonrepaux, Count de, 79, 80.
Book-trade of the refugees at Amsterdam 59.
Bordage, Marq. de, his flight 32 n. 1.
Bosc, P. du, at Rotterdam, 52 n. 1, 54.
Bostaquet, I. D. de, his flight 179; in Ireland 110.
Brandenburg, character of French colony 148, 153.
Briquemault, H. de, at Lippstadt, 149, 158.
Brousson, C., 132.
Burlamachi, at Geneva 120 n. 2.
Caen; injury from the emigration 171 n. 2.

Calvinism, tendencies of, 1 f., 17 n. 3, 54 f., 176.
Cambric, see *Linen*.
Caméron at Saumur 7.
Cappel, L., 7, 119.
Cavéirac, Abbé de, 65 n., 165 f.
Chaise, Père La, 23, 25 n. 4, 73.
Charles II 74-78.
Charles, P., at Orthèz 6 n. 1.
Chaufepié, S. de, 176 n. 3.
Chauvain, E., at Berlin, 161 f.
Chouet at Geneva 120.
Christina, Queen, on the Recall 15 n. 4.
Churches, protestant, destroyed 13, 21 n. 4, 27.
Claude, J., at Nîmes 6 n. 2, at the Hague 52, 57; his *Plaintes des Protestants* 27 n. 6, 80; his judgement of the persecution 13 f.
Clockmaking, at Canterbury 91 n. 6, Geneva 119, Norwich 91 n. 2.
Colbert, 9 f., 22, 27; diffusion of his system 156 f., 173.
Commerce of the refugees at Berlin 147 & n. 2, Frankfurt-am-Main 126 n. 6, in Prussian dependencies 152 :—Decline in France 170 ff. See also *Shipping*.
Compton, H., bp. of London, 105, 75.
Cotton-trade promoted by the refugees at Bideford 89, Bromley 93, Geneva 119.
Croze, M. V. de la, 178 n. 6.

Daillé, J., 123 n. 4.
Daillon 82 n. 2.
Daneau, L., at Orthèz 6 n. 1.
Dauphiné; its element in the Dispersion 57 n. 3; at Berlin 155 n. 3; Bern 123; Geneva 117, 119; Hesse 137, 140 n. 3, 141 notes, 142; Yverdun 121.
Desaguliers 178.
Die, protestant college 5.
Dollond, J., 178 n. 3.
Dragonnades 26 f., 186 f.

Duplessis-Mornay, his scheme of church-union 7.
Duquesne, family of, 43, 124.
Emigration of the huguenots 11, 12, 14, 26, 28 ff.; forbidden 14 n. 4, 76 n. 5;—to America 95-100, Baden 133, Brandenburg 131, 148 ff., Brunswick 70 ff., Cape Colony 43 f., Carolina 97 f., Denmark 65, England 76 f., 80, 87 f., 99, 106 f., Frankfurt 126 f. (cp. 117 f., 125), Friesland 34 ff., 37 ff., Gaasterland 38 (cp. 35 n. 5), S Gallen 123 n. 6, Geneva 115 ff., the German seaports 63 ff., Glarus 123 n. 6, Hesse 137-143, Lippe-Detmold 129 n. 3, Maryland 93, Mecklenburg 70, Nassau 129 n. 3, the Netherlands 37 f., 39, 41, 42, 43, 45, 50 f., Overijssel 39, Pennsylvania 100, Russia 67 f., Sachsen-Hildburghausen 128 f., Solms-Braunfels 129 n. 3, Sweden 70, Switzerland 114, the Uckermark 151 f., Vaud 114 f., Virginia 97 f. (cp. 100 n. 3), Westphalia 150 ff., Wuerttemberg 129 ff., Zeeland 41; —total numbers 165-169.
Erman and Reclam, their history of the colony in Brandenburg 144 f., cp. vi.
Exportation of capital 31 f., 169 f., 59 n. 4.
Fisheries, engaged in by refugees, at Bearhaven 115, Dordrecht 60, Holstein 65.
Fontaine, J., in England 89 f., in Ireland 113; his memoirs 19 n. 1.
Frederick 1, king of Prussia 154 f.; relations with Neuchâtel 124.
Frederick William 1, 160.
French language diffused by the refugees at Berlin 158, Geneva 119, Hanover 72, Lausanne 119. Cp. *Huguenots*.
Friedrich Wilhelm, the Great Elector, 145 f., 150, 154, 163.
Gallican Church; its support of Lewis XIV 16 f.; condition after the emigration 181 f.
Galway, Lord, 87 f., 109 f.
Gaylen at Amsterdam 59 n. 4.
Geneva, French society of, 119 ff.; relations with S Petersburg 68.

Gex, Pays de, emigration to Geneva 117, to the Pays de Vaud 114 f.
Glass, manufactured at Berlin 155. London 93. Neustadt-an-der-Dosse 155; in Sussex 93.
Grumkow 150.
Guiraud, C., at Nîmes 6.
Halifax, Marquess of, 74, 197 n. 4.
Harlay, abp of Paris, 23 n. 3, 73.
Hats manufactured at Berlin 155, Frankfurt-am-Oder and Magdeburg 155 n. 3, Rotterdam 60, Wandsworth 92.
Hérault, L., 192 n. 5.
Holland, relations with Brandenburg 149 n. 8, Hanover 72, Neu-Isenburg 135, Sweden 70, Switzerland 118, 122. See *Orange* and *William III*.
Huber, Marie, at Geneva 121.
Huguenots: the name 2 n. 1; number 25 n. 1, 168; religion 3 f.; education 5-8; politics 2 f.; condition under Mazarin 11; presumed disaffection 17 f.; yet nonresistance 18 f.; provincial strength 20 f.; oppressed 26 f.; see *Emigration*: their social influence 179 f.; in Berlin 163 f., 154 f.; Carolina 98; England 104 f.; Holland 60 ff.; Ireland 111 f. Cp. *Calvinism*.
Icard, C., at Bremen 64.
Industries of the huguenots 8 f.; promoted by their emigrants in Amsterdam 59, Berlin 155, Brandenburg 156 f., Cassel 139, Erlangen 131, Frankenhain 142 n. 5, Neu-Isenburg 136; lost to France 171 f. See also *Clockmaking, Cotton, Glass, Hats, Jewellery, Linen, Paper, Silk, Tapestry, Wool*.
Inguenheim at Schwabach 131 n. 1.
James II 78 ff.
Jenkyns, Sir L., 75.
Jesuits, the, and the Recall 24 n. 1, 25 n. 4; cp. 197 n. 4.
Jewellery at Berlin 155 n. 3, Geneva 119, Hanau 137.
Jurieu in Holland 39 n. 2, 48 f., 52 f.; judgement of the persecution 28.
Larrey, I. de, 162, 178.
Lenfant 178; at Cassel 138, at Berlin 163.
Lewis XIV: his aims 15; their results

181 ff.; suspicion of the huguenots 17 f., 19 f.; relations with England 78, Geneva 116 f.; Western Germany 128, Turkey 119 n. 3; his conversion and crusade 24 ff.
Linen-trade promoted in Gelderland 40; Groningen 39; Hamburg 64; Ipswich 93; Lisburn 111 f.; Overijssel 39; Waterford 112.
Liotard, E. and M., at Geneva, 119 n. 5.
Literature of the refugees 177 f., 57 n. 3; at Berlin 158–164; the Hague 57; Rotterdam 56.
London, growth of, 82 ff.
Louvois and the huguenots 21 f.
Lutherans, their jealousy of the refugees 64, 66, 125 f.; cp. 50, 127, 72.
Lyons; emigration to Geneva 116; decay of trade 171.

Maintenon, Mme de, 24, 27.
Mariet, his escape 31 n. 3.
Marillac in Poitou 24, 25 n. 4, 76.
Marsilly, C. R. de, 18 n. 1.
Martin, D., 180 n. 1.
Ménard, J., 57, 66 n. 2; P., 66.
Metz, emigration from, 149, 155 n. 3; the loss 171.
Military emigration 175 f.; in Brandenburg 157 f., Denmark 67, England 102 ff., Holland 101 f., Ireland 110 f., Russia 68 f.
Ministers in Brandenburg 158 f.; Denmark 66; England 81 ff.; Holland 51 f.
Mirmand, M de, 122 n. 4.
Moine, Le, in Spitalfields 108 n. 3, 109 n. 1.
Moivre, A. de, 178.
Monfreton, Le N. de, 38 n. 1.
Montauban, protestant college 7.
Montpellier, protestant college 6.
Mousquetaires, Grands, 157.

Nantes, Edict of, confirmed 11 f.; steps to its recall 12 ff.; recalled 27 and n. 7.
Naturalisation accorded to the refugees in Bern 123, Carolina 98, Ireland 109, the Netherlands 37, New York and Virginia 97, Zeeland 41; proposed in England 74 f., cp. 107 & n. 4.
Navy, huguenots in the, 18.
Netherlands, French churches in, 187-190: see *Holland*.

Nîmes, protestant college 6; persecution at 6 n. 5; emigration to Geneva 119; loss thereby 172.
Normandy, under dragoons 21 n. 3, 185, 186; emigration to London 108, Rotterdam 50, Southampton 88.
Orange, persecution in, 42 and n. 2, 152 and n. 4.; Prince of Orange, his party in the Netherlands 35 f., 36 n. 2, 190; see *William III*.
Orthèz, royal university 6 n. 1.

Paets and the Rotterdam Athenaeum 48 & 54.
Palatinate, the, refuge in, 129; its churches, 130 n. 5; desolation by Lewis XIV 129, second immigration 130, and dispersion into England 99, and America 100.
Papacy, the, and Lewis XIV 15 and n. 4.
Paper made by refugees at Amsterdam 59, Berlin 155, Glasgow, Kent, Laverstoke 93, Zaandam 59.
Papin, D., 140, 178.
Petitot, J., at Geneva 119.
Philosophy diffused by refugees 177, at Berlin 161, Geneva 119 f., Rotterdam 54 ff.
Picardy, emigration to Carolina 98, and Edinburgh 94.
Place, J. de la, 7, 120.
Placette, J. de la, at Copenhagen 66.
Poitou, initial persecution in, 13, 17, 24, 25, 34 f., 76, 88, 89, 94, 149; condition after the emigration 171 f.
Polyandre, J., at Dordrecht 49.
Potsdam, Edict of, 145 f.
Pusey, E. B., 180.
Puylaurens, protestant college 7 n. 4.

Rapin, P. de, 178, 104 n. 2.
Raselle and the Irish refuge 109 n. 3.
Refugees,—in Altona 65, Amsterdam 45. 36 n. 7, 37, 50 f., 59, Arnemuiden 37, Balk 38, Barnstaple 89, Basel 123, Berlin 149, 155 f., Bern 116, 122 f., Boston *U.S.A.* 95 f., Brandenburg 156, Bremen 64, Bristol 89, Canterbury 91 f., Carlshafen 141 (cp. 72 n. 2), Cassel 138 ff., 143, Celle 72, Charleston 98, Constantinople 119 n. 3, Copenhagen 65 ff. (cp. 135), Dantzig 69, Dordrecht 49 f., Dresden

128, Dublin 111, Edinburgh 94, Emden 63, Erlangen 131, Frankfurt-am-Main 125 ff., Frankfurt-am-Oder 156, Friedrichsdorf 137 f., Geneva 118 f., Glueckstadt 65, Greenwich 87, Groningen 36, 39, Haarlem 36 n. 7, 37, 46 ff., 58, the Hague 47, 57, Hamburg 64 f., Hameln 72, Hanau 137 f., Hanover 72, Koepenick 156, Lausanne 115, 119, Leeuwarden 38 f., Leipzig 128, Leyden 58 f., Lisburn 111 f., London 80-86, 107 f., Luebeck 64, Maastricht 42 f., Magdeburg 151, 156, Middelburg 41, 36 n. 7, Moscow 68, Neuchâtel 123 f. (cp. I n. 1), Neu-Isenburg 134 ff., New York 96, 100, Norwich 90 f., S Petersburg 68, Portarlington 110, Rotterdam 47, 50, 54 ff., Rye 90, 77 n. 4, Schaffhausen 117, 123, Schwabach 131, Southampton 88, Surinam 59, Utrecht 47, 36, 40, Wandsworth 92, Waterford 112, Youghal 111, Zuerich 123, 115 n. 4, Zwolle 40 :—suspected in Bern 122, in England 77, 79, 90, Lausanne 122 :—see *Emigration.*

Revolution in England supported by the refugees 80, 100-105, 176.

Reynier, J. L., 119 n. 4.

Richelieu 3, 11.

Robillard, S. de, 107 n. 5.

Rochefoucault, F. C. de la, 67.

Rochelle, La, persecution at, 49 n. 4; emigration from 77, 89; condition afterwards 170, 171 n. 3.

Roger at Berlin 163.

Rou, J., 57, 48. 161 n. 7.

Rulhière, his *Eclaircissements Historiques* 10 n. 1, 12, 24.

Russell, Lady, on the exodus 28 n. 3.

Ruvigny, Marquess de, 87.

Sage, Le, at Geneva 121.

Saintonge, emigrants from, in England 89, at Neuchâtel 123 n. 8.

Saint-Simon, Duke de, 16 n. 1.

Saumur, protestant college 7; cp. *Beausobre and Lenfant* 162 f., *Rou* 119.

Saurin, E., 57.

Savile, H., 73 f.

Schomberg, Marshal, 102, 104, 157.

Science of the refugees 177 f., at Berlin 160 f., Geneva 120, Marburg 140.

Sedan, protestant college 7; cp. *Bayle, Jurieu*; persecution at 42.

Seignelay, minister of marine, 18, 32.

Seven Dials 84, 86.

Shipping, in England 87, 89; see *Commerce, Fisheries.*

Silk-trade promoted by the refugees, in Amersfoort 40, Amsterdam 59, Berlin 155, Bern 122, Bideford 89, Canterbury 91, England 91 n. 2, Geneva 118, London 93, Spitalfields 83, Utrecht 40; in France after the emigration 171.

Soho 84 ff.

Spanheim, E., at Versailles 146, 23; at Berlin 163.

Spitalfields 81 ff.

Superville, D. de, at Rotterdam 54.

Switzerland, refugees sent on from, to Ireland 109, to Saxony 129 n. 3.

Tapestry-workers at Bern 123, Exeter 89, Fulham 93.

Thynne, T., 73.

Tobacco planted by the refugees in Brandenburg 152, Denmark 67.

Valkenier 137.

Varennes, Marquess de, 158.

Vauban, Marshal, 165.

Vaudois, confused with huguenots, 127 f., 132, 133 n. 5, 136 n. 2, 137 notes, 142 n. 5 ;—in Brandenburg 151; Hesse 139, 141, 142; the Palatinate 130; Wuerttemberg 132.

Venours, Marq. de, at Haarlem, 46 ff.

Vines grown by the refugees at the Cape 43 n. 8, 44 & n. 3; in Carolina 97.

Weiss C., vii, 9 n. 1, 67 n. 5, 69 n. 4.

William III, interest in the American 97 and Irish refugees 107; in the exiled soldiery 101 f.; relations with Lewis XIV 42.

Wool-manufacture promoted by the refugees at Amsterdam 59, Berlin 155, Bern 122, Brandenburg 156 n. 4, Friedrichsdorf 137, Geneva 118, Haarlem 47, 58, Leyden 58 f., Neuchâtel 123 n. 8, Norwich 91, Yverdun 121.

Yperen, Dood van, 60 n. 3.

BEDFORD STREET, STRAND, LONDON, W.C.
December, 1879.

MACMILLAN & CO.'S CATALOGUE of Works in the Departments of History, Biography, Travels, Critical and Literary Essays, Politics, Political and Social Economy, Law, etc.; and Works connected with Language.

HISTORY, BIOGRAPHY, TRAVELS, &c.

Albemarle.—FIFTY YEARS OF MY LIFE. By GEORGE THOMAS, Earl of Albemarle. With Steel Portrait of the first Earl of Albemarle, engraved by JEENS. Third and Cheaper Edition. Crown 8vo. 7s. 6d.

"*The book is one of the most amusing of its class. . . . These reminiscences have the charm and flavour of personal experience, and they bring us into direct contact with the persons they describe.*"—EDINBURGH REVIEW.

Anderson.—MANDALAY TO MOMIEN; a Narrative of the Two Expeditions to Western China, of 1868 and 1875, under Colonel E. B. Sladen and Colonel Horace Browne. By Dr. ANDERSON, F.R.S.E., Medical and Scientific Officer to the Expeditions. With numerous Maps and Illustrations. 8vo. 21s.

"*A pleasant, useful, carefully-written, and important work.*"—ATHENÆUM.

Appleton.—Works by T. G. APPLETON :—

A NILE JOURNAL. Illustrated by EUGENE BENSON. Crown 8vo. 6s.

SYRIAN SUNSHINE. Crown 8vo. 6s.

Arnold (M.)—ESSAYS IN CRITICISM. By MATTHEW ARNOLD. New Edition, Revised and Enlarged. Crown 8vo. 9s.

Arnold (W. T.)—THE ROMAN SYSTEM OF PROVINCIAL ADMINISTRATION TO THE ACCESSION OF CONSTANTINE THE GREAT. Being the Arnold Prize Essay for 1879. By W. T. Arnold, B.A. Crown 8vo. 6s.

15,000.12.79. A

Atkinson.—AN ART TOUR TO NORTHERN CAPITALS OF EUROPE, including Descriptions of the Towns, the Museums, and other Art Treasures of Copenhagen, Christiania, Stockholm, Abo, Helsingfors, Wiborg, St. Petersburg, Moscow, and Kief. By J. BEAVINGTON ATKINSON. 8vo. 12s.

Bailey.—THE SUCCESSION TO THE ENGLISH CROWN. A Historical Sketch. By A. BAILEY, M.A., Barrister-at-Law. Crown 8vo. 7s. 6d.

Baker (Sir Samuel W.)—Works by Sir SAMUEL BAKER, Pacha, M.A., F.R.S., F.R.G.S. :—

CYPRUS AS I SAW IT IN 1879. With Frontispiece. 8vo. 12s. 6d.

ISMAILIA: A Narrative of the Expedition to Central Africa for the Suppression of the Slave Trade, organised by Ismail, Khedive of Egypt. With Portraits, Map, and fifty full-page Illustrations by ZWECKER and DURAND. New and Cheaper Edition. With New Preface. Crown 8vo. 6s.

"*A book which will be read with very great interest.*"—TIMES. "*Well written and full of remarkable adventures.*"—PALL MALL GAZETTE. "*Adds another thrilling chapter to the history of African adventure.*"—DAILY NEWS. "*Reads more like a romance.... incomparably more entertaining than books of African travel usually are.*"—MORNING POST.

THE ALBERT N'YANZA Great Basin of the Nile, and Exploration of the Nile Sources. Fifth Edition. Maps and Illustrations. Crown 8vo. 6s.

"*Charmingly written;*" says the SPECTATOR, "*full, as might be expected, of incident, and free from that wearisome reiteration of useless facts which is the drawback to almost all books of African travel.*"

THE NILE TRIBUTARIES OF ABYSSINIA, and the Sword Hunters of the Hamran Arabs. With Maps and Illustrations. Sixth Edition. Crown 8vo. 6s.

The TIMES *says: "It adds much to our information respecting Egyptian Abyssinia and the different races that spread over it. It contains, moreover, some notable instances of English daring and enterprising skill; it abounds in animated tales of exploits dear to the heart of the British sportsman; and it will attract even the least studious reader, as the author tells a story well, and can describe nature with uncommon power."*

Bancroft.—THE HISTORY OF THE UNITED STATES OF AMERICA, FROM THE DISCOVERY OF THE CONTINENT. By GEORGE BANCROFT. New and thoroughly Revised Edition. Six Vols. Crown 8vo. 54s.

Barker (Lady).—Works by LADY BARKER :—
A YEAR'S HOUSEKEEPING IN SOUTH AFRICA. With Illustrations. New and Cheaper Edition. Crown 8vo. 6s.

"*We have to thank Lady Barker for a very amusing book, over which we have spent many a delightful hour, and of which we will not take leave without alluding to the ineffably droll illustrations which add so very much to the enjoyment of her clear and sparkling descriptions.*"—MORNING POST.

Beesly.—STORIES FROM THE HISTORY OF ROME. By Mrs. BEESLY. Extra fcap. 8vo. 2s. 6d.

"*A little book for which every cultivated and intelligent mother will be grateful for.*"—EXAMINER.

Bismarck.—IN THE FRANCO-GERMAN WAR. An Authorized Translation from the German of Dr. MORITZ BUSCH. Two Vols. Crown 8vo. 18s.

The TIMES *says* :—"*The publication of Bismarck's after-dinner talk, whether discreet or not, will be of priceless biographical value, and Englishmen, at least, will not be disposed to quarrel with Dr. Busch for giving a picture as true to life as Boswell's 'Johnson' of the foremost practical genius that Germany has produced since Frederick the Great.*"

Blackburne.—BIOGRAPHY OF THE RIGHT HON. FRANCIS BLACKBURNE, Late Lord Chancellor of Ireland. Chiefly in connexion with his Public and Political Career. By his Son, EDWARD BLACKBURNE, Q.C. With Portrait Engraved by JEENS. 8vo. 12s.

Blanford (W. T.)—GEOLOGY AND ZOOLOGY OF ABYSSINIA. By W. T. BLANFORD. 8vo. 21s.

Brontë.—CHARLOTTE BRONTË. A Monograph. By T. WEMYSS REID. With Illustrations. Third Edition. Crown 8vo. 6s.

Brooke.—THE RAJA OF SARAWAK : an Account of Sir James Brooke, K.C.B., LL.D. Given chiefly through Letters or Journals. By GERTRUDE L. JACOB. With Portrait and Maps. Two Vols. 8vo. 25s.

Bryce.—Works by JAMES BRYCE, D.C.L., Regius Professor of Civil Law, Oxford :—
THE HOLY ROMAN EMPIRE. Sixth Edition, Revised and Enlarged. Crown 8vo. 7s. 6d.

"*It exactly supplies a want : it affords a key to much which men read of in their books as isolated facts, but of which they have hitherto had no connected exposition set before them.*"—SATURDAY REVIEW.

Bryce.—*continued.*

TRANSCAUCASIA AND ARARAT: being Notes of a Vacation Tour in the Autumn of 1876. With an Illustration and Map. Third Edition. Crown 8vo. 9s.

"*Mr. Bryce has written a lively and at the same time an instructive description of the tour he made last year in and about the Caucasus. When so well-informed a jurist travels into regions seldom visited, and even walks up a mountain so rarely scaled as Ararat, he is justified in thinking that the impressions he brings home are worthy of being communicated to the world at large, especially when a terrible war is casting a lurid glow over the countries he has lately surveyed.*"—ATHENÆUM.

Burgoyne.—POLITICAL AND MILITARY EPISODES DURING THE FIRST HALF OF THE REIGN OF GEORGE III. Derived from the Life and Correspondence of the Right Hon. J. Burgoyne, Lieut.-General in his Majesty's Army, and M.P. for Preston. By E. B. DE FONBLANQUE. With Portrait, Heliotype Plate, and Maps. 8vo. 16s.

Burke.—EDMUND BURKE, a Historical Study. By JOHN MORLEY, B.A., Oxon. Crown 8vo. 7s. 6d.

Burrows.—WORTHIES OF ALL SOULS: Four Centuries of English History. Illustrated from the College Archives. By MONTAGU BURROWS, Chichele Professor of Modern History at Oxford, Fellow of All Souls. 8vo. 14s.

"*A most amusing as well as a most instructive book.*—GUARDIAN.

Cameron.—OUR FUTURE HIGHWAY. By V. LOVETT CAMERON, C.B., Commander R.N. With Illustrations. 2 vols. Crown 8vo. [*Shortly.*

Campbell.—LOG-LETTERS FROM THE "CHALLENGER." By LORD GEORGE CAMPBELL. With Map. Fifth and cheaper Edition. Crown 8vo. 6s.

"*A delightful book, which we heartily commend to the general reader.*" —SATURDAY REVIEW.

"*We do not hesitate to say that anything so fresh, so picturesque, so generally delightful, as these log-letters has not appeared among books o travel for a long time.*"—EXAMINER.

Campbell.—MY CIRCULAR NOTES: Extracts from Journals; Letters sent Home; Geological and other Notes, written while Travelling Westwards round the World, from July 6th, 1874, to July 6th, 1875. By J. F. CAMPBELL, Author of "Frost and Fire." Cheaper Issue. Crown 8vo. 6s.

Campbell.—TURKS AND GREEKS. Notes of a recent Excursion. By the Hon. DUDLEY CAMPBELL, M.A. With Coloured Map. Crown 8vo. 3s. 6d.

Carpenter.—LIFE AND WORK OF MARY CARPENTER By the Rev. J. E. CARPENTER. With Portrait engraved by JEENS. Crown 8vo. [*Shortly*.

Carstares.—WILLIAM CARSTARES: a Character and Career of the Revolutionary Epoch (1649—1715). By ROBERT STORY, Minister of Rosneath. 8vo. 12s.

Chatterton: A BIOGRAPHICAL STUDY. By DANIEL WILSON, LL.D., Professor of History and English Literature in University College, Toronto. Crown 8vo. 6s. 6d.

Chatterton: A STORY OF THE YEAR 1770. By Professor MASSON, LL.D. Crown 8vo. 5s.

Clark.—MEMORIALS FROM JOURNALS AND LETTERS OF SAMUEL CLARK, M.A., formerly Principal of the National Society's Training College, Battersea. Edited with Introduction by his WIFE. With Portrait. Crown 8vo. 7s. 6d.

Clifford (W. K.)—LECTURES AND ESSAYS. Edited by LESLIE STEPHEN and FREDERICK POLLOCK, with Introduction by F. POLLOCK. Two Portraits. 2 vols. 8vo. 25s.

The TIMES *of October 22, 1879, says:*—"*Many a friend of the author on first taking up these volumes and remembering his versatile genius and his keen enjoyment of all realms of intellectual activity must have trembled lest they should be found to consist of fragmentary pieces of work, too disconnected to do justice to his powers of consecutive reasoning and too varied to have any effect as a whole. Fortunately those fears are groundless . . . . It is not only in subject that the various papers are closely related. There is also a singular consistency of view and of method throughout . . . . It is in the social and metaphysical subjects that the richness of his intellect shows itself most forcibly in the variety and originality of the ideas which he presents to us. To appreciate this variety, it is necessary to read the book itself, for it treats, in some form or other, of nearly all the subjects of deepest interest in this age of questioning.*"

Combe.—THE LIFE OF GEORGE COMBE, Author of "The Constitution of Man." By CHARLES GIBBON. With Three Portraits engraved by JEENS. Two Vols. 8vo. 32s.

"*A graphic and interesting account of the long life and indefatigable labours of a very remarkable man.*"—SCOTSMAN.

Cooper.—ATHENÆ CANTABRIGIENSES. By CHARLES HENRY COOPER, F.S.A., and THOMPSON COOPER, F.S.A. Vol. I. 8vo., 1500—85, 18s.; Vol. II., 1586—1609, 18s.

Correggio.—ANTONIO ALLEGRI DA CORREGGIO. From the German of Dr. JULIUS MEYER, Director of the Royal Gallery, Berlin. Edited, with an Introduction, by Mrs. HEATON. Containing Twenty Woodbury-type Illustrations. Royal 8vo. Cloth elegant. 31s. 6d.

Cox (G. V.)—RECOLLECTIONS OF OXFORD. By G. V. Cox, M.A., New College, late Esquire Bedel and Coroner in the University of Oxford. *Cheaper Edition.* Crown 8vo. 6s.

Cunynghame (Sir A. T.)—MY COMMAND IN SOUTH AFRICA, 1874—78. Comprising Experiences of Travel in the Colonies of South Africa and the Independent States. By Sir ARTHUR THURLOW CUNYNGHAME, G.C.B., then Lieutenant-Governor and Commander of the Forces in South Africa. Third Edition. 8vo. 12s. 6d.

The TIMES *says:—"It is a volume of great interest, ... full of incidents which vividly illustrate the condition of the Colonies and the character and habits of the natives. .... It contains valuable illustrations of Cape warfare, and at the present moment it cannot fail to command wide-spread attention."*

"Daily News."—THE DAILY NEWS' CORRESPONDENCE of the War between Germany and France, 1870—1. Edited with Notes and Comments. New Edition. Complete in One Volume. With Maps and Plans. Crown 8vo. 6s.

THE DAILY NEWS' CORRESPONDENCE of the War between Russia and Turkey, to the fall of Kars. Including the letters of Mr. Archibald Forbes, Mr. J. E. McGahan, and other Special Correspondents in Europe and Asia. Second Edition, enlarged. Cheaper Edition. Crown 8vo. 6s.

FROM THE FALL OF KARS TO THE CONCLUSION OF PEACE. Cheaper Edition. Crown 8vo. 6s.

Davidson.—THE LIFE OF A SCOTTISH PROBATIONER; being a Memoir of Thomas Davidson, with his Poems and Letters. By JAMES BROWN, Minister of St. James's Street Church, Paisley. Second Edition, revised and enlarged, with Portrait. Crown 8vo. 7s. 6d.

Deas.—THE RIVER CLYDE. An Historical Description of the Rise and Progress of the Harbour of Glasgow, and of the Improvement of the River from Glasgow to Port Glasgow. By J. DEAS, M. Inst. C.E. 8vo. 10s. 6d.

Denison.—A HISTORY OF CAVALRY FROM THE EARLIEST TIMES. With Lessons for the Future. By Lieut.-Col. GEORGE DENISON, Commanding the Governor-General's Body Guard, Canada, Author of "Modern Cavalry." With Maps and Plans. 8vo. 18s.

Dilke.—GREATER BRITAIN. A Record of Travel in English-speaking Countries during 1866-7. (America, Australia, India. By Sir CHARLES WENTWORTH DILKE, M.P. Sixth Edition. Crown 8vo. 6s.

"*Many of the subjects discussed in these pages,*" *says the* DAILY NEWS, "*are of the widest interest, and such as no man who cares for the future of his race and of the world can afford to treat with indifference.*"

Doyle.—HISTORY OF AMERICA. By J. A. DOYLE. With Maps. 18mo. 4s. 6d.

"*Mr. Doyle's style is clear and simple, his facts are accurately stated, and his book is meritoriously free from prejudice on questions where partisanship runs high amongst us.*"—SATURDAY REVIEW.

Drummond of Hawthornden: THE STORY OF HIS LIFE AND WRITINGS. By PROFESSOR MASSON. With Portrait and Vignette engraved by C. H. JEENS. Crown 8vo. 10s. 6d.

Duff.—Works by M. E. GRANT-DUFF, M.P., late Under Secretary of State for India :—

NOTES OF AN INDIAN JOURNEY. With Map. 8vo. 10s. 6d.

MISCELLANIES POLITICAL AND LITERARY. 8vo. 10s. 6d.

Eadie.—LIFE OF JOHN EADIE, D.D., LL.D. By JAMES BROWN, D.D., Author of "The Life of a Scottish Probationer." With Portrait. Second Edition. Crown 8vo. 7s. 6d.

"*An ably written and characteristic biography.*"—TIMES.

Elliott.—LIFE OF HENRY VENN ELLIOTT, of Brighton. By JOSIAH BATEMAN, M.A. With Portrait, engraved by JEENS. Extra fcap. 8vo. Third and Cheaper Edition. 6s.

Elze.—ESSAYS ON SHAKESPEARE. By Dr. KARL ELZE. Translated with the Author's sanction by L. DORA SCHMITZ. 8vo. 12s.

English Men of Letters. Edited by JOHN MORLEY. A Series of Short Books to tell people what is best worth knowing as to the Life, Character, and Works of some of the great English Writers. In crown 8vo. Price 2s. 6d. each.

English Men of Letters.—*continued.*

I. DR. JOHNSON. By LESLIE STEPHEN.

"The new series opens well with Mr. Leslie Stephen's sketch of Dr. Johnson. It could hardly have been done better; and it will convey to the readers for whom it is intended a juster estimate of Johnson than either of the two essays of Lord Macaulay"—PALL MALL GAZETTE.

II. SIR WALTER SCOTT. By R. H. HUTTON.

"The tone of the volume is excellent throughout."—ATHENÆUM.

"We could not wish for a more suggestive introduction to Scott and his poems and novels."—EXAMINER.

III. GIBBON. By J. C. MORISON.

"As a clear, thoughtful, and attractive record of the life and works of the greatest among the world's historians, it deserves the highest praise."—EXAMINER.

IV. SHELLEY. By J. A. SYMONDS.

"The lovers of this great poet are to be congratulated on having at their command so fresh, clear, and intelligent a presentment of the subject, written by a man of adequate and wide culture."—ATHENÆUM.

V. HUME. By Professor HUXLEY.

"It may fairly be said that no one now living could have expounded Hume with more sympathy or with equal perspicuity."—ATHENÆUM.

VI. GOLDSMITH. By WILLIAM BLACK.

"Mr. Black brings a fine sympathy and taste to bear in his criticism of Goldsmith's writings as well as in his sketch of the incidents of his life." ATHENÆUM.

VII. DEFOE. By W. MINTO.

"Mr. Minto's book is careful and accurate in all that is stated, and faithful in all that it suggests. It will repay reading more than once." ATHENÆUM.

VIII. BURNS. By Principal SHAIRP, Professor of Poetry in the University of Oxford.

"It is impossible to desire fairer criticism than Principal Shairp's on Burns's poetry . . . . None of the series has given a truer estimate either of character or of genius than this little volume . . . . and all who read it will be thoroughly grateful to the author for this monument to the genius of Scotland's greatest poet."—SPECTATOR.

IX. SPENSER. By the Very Rev. the DEAN OF ST. PAUL'S.

"Dr. Church is master of his subject, and writes always with good taste."—ACADEMY.

X. THACKERAY. By ANTHONY TROLLOPE.

"Mr. Trollope's sketch is excellently adapted to fulfil the purpose of the series in which it appears."—ATHENÆUM.

XI. BURKE. By JOHN MORLEY.

"Perhaps the best criticism yet published on the life and character of

English Men of Letters.—*continued.*

Burke is contained in Mr. Morley's compendious biography. His style is vigorous and polished, and both his political and personal judgment, and his literary criticisms are just, generous, subtle, and in a high degree interesting."—SATURDAY REVIEW.

MILTON. By MARK PATTISON. [*Just ready.*]
HAWTHORNE. By HENRY JAMES.
SOUTHEY. By Professor DOWDEN.
CHAUCER. By Professor WARD.
COWPER. By GOLDWIN SMITH. [*In preparation.*]
BUNYAN. By J. A. FROUDE.
WORDSWORTH. By F. W. H. MYERS.
Others in preparation.

Eton College, History of. By H. C. MAXWELL LYTE,
M.A. With numerous Illustrations by Professor DELAMOTTE, Coloured Plates, and a Steel Portrait of the Founder, engraved by C. H. JEENS. New and cheaper Issue, with Corrections. Medium 8vo. Cloth elegant. 21*s.*

" *We are at length presented with a work on England's greatest public school, worthy of the subject of which it treats. . . . A really valuable and authentic history of Eton College."*—GUARDIAN.

European History, Narrated in a Series of Historical
Selections from the best Authorities. Edited and arranged by E. M. SEWELL and C. M. YONGE. First Series, crown 8vo. 6*s.*; Second Series, 1088-1228, crown 8vo. 6*s.* Third Edition.

" *We know of scarcely anything,*" says the GUARDIAN, *of this volume,* "*which is so likely to raise to a higher level the average standard of English education."*

Faraday.—MICHAEL FARADAY. By J. H. GLADSTONE,
Ph.D., F.R.S. Second Edition, with Portrait engraved by JEENS from a photograph by J. WATKINS. Crown 8vo. 4*s.* 6*d.*
PORTRAIT. Artist's Proof. 5*s.*

Forbes.—LIFE AND LETTERS OF JAMES DAVID
FORBES, F.R.S., late Principal of the United College in the University of St. Andrews. By J. C. SHAIRP, LL.D., Principal of the United College in the University of St. Andrews; P. G. TAIT, M.A., Professor of Natural Philosophy in the University of Edinburgh; and A. ADAMS-REILLY, F.R.G.S. 8vo. with Portraits, Map, and Illustrations, 16*s.*

Freeman.—Works by EDWARD A. FREEMAN, D.C.L., LL.D. :—
HISTORICAL ESSAYS. Third Edition. 8vo. 10*s.* 6*d.*
CONTENTS :—*I.* "*The Mythical and Romantic Elements in Early English History;*" *II.* "*The Continuity of English History;*" *III.* "*The Relations between the Crowns of England and Scotland;*" *IV.*

Freeman—*continued.*

"*St. Thomas of Canterbury and his Biographers;*" V. "*The Reign of Edward the Third:*" VI. "*The Holy Roman Empire;*" VII. "*The Franks and the Gauls;*" VIII. "*The Early Sieges of Paris;*" IX. "*Frederick the First, King of Italy;*" X. "*The Emperor Frederick the Second:*" XI. "*Charles the Bold;*" XII. "*Presidential Government.*

HISTORICAL ESSAYS. SECOND SERIES. 8vo. 10s. 6d.
The principal Essays are:—"*Ancient Greece and Mediæval Italy:*" "*Mr. Gladstone's Homer and the Homeric Ages:*" "*The Historians of Athens:*" "*The Athenian Democracy:*" "*Alexander the Great:*" "*Greece during the Macedonian Period:*" "*Mommsen's History of Rome:*" "*Lucius Cornelius Sulla:*" "*The Flavian Cæsars.*"

HISTORICAL ESSAYS. Third Series. 8vo. 12s.
CONTENTS:—"*First Impressions of Rome.*" "*The Illyrian Emperors and their Land.*" "*Augusta Treverorum.*" "*The Goths at Ravenna.*" "*Race and Language.*" "*The Byzantine Empire.*" "*First Impressions of Athens.*" "*Mediæval and Modern Greece.*" "*The Southern Slaves.*" "*Sicilian Cycles.*" "*The Normans at Palermo.*"

COMPARATIVE POLITICS.—Lectures at the Royal Institution. To which is added the "Unity of History," the Rede Lecture at Cambridge, 1872. 8vo. 14s.

THE HISTORY AND CONQUESTS OF THE SARACENS. Six Lectures. Third Edition, with New Preface. Crown 8vo. 3s. 6d.

HISTORICAL AND ARCHITECTURAL SKETCHES: chiefly Italian. With Illustrations by the Author. Crown 8vo. 10s. 6d.

HISTORY OF FEDERAL GOVERNMENT, from the Foundation of the Achaian League to the Disruption of the United States. Vol. I. General Introduction. History of the Greek Federations. 8vo. 21s.

OLD ENGLISH HISTORY. With *Five Coloured Maps.* Fourth Edition. Extra fcap. 8vo., half-bound. 6s.
"*The book indeed is full of instruction and interest to students of all ages, and he must be a well-informed man indeed who will not rise from its perusal with clearer and more accurate ideas of a too much neglected portion of English history.*"—SPECTATOR.

HISTORY OF THE CATHEDRAL CHURCH OF WELLS, as illustrating the History of the Cathedral Churches of the Old Foundation. Crown 8vo. 3s. 6d.
"*The history assumes in Mr. Freeman's hands a significance, and, we may add, a practical value as suggestive of what a cathedral ought to be, which make it well worthy of mention.*"—SPECTATOR.

Freeman—*continued.*

THE GROWTH OF THE ENGLISH CONSTITUTION FROM THE EARLIEST TIMES. Crown 8vo. 5s. Third Edition, revised.

GENERAL SKETCH OF EUROPEAN HISTORY. Being Vol. I. of a Historical Course for Schools edited by E. A. FREEMAN. New Edition, enlarged with Maps, Chronological Table, Index, &c. 18mo. 3s. 6d.

"*It supplies the great want of a good foundation for historical teaching. The scheme is an excellent one, and this instalment has been accepted in a way that promises much for the volumes that are yet to appear.*"—EDUCATIONAL TIMES.

THE OTTOMAN POWER IN EUROPE : its Nature, its Growth, and its Decline. With Three Coloured Maps. Crown 8vo. 7s. 6d.

Galileo.—THE PRIVATE LIFE OF GALILEO. Compiled principally from his Correspondence and that of his eldest daughter, Sister Maria Celeste, Nun in the Franciscan Convent of S. Matthew in Arcetri. With Portrait. Crown 8vo. 7s. 6d.

Geddes.—THE PROBLEM OF THE HOMERIC POEMS. By W. D. GEDDES, LL.D., Professor of Greek in the University of Aberdeen. 8vo. 14s.

Gladstone—Works by the Right Hon. W. E. GLADSTONE, M.P.:—
JUVENTUS MUNDI. The Gods and Men of the Heroic Age. Crown 8vo. cloth. With Map. 10s. 6d. Second Edition.

"*Seldom,*" says the ATHENÆUM, "*out of the great poems themselves, have these Divinities looked so majestic and respectable. To read these brilliant details is like standing on the Olympian threshold and gazing at the ineffable brightness within.*"

HOMERIC SYNCHRONISM. An inquiry into the Time and Place of Homer. Crown 8vo. 6s.

"*It is impossible not to admire the immense range of thought and inquiry which the author has displayed.*"—BRITISH QUARTERLY REVIEW.

Goethe and Mendelssohn (1821—1831). Translated from the German of Dr. KARL MENDELSSOHN, Son of the Composer, by M. E. VON GLEHN. From the Private Diaries and Home Letters of Mendelssohn, with Poems and Letters of Goethe never before printed. Also with two New and Original Portraits, Facsimiles, and Appendix of Twenty Letters hitherto unpublished. Crown 8vo. 5s. Second Edition, enlarged.

"... Every page is full of interest, not merely to the musician, but to the general reader. The book is a very charming one, on a topic of deep and lasting interest."—STANDARD.

Goldsmid.—TELEGRAPH AND TRAVEL. A Narrative of the Formation and Development of Telegraphic Communication between England and India, under the orders of Her Majesty's Government, with incidental Notices of the Countries traversed by the Lines. By Colonel Sir FREDERIC GOLDSMID, C.B., K.C.S.I., late Director of the Government Indo-European Telegraph. With numerous Illustrations and Maps. 8vo. 21s.

"The merit of the work is a total absence of exaggeration, which does not, however, preclude a vividness and vigour of style not always characteristic of similar narratives."—STANDARD.

Gordon.—LAST LETTERS FROM EGYPT, to which are added Letters from the Cape. By LADY DUFF GORDON. With a Memoir by her Daughter, Mrs. Ross, and Portrait engraved by JEENS. Second Edition. Crown 8vo. 9s.

"The intending tourist who wishes to acquaint himself with the country he is about to visit, stands embarrassed amidst the riches presented for his choice, and in the end probably rests contented with the sober usefulness of Murray. He will not, however, if he is well advised, grudge a place in his portmanteau to this book."—TIMES.

Gray.—CHINA. A History of the Laws, Manners, and Customs of the People. By the VENERABLE JOHN HENRY GRAY. LL.D., Archdeacon of Hong Kong, formerly H.B.M. Consular Chaplain at Canton. Edited by W. Gow Gregor. With 150 Full-page Illustrations, being Facsimiles of Drawings by a Chinese Artist. 2 Vols. Demy 8vo. 32s.

"Its pages contain the most truthful and vivid picture of Chinese life which has ever been published."—ATHENÆUM.

"The only elaborate and valuable book we have had for many years treating generally of the people of the Celestial Empire."—ACADEMY.

Green.—Works by JOHN RICHARD GREEN :—

HISTORY OF THE ENGLISH PEOPLE. Vol. I.—Early England—Foreign Kings—The Charter—The Parliament. With 8 Coloured Maps. 8vo. 16s. Vol. II.—The Monarchy, 1461—1540 ; the Restoration, 1540—1603. 8vo. 16s. Vol. III.—Puritan England, 1603—1660 ; the Revolution, 1660—1688. With 4 Maps. 8vo. 16s. [Vol. IV. in the press.

"Mr. Green has done a work which probably no one but himself could have done. He has read and assimilated the results of all the labours of students during the last half century in the field of English history, and has given them a fresh meaning by his own independent study. He has fused together by the force of sympathetic imagination all that he has so

Green.—*continued.*

collected, and has given us a vivid and forcible sketch of the march of English history. His book, both in its aims and its accomplishments, rises far beyond any of a similar kind, and it will give the colouring to the popular view to English history for some time to come."—EXAMINER.

A SHORT HISTORY OF THE ENGLISH PEOPLE. With Coloured Maps, Genealogical Tables, and Chronological Annals. Crown 8vo. 8s. 6d. Sixty-third Thousand.

" To say that Mr. Green's book is better than those which have preceded it, would be to convey a very inadequate impression of its merits. It stands alone as the one general history of the country, for the sake of which all others, if young and old are wise, will be speedily and surely set aside."

STRAY STUDIES FROM ENGLAND AND ITALY. Crown 8vo. 8s. 6d. Containing : Lambeth and the Archbishops—The Florence of Dante—Venice and Rome—Early History of Oxford—The District Visitor—Capri—Hotels in the Clouds—Sketches in Sunshine, &c.

" One and all of the papers are eminently readable."—ATHENÆUM.

Guest.—LECTURES ON THE HISTORY OF ENGLAND. By M. J. GUEST. With Maps. Crown 8vo. 6s.

" The book is pleasant reading, it is full of information, much of it is valuable, most of it is correct, told in a gossipy and intelligible way."—ATHENÆUM.

Hamerton.—Works by P. G. HAMERTON :—

THE INTELLECTUAL LIFE. With a Portrait of Leonardo da Vinci, etched by LEOPOLD FLAMENG. Second Edition. Crown 8vo. 10s. 6d.

" We have read the whole book with great pleasure, and we can recommend it strongly to all who can appreciate grave reflections on a very important subject, excellently illustrated from the resources of a mind stored with much reading and much keen observation of real life."—SATURDAY REVIEW.

THOUGHTS ABOUT ART. New Edition, revised, with an Introduction. Crown 8vo. 8s. 6d.

" A manual of sound and thorough criticism on art."—STANDARD.

Hill.—THE RECORDER OF BIRMINGHAM. A Memoir of Matthew Davenport Hill, with Selections from his Correspondence. By his Daughters ROSAMOND and FLORENCE DAVENPORT-HILL. With Portrait engraved by C. H. JEENS. 8vo. 16s.

Hill.—WHAT WE SAW IN AUSTRALIA. By ROSAMOND and FLORENCE HILL. Crown 8vo. 10s. 6d.

"*May be recommended as an interesting and truthful picture of the condition of those lands which are so distant and yet so much like home.*" —SATURDAY REVIEW.

Hodgson.—MEMOIR OF REV. FRANCIS HODGSON, B.D., Scholar, Poet, and Divine. By his Son, the Rev. JAMES T. HODGSON, M.A. Containing numerous Letters from Lord Byron and others. With Portrait engraved by JEENS. Two Vols. Crown 8vo. 18s.

"*A book that has added so much of a healthy nature to our knowledge of Byron, and that contains so rich a store of delightful correspondence.*" —ATHENÆUM.

Hole.—A GENEALOGICAL STEMMA OF THE KINGS OF ENGLAND AND FRANCE. By the Rev. C. HOLE, M.A., Trinity College, Cambridge. On Sheet, 1s.

A BRIEF BIOGRAPHICAL DICTIONARY. Compiled and Arranged by the Rev. CHARLES HOLE, M.A. Second Edition. 18mo. 4s. 6d.

Hooker and Ball.—MAROCCO AND THE GREAT ATLAS: Journal of a Tour in. By Sir JOSEPH D. HOOKER, K.C.S.I., C.B., F.R.S., &c., and JOHN BALL, F.R.S. With an Appendix, including a Sketch of the Geology of Marocco, by G. MAW, F.L.S., F.G.S. With Illustrations and Map. 8vo. 21s.

"*It is long since any more interesting book of travels has issued from our press.*"—SATURDAY REVIEW. "*This is, without doubt, one of the most interesting and valuable books of travel published for many years.*" —SPECTATOR.

Hozier (H. M.)—Works by CAPTAIN HENRY M. HOZIER, late Assistant Military Secretary to Lord Napier of Magdala:—

THE SEVEN WEEKS' WAR; Its Antecedents and Incidents. *New and Cheaper Edition.* With New Preface, Maps, and Plans. Crown 8vo. 6s.

THE INVASIONS OF ENGLAND: a History of the Past, with Lessons for the Future. Two Vols. 8vo. 28s.

Hübner.—A RAMBLE ROUND THE WORLD IN 1871. By M. LE BARON HÜBNER, formerly Ambassador and Minister. Translated by LADY HERBERT. New and Cheaper Edition. With numerous Illustrations. Crown 8vo. 6s.

"*It is difficult to do ample justice to this pleasant narrative of travel .... it does not contain a single dull paragraph.*"—MORNING POST.

Hughes.—Works by THOMAS HUGHES, Q.C., Author of "Tom Brown's School Days."

ALFRED THE GREAT. New Edition. Crown 8vo. 6s.

MEMOIR OF A BROTHER. With Portrait of GEORGE HUGHES, after WATTS. Engraved by JEENS. Crown 8vo. 5s. Sixth Edition.

"*The boy who can read this book without deriving from it some additional impulse towards honourable, manly, and independent conduct, has no good stuff in him.*"—DAILY NEWS.

Hunt.—HISTORY OF ITALY. By the Rev. W. HUNT, M.A. Being the Fourth Volume of the Historical Course for Schools. Edited by EDWARD A. FREEMAN, D.C.L. 18mo. 3s.

"*Mr. Hunt gives us a most compact but very readable little book, containing in small compass a very complete outline of a complicated and perplexing subject. It is a book which may be safely recommended to others besides schoolboys.*"—JOHN BULL.

Irving.—THE ANNALS OF OUR TIME. A Diurnal of Events, Social and Political, Home and Foreign, from the Accession of Queen Victoria to the Peace of Versailles. By JOSEPH IRVING. *Fourth Edition.* 8vo. half-bound. 16s.

ANNALS OF OUR TIME. Supplement. From Feb. 28, 1871, to March 19, 1874. 8vo. 4s. 6d.

ANNALS OF OUR TIME. Second Supplement. From March, 1874, to the Occupation of Cyprus. 8vo. 4s. 6d.

"*We have before us a trusty and ready guide to the events of the past thirty years, available equally for the statesman, the politician, the public writer, and the general reader.*"—TIMES.

James.—Works by HENRY JAMES, Jun. FRENCH POETS AND NOVELISTS. Crown 8vo. 8s. 6d.

CONTENTS:—*Alfred de Musset; Théophile Gautier; Baudelaire; Honoré de Balzac; George Sand; The Two Ampères; Turgenieff, &c.*

Johnson's Lives of the Poets.—The Six Chief Lives—Milton, Dryden, Swift, Addison, Pope, Gray. With Macaulay's "Life of Johnson." Edited, with Preface, by MATTHEW ARNOLD. Crown 8vo. 6s.

Killen.—ECCLESIASTICAL HISTORY OF IRELAND, from the Earliest Date to the Present Time. By W. D. KILLEN, D.D., President of Assembly's College, Belfast, and Professor of Ecclesiastical History. Two Vols. 8vo. 25s.

"*Those who have the leisure will do well to read these two volumes. They are full of interest, and are the result of great research. . . . We* have no hesitation in recommending the work to all who wish to improve their acquaintance with Irish history."—SPECTATOR.

Kingsley (Charles).—Works by the Rev. CHARLES KINGSLEY, M.A., Rector of Eversley and Canon of Westminster. (For other Works by the same Author, see THEOLOGICAL and BELLES LETTRES Catalogues.)

ON THE ANCIEN RÉGIME as it existed on the Continent before the FRENCH REVOLUTION. Three Lectures delivered at the Royal Institution. Crown 8vo. 6s.

AT LAST: A CHRISTMAS in the WEST INDIES. With nearly Fifty Illustrations. Sixth Edition. Crown 8vo. 6s.
*Mr. Kingsley's dream of forty years was at last fulfilled, when he started on a Christmas expedition to the West Indies, for the purpose of becoming personally acquainted with the scenes which he has so vividly described in "Westward Ho!" These two volumes are the journal of his voyage. Records of natural history, sketches of tropical landscape, chapters on education, views of society, all find their place. "We can only say that Mr. Kingsley's account of a 'Christmas in the West Indies' is in every way worthy to be classed among his happiest productions."—*STANDARD.

THE ROMAN AND THE TEUTON. A Series of Lectures delivered before the University of Cambridge. New and Cheaper Edition, with Preface by Professor MAX MÜLLER. Crown 8vo. 6s.

PLAYS AND PURITANS, and other Historical Essays. With Portrait of Sir WALTER RALEIGH. New Edition. Crown 8vo. 6s.
In addition to the Essay mentioned in the title, this volume contains other two—one on "Sir Walter Raleigh and his Time," and one on Froude's "History of England."

Kingsley (Henry).—TALES OF OLD TRAVEL. Re-narrated by HENRY KINGSLEY, F.R.G.S. With *Eight Illustrations* by HUARD. Fifth Edition. Crown 8vo. 5s.
*"We know no better book for those who want knowledge or seek to refresh it. As for the 'sensational,' most novels are tame compared with these narratives."—*ATHENÆUM.

Lang.—CYPRUS: Its History, its Present Resources and Future Prospects. By R. HAMILTON LANG, late H.M. Consul for the Island of Cyprus. With Two Illustrations and Four Maps. 8vo. 14s.
*"The fair and impartial account of her past and present to be found in these pages has an undoubted claim on the attention of all intelligent readers."—*MORNING POST.

Laocoon.—Translated from the Text of Lessing, with Preface and Notes by the Right Hon. SIR ROBERT J. PHILLIMORE, D.C.L. With Photographs. 8vo. 12s.

Leonardo da Vinci and his Works.—Consisting of a Life of Leonardo Da Vinci, by MRS. CHARLES W. HEATON, Author of "Albrecht Dürer of Nürnberg," &c., an Essay on his Scientific and Literary Works by CHARLES CHRISTOPHER BLACK, M.A., and an account of his more important Paintings and Drawings. Illustrated with Permanent Photographs. Royal 8vo, cloth, extra gilt. 31s. 6d.

Liechtenstein.—HOLLAND HOUSE. By Princess MARIE LIECHTENSTEIN. With Five Steel Engravings by C. H. JEENS, after Paintings by WATTS and other celebrated Artists, and numerous Illustrations drawn by Professor P. H. DELAMOTTE, and engraved on Wood by J. D. COOPER, W. PALMER, and JEWITT & Co. Third and Cheaper Edition. Medium 8vo. cloth elegant. 16s.

Also, an Edition containing, in addition to the above, about 40 Illustrations by the Woodbury-type process, and India Proofs of the Steel Engravings. Two vols. medium 4to. half morocco elegant. 4l. 4s.

Lloyd.—THE AGE OF PERICLES. A History of the Arts and Politics of Greece from the Persian to the Peloponnesian War. By W. WATKISS LLOYD. Two Vols. 8vo. 21s.

"*No such account of Greek art of the best period has yet been brought together in an English work. . . . . Mr. Lloyd has produced a book of unusual excellence and interest.*"—PALL MALL GAZETTE.

Loch Etive and the Sons of Uisnach.—With Illustrations. 8vo. 14s.

"*Not only have we Loch Etive of the present time brought before us in colours as true as they are vivid, but stirring scenes which happened on the borders of the beautiful lake in semi-mythical times are conjured up with singular skill. Nowhere else do we remember to have met with such a well-written account of the invasion of Scotland by the Irish.*"—GLOBE.

Loftie.—A RIDE IN EGYPT FROM SIOOT TO LUXOR, IN 1879; with Notes on the Present State and Ancient History of the Nile Valley, and some account of the various ways of making the voyage out and home. By the Rev. W. J. LOFTIE. With Illustrations. Crown 8vo. 10s. 6d.

"*We prophesy that Mr. Loftie's little book will accompany many travellers on the Nile in the coming winters.*"—TIMES.

Lubbock.— ADDRESSES, POLITICAL AND EDUCATIONAL. By Sir JOHN LUBBOCK, Bart., M.P., D.C.L., F.R.S. 8vo. 8s. 6d.

Macdonell.—FRANCE SINCE THE FIRST EMPIRE. By JAMES MACDONELL. Edited with Preface by his Wife. Crown 8vo. [*Shortly.*

Macarthur.—HISTORY OF SCOTLAND, By MARGARET MACARTHUR. Being the Third Volume of the Historical Course for Schools, Edited by EDWARD A. FREEMAN, D.C.L. Second Edition. 18mo. 2s.

"*It is an excellent summary, unimpeachable as to facts, and putting them in the clearest and most impartial light attainable.*"—GUARDIAN.
"*No previous History of Scotland of the same bulk is anything like so trustworthy, or deserves to be so extensively used as a text-book.*"—GLOBE.

Macmillan (Rev. Hugh).—For other Works by same Author, see THEOLOGICAL and SCIENTIFIC CATALOGUES.

HOLIDAYS ON HIGH LANDS; or, Rambles and Incidents in search of Alpine Plants. Second Edition, revised and enlarged. Globe 8vo. cloth. 6s.

"*Botanical knowledge is blended with a love of nature, a pious enthusiasm, and a rich felicity of diction not to be met with in any works of kindred character, if we except those of Hugh Miller.*"—TELEGRAPH.

Macready.—MACREADY'S REMINISCENCES AND SELECTIONS FROM HIS DIARIES AND LETTERS. Edited by Sir F. POLLOCK, Bart., one of his Executors. With Four Portraits engraved by JEENS. New and Cheaper Edition. Crown 8vo. 7s. 6d.

"*As a careful and for the most part just estimate of the stage during a very brilliant period, the attraction of these volumes can scarcely be surpassed. . . . Readers who have no special interest in theatrical matters, but enjoy miscellaneous gossip, will be allured from page to page, attracted by familiar names and by observations upon popular actors and authors.*"—SPECTATOR.

Mahaffy.—Works by the Rev. J. P. MAHAFFY, M.A., Fellow of Trinity College, Dublin :—

SOCIAL LIFE IN GREECE FROM HOMER TO MENANDER. Third Edition, revised and enlarged, with a new chapter on Greek Art. Crown 8vo. 9s.

"*It should be in the hands of all who desire thoroughly to understand and to enjoy Greek literature, and to get an intelligent idea of the old Greek life, political, social, and religious.*"—GUARDIAN.

Mahaffy.—*continued.*
> RAMBLES AND STUDIES IN GREECE. With Illustrations. Crown 8vo. 10s. 6d. New and enlarged Edition, with Map and Illustrations.
>
> "*A singularly instructive and agreeable volume.*"—ATHENÆUM.

"Maori."—SPORT AND WORK ON THE NEPAUL FRONTIER; or, Twelve Years' Sporting Reminiscences of an Indigo Planter. By "MAORI." With Illustrations. 8vo. 14s.
> "*Every day's adventures, with all the joys and perils of the chase, are told as only a keen and cunning sportsman can tell them.*"—STANDARD.

Margary.—THE JOURNEY OF AUGUSTUS RAYMOND MARGARY FROM SHANGHAE TO BHAMO AND BACK TO MANWYNE. From his Journals and Letters, with a brief Biographical Preface, a concluding chapter by Sir RUTHERFORD ALCOCK, K.C.B., and a Steel Portrait engraved by JEENS, and Map. 8vo. 10s. 6d.
> "*There is a manliness, a cheerful spirit, an inherent vigour which was never overcome by sickness or debility, a tact which conquered the prejudices of a strange and suspicious population, a quiet self-reliance, always combined with deep religious feeling, unalloyed by either priggishness, cant, or superstition, that ought to commend this volume to readers sitting quietly at home who feel any pride in the high estimation accorded to men of their race at Yarkand or at Khiva, in the heart of Africa, or on the shores of Lake Seri-kul.*"—SATURDAY REVIEW.

Markham.—NORTHWARD HO! By Captain ALBERT H. MARKHAM, R.N., Author of "The Great Frozen Sea," &c. Including a Narrative of Captain Phipps's Expedition, by a Midshipman. With Illustrations. Crown 8vo. 10s. 6d.
> "*Captain Markham's interesting volume has the advantage of being written by a man who is practically conversant with the subject.*"—PALL MALL GAZETTE.

Martin.—THE HISTORY OF LLOYD'S, AND OF MARINE INSURANCE IN GREAT BRITAIN. With an Appendix containing Statistics relating to Marine Insurance. By FREDERICK MARTIN, Author of "The Statesman's Year Book." 8vo. 14s.

Martineau.—BIOGRAPHICAL SKETCHES, 1852—1875. By HARRIET MARTINEAU. With Additional Sketches, and Autobiographical Sketch. Fifth Edition. Crown 8vo. 6s.

Masson (David).—For other Works by same Author, see PHILOSOPHICAL and BELLES LETTRES CATALOGUES.

Masson (David).—*continued.*

CHATTERTON: A Story of the Year 1770. By DAVID MASSON, LL.D., Professor of Rhetoric and English Literature in the University of Edinburgh. Crown 8vo. 5s.

THE THREE DEVILS: Luther's, Goethe's, and Milton's; and other Essays. Crown 8vo. 5s.

WORDSWORTH, SHELLEY, AND KEATS; and other Essays. Crown 8vo. 5s.

Mathews.—LIFE OF CHARLES J. MATHEWS, Chiefly Autobiographical. With Selections from his Correspondence and Speeches. Edited by CHARLES DICKENS.

"*One of the pleasantest and most readable books of the season. From first to last these two volumes are alive with the inimitable artist and comedian. ... The whole book is full of life, vigour, and wit, and even through some of the gloomy episodes of volume two, will repay most careful study. So complete, so varied a picture of a man's life is rarely to be met with.*"—STANDARD.

Maurice.—THE FRIENDSHIP OF BOOKS; AND OTHER LECTURES. By the REV. F. D. MAURICE. Edited with Preface, by THOMAS HUGHES, Q.C. Crown 8vo. 10s. 6d.

Mayor (J. E. B.)—WORKS edited by JOHN E. B. MAYOR, M.A., Kennedy Professor of Latin at Cambridge :—

CAMBRIDGE IN THE SEVENTEENTH CENTURY. Part II Autobiography of Matthew Robinson. Fcap. 8vo. 5s. 6d.

LIFE OF BISHOP BEDELL. By his SON. Fcap. 8vo. 3s. 6d.

Melbourne.—MEMOIRS OF THE RT. HON. WILLIAM, SECOND VISCOUNT MELBOURNE. By W. M. TORRENS, M.P. With Portrait after Sir. T. Lawrence. Second Edition. 2 Vols. 8vo. 32s.

"*As might be expected, he has produced a book which will command and reward attention. It contains a great deal of valuable matter and a great deal of animated, elegant writing.*"—QUARTERLY REVIEW.

Mendelssohn.—LETTERS AND RECOLLECTIONS. By FERDINAND HILLER. Translated by M. E. VON GLEHN. With Portrait from a Drawing by KARL MÜLLER, never before published. Second Edition. Crown 8vo. 7s. 6d.

"*This is a very interesting addition to our knowledge of the great German composer. It reveals him to us under a new light, as the warm-hearted comrade, the musician whose soul was in his work, and the home-loving, domestic man.*"—STANDARD.

Merewether.—BY SEA AND BY LAND. Being a Trip through Egypt, India, Ceylon, Australia, New Zealand, and America—all Round the World. By HENRY ALWORTH MEREWETHER, one of Her Majesty's Counsel. Crown 8vo. 8s. 6d.

Michael Angelo Buonarotti; Sculptor, Painter, Architect. The Story of his Life and Labours. By C. C. BLACK, M.A. Illustrated by 20 Permanent Photographs. Royal 8vo. cloth elegant, 31s. 6d.

"*The story of Michael Angelo's life remains interesting whatever be the manner of telling it, and supported as it is by this beautiful series of photographs, the volume must take rank among the most splendid of Christmas books, fitted to serve and to outlive the season.*"—PALL MALL GAZETTE.

Michelet.—A SUMMARY OF MODERN HISTORY. Translated from the French of M. MICHELET, and continued to the present time by M. C. M. SIMPSON. Globe 8vo. 4s. 6d.

Milton.—LIFE OF JOHN MILTON. Narrated in connection with the Political, Ecclesiastical, and Literary History of his Time. By DAVID MASSON, M.A., LL.D., Professor of Rhetoric and English Literature in the University of Edinburgh. With Portraits. Vol. I. 18s. Vol. II., 1638—1643. 8vo. 16s. Vol. III. 1643—1649. 8vo. 18s. Vols. IV. and V. 1649—1660. 32s. Vol. VI. concluding the work in the press.

This work is not only a Biography, but also a continuous Political, Ecclesiastical, and Literary History of England through Milton's whole time.

Mitford (A. B.)—TALES OF OLD JAPAN. By A. B. MITFORD, Second Secretary to the British Legation in Japan. With upwards of 30 Illustrations, drawn and cut on Wood by Japanese Artists. New and Cheaper Edition. Crown 8vo. 6s.

"*These very original volumes will always be interesting as memorials of a most exceptional society, while regarded simply as tales, they are sparkling, sensational, and dramatic.*"—PALL MALL GAZETTE.

Monteiro.—ANGOLA AND THE RIVER CONGO. By JOACHIM MONTEIRO. With numerous Illustrations from Sketches taken on the spot, and a Map. Two Vols. crown 8vo. 21s.

Morison.—THE LIFE AND TIMES OF SAINT BERNARD, Abbot of Clairvaux. By JAMES COTTER MORISON, M.A. New Edition. Crown 8vo. 6s.

Moseley.—NOTES BY A NATURALIST ON THE *CHALLENGER*: being an Account of various Observations made during the Voyage of H.M.S. *Challenger*, Round the World, in 1872-76. By H. N. MOSELEY, F.R.S., Member of the Scientific Staff of the *Challenger*. 8vo. with Maps, Coloured Plates, and Woodcuts. 21s.

"This is certainly the most interesting and suggestive book, descriptive of a naturalist's travels, which has been published since Mr. Darwin's '*Journal of Researches*' appeared, more than forty years ago."—NATURE. "We cannot point to any book of travels in our day more vivid in its powers of description, more varied in its subject matter, or more attractive to every educated reader."—SATURDAY REVIEW.

Murray.—ROUND ABOUT FRANCE. By E. C. GRENVILLE MURRAY. Crown 8vo. 7s. 6d.

"These short essays are a perfect mine of information as to the present condition and future prospects of political parties in France. . . . It is at once extremely interesting and exceptionally instructive on a subject on which few English people are well informed."—SCOTSMAN.

Napier.—MACVEY NAPIER'S SELECTED CORRESPONDENCE. Edited by his Son, MACVEY NAPIER. 8vo. 14s.

The TIMES says:—"It is replete with useful material for the biographers of many distinguished writers of the generation which is passing away. Since reading it we understand several noteworthy men, and Brougham in particular, far better than we did before." "It would be useless to attempt within our present limits to give any adequate idea of the abundance of interesting passages which meet us in the letters of Macaulay, Brougham, Carlyle, Jeffrey, Senior, and many other well-known writers. Especially piquant are Jeffrey's periodical criticisms on the contents of the Review which he had formerly edited."—PALL MALL GAZETTE.

Napoleon.—THE HISTORY OF NAPOLEON I. By P. LANFREY. A Translation with the sanction of the Author. 4 vols. 8vo. Vols. I. II. and III. price 12s. each. Vol. IV. 6s.

The PALL MALL GAZETTE says it is "one of the most striking pieces of historical composition of which France has to boast," and the SATURDAY REVIEW calls it "an excellent translation of a work on every ground deserving to be translated. It is unquestionably and immeasurably the best that has been produced. It is in fact the only work to which we can turn for an accurate and trustworthy narrative of that extraordinary career. . . . The book is the best and indeed the only trustworthy history of Napoleon which has been written."

Nichol.—TABLES OF EUROPEAN LITERATURE AND HISTORY, A.D. 200—1876. By J. NICHOL, LL.D., Professor of English Language and Literature, Glasgow. 4to. 6s. 6d.

TABLES OF ANCIENT LITERATURE AND HISTORY, B.C. 1500—A.D. 200. By the same Author. 4to. 4s. 6d.

HISTORY, BIOGRAPHY, TRAVELS, ETC. 23

Nordenskiöld's Arctic Voyages, 1858-79. — With Maps and numerous Illustrations. 8vo. 16s.
"*A volume of great interest and much scientific value.*"—NATURE.

Oliphant (Mrs.).—THE MAKERS OF FLORENCE: Dante Giotto, Savonarola, and their City. By Mrs. OLIPHANT. With numerous Illustrations from drawings by Professor DELAMOTTE, and portrait of Savonarola, engraved by JEENS. Second Edition. Medium 8vo. Cloth extra. 21s.
"*We are grateful to Mrs. Oliphant for her eloquent and beautiful sketches of Dante, Fra Angelico, and Savonarola. They are picturesque, full of life, and rich in detail, and they are charmingly illustrated by the art of the engraver.*"—SPECTATOR.

Oliphant.—THE DUKE AND THE SCHOLAR; and other Essays. By T. L. KINGTON OLIPHANT. 8vo. 7s. 6d.
"*This volume contains one of the most beautiful biographical essays we have seen since Macaulay's days.*"—STANDARD.

Otte.—SCANDINAVIAN HISTORY. By E. C. OTTE. With Maps. Extra fcap. 8vo. 6s.

Owens College Essays and Addresses.—By PROFESSORS AND LECTURERS OF OWENS COLLEGE, MANCHESTER. Published in Commemoration of the Opening of the New College Buildings, October 7th, 1873. 8vo. 14s.

Palgrave (R. F. D.)—THE HOUSE OF COMMONS; Illustrations of its History and Practice. By REGINALD F. D. PALGRAVE, Clerk Assistant of the House of Commons. New and Revised Edition. Crown 8vo. 2s. 6d.

Palgrave (Sir F.)—HISTORY OF NORMANDY AND OF ENGLAND. By Sir FRANCIS PALGRAVE, Deputy Keeper of Her Majesty's Public Records. Completing the History to the Death of William Rufus. 4 Vols. 8vo. 4l. 4s.

Palgrave (W. G.)—A NARRATIVE OF A YEAR'S JOURNEY THROUGH CENTRAL AND EASTERN ARABIA, 1862-3. By WILLIAM GIFFORD PALGRAVE, late of the Eighth Regiment Bombay N. I. Sixth Edition. With Maps, Plans, and Portrait of Author, engraved on steel by Jeens. Crown 8vo. 6s.
"*He has not only written one of the best books on the Arabs and one of the best books on Arabia, but he has done so in a manner that must command the respect no less than the admiration of his fellow-countrymen.*"—FORTNIGHTLY REVIEW.

Palgrave.—*continued.*

ESSAYS ON EASTERN QUESTIONS. By W. GIFFORD PALGRAVE. 8vo. 10s. 6d.

"*These essays are full of anecdote and interest. The book is decidedly a valuable addition to the stock of literature on which men must base their opinion of the difficult social and political problems suggested by the designs of Russia, the capacity of Mahometans for sovereignty, and the good government and retention of India.*"—SATURDAY REVIEW.

DUTCH GUIANA. With Maps and Plans. 8vo. 9s.

"*His pages are nearly exhaustive as far as facts and statistics go, while they are lightened by graphic social sketches as well as sparkling descriptions of scenery.*"—SATURDAY REVIEW.

Patteson.—LIFE AND LETTERS OF JOHN COLERIDGE PATTESON, D.D., Missionary Bishop of the Melanesian Islands. By CHARLOTTE M. YONGE, Author of "The Heir of Redclyffe." With Portraits after RICHMOND and from Photograph, engraved by JEENS. With Map. Fifth Edition. Two Vols. Crown 8vo. 12s.

"*Miss Yonge's work is in one respect a model biography. It is made up almost entirely of Patteson's own letters. Aware that he had left his home once and for all, his correspondence took the form of a diary, and as we read on we come to know the man, and to love him almost as if we had seen him.*"—ATHENÆUM. "*Such a life, with its grand lessons of unselfishness, is a blessing and an honour to the age in which it is lived; the biography cannot be studied without pleasure and profit, and indeed we should think little of the man who did not rise from the study of it better and wiser. Neither the Church nor the nation which produces such sons need ever despair of its future.*"—SATURDAY REVIEW.

Pauli.—PICTURES OF OLD ENGLAND. By Dr. REINHOLD PAULI. Translated, with the approval of the Author, by E. C. OTTÉ. Cheaper Edition. Crown 8vo. 6s.

Payne.—A HISTORY OF EUROPEAN COLONIES. By E. J. PAYNE, M.A. With Maps. 18mo. 4s. 6d.

The TIMES says:—"*We have seldom met with a historian capable of forming a more comprehensive, far-seeing, and unprejudiced estimate of events and peoples, and we can commend this little work as one certain to prove of the highest interest to all thoughtful readers.*"

Persia.—EASTERN PERSIA. An Account of the Journeys of the Persian Boundary Commission, 1870-1-2.—Vol. I. The Geography, with Narratives by Majors ST. JOHN, LOVETT, and EUAN SMITH, and an Introduction by Major-General Sir FREDERIC GOLDSMID, C.B., K.C.S.I., British Commissioner and Arbitrator.

With Maps and Illustrations.—Vol. II. The Zoology and Geology. By W. T. BLANFORD, A.R.S.M., F.R.S. With Coloured Illustrations. Two Vols. 8vo. 42s.

"*The volumes largely increase our store of information about countries with which Englishmen ought to be familiar. . . . They throw into the shade all that hitherto has appeared in our tongue respecting the local features of Persia, its scenery, its resources, even its social condition. They contain also abundant evidence of English endurance, daring, and spirit.*"—TIMES.

Prichard.—THE ADMINISTRATION OF INDIA. From 1859 to 1868. The First Ten Years of Administration under the Crown. By I. T. PRICHARD, Barrister-at-Law. Two Vols. Demy 8vo. With Map. 21s.

Raphael.—RAPHAEL OF URBINO AND HIS FATHER GIOVANNI SANTI. By J. D. PASSAVANT, formerly Director of the Museum at Frankfort. With Twenty Permanent Photographs. Royal 8vo. Handsomely bound. 31s. 6d.

The SATURDAY REVIEW *says of them*, "*We have seen not a few elegant specimens of Mr. Woodbury's new process, but we have seen none that equal these.*"

Reynolds.—SIR JOSHUA REYNOLDS AS A PORTRAIT PAINTER. AN ESSAY. By J. CHURTON COLLINS, B.A. Balliol College, Oxford. Illustrated by a Series of Portraits of distinguished Beauties of the Court of George III.; reproduced in Autotype from Proof Impressions of the celebrated Engravings, by VALENTINE GREEN, THOMAS WATSON, F. R. SMITH, E. FISHER, and others. Folio half-morocco. £5 5s.

Rogers (James E. Thorold).—HISTORICAL GLEANINGS: A Series of Sketches. Montague, Walpole, Adam Smith, Cobbett. By Prof. ROGERS. Crown 8vo. 4s. 6d. Second Series. Wiklif, Laud, Wilkes, and Horne Tooke. Crown 8vo. 6s.

Routledge.—CHAPTERS IN THE HISTORY OF POPULAR PROGRESS IN ENGLAND, chiefly in Relation to the Freedom of the Press and Trial by Jury, 1660—1820. With application to later years. By J. ROUTLEDGE. 8vo. 16s.

"*The volume abounds in facts and information, almost always useful and often curious.*"—TIMES.

Rumford.—COUNT RUMFORD'S COMPLETE WORKS, with Memoir, and Notices of his Daughter. By GEORGE ELLIS. Five Vols. 8vo. 4l. 14s. 6d.

Seeley (Professor).—LECTURES AND ESSAYS. By J. R. SEELEY, M.A. Professor of Modern History in the University of Cambridge. 8vo. 10s. 6d.
CONTENTS:—*Roman Imperialism:* 1. *The Great Roman Revolution;* 2. *The Proximate Cause of the Fall of the Roman Empire; The Later Empire.* — *Milton's Political Opinions* — *Milton's Poetry* — *Elementary Principles in Art* — *Liberal Education in Universities* — *English in Schools* — *The Church as a Teacher of Morality* — *The Teaching of Politics: an Inaugural Lecture delivered at Cambridge.*

Shelburne.—LIFE OF WILLIAM, EARL OF SHELBURNE, AFTERWARDS FIRST MARQUIS OF LANSDOWNE. With Extracts from his Papers and Correspondence. By Lord EDMOND FITZMAURICE. In Three Vols. 8vo. Vol. I. 1737—1766, 12s.; Vol. II. 1766—1776, 12s.; Vol. III. 1776—1805. 16s.
"*Lord Edmond Fitzmaurice has succeeded in placing before us a wealth of new matter, which, while casting valuable and much-needed light on several obscure passages in the political history of a hundred years ago, has enabled us for the first time to form a clear and consistent idea of his ancestor.*"—SPECTATOR.

Sime.—HISTORY OF GERMANY. By JAMES SIME, M.A. 18mo. 3s. Being Vol. V. of the Historical Course for Schools: Edited by EDWARD A. FREEMAN, D.C.L.
"*This is a remarkably clear and impressive History of Germany.*"—STANDARD.

Squier.—PERU: INCIDENTS OF TRAVEL AND EXPLORATION IN THE LAND OF THE INCAS. By E. G. SQUIER, M.A., F.S.A., late U.S. Commissioner to Peru. With 300 Illustrations. Second Edition. 8vo. 21s.
The TIMES *says:*—"*No more solid and trustworthy contribution has been made to an accurate knowledge of what are among the most wonderful ruins in the world. The work is really what its title implies. While of the greatest importance as a contribution to Peruvian archæology, it is also a thoroughly entertaining and instructive narrative of travel. Not the least important feature must be considered the numerous well executed illustrations.*"

Strangford.—EGYPTIAN SHRINES AND SYRIAN SEPULCHRES, including a Visit to Palmyra. By EMILY A. BEAUFORT (Viscountess Strangford), Author of "The Eastern Shores of the Adriatic." New Edition. Crown 8vo. 7s. 6d.

Tait.—AN ANALYSIS OF ENGLISH HISTORY, based upon Green's "Short History of the English People." By C. W. A. TAIT, M.A., Assistant Master, Clifton College. Crown 8vo. 3s. 6d.

HISTORY, BIOGRAPHY, TRAVELS, ETC.

Tait.—CATHARINE AND CRAUFURD TAIT, WIFE AND SON OF ARCHIBALD CAMPBELL, ARCHBISHOP OF CANTERBURY : a Memoir, Edited, at the request of the Archbishop, by the Rev. W. BENHAM, B.D., Vicar of Margate, and One of the Six Preachers of Canterbury Cathedral. With Two Portraits engraved by JEENS. Crown 8vo. 12s. 6d.

"*The volume can scarcely fail to be read widely and with deep interest. . . . It is difficult to put it down when once taken in hand, still more difficult to get through it without emotion. . . . We commend the volume to those who knew Catharine and Craufurd Tait as one which will bring back to their minds recollections of their characters as true as the recollections of the faces brought back by the two excellent portraits which adorn the book; while to those who knew them not, we commend it as containing the record of two noble Christian lives, which it will be a pleasure to them to contemplate and an advantage to emulate.*"—TIMES.

Thomas.—THE LIFE OF JOHN THOMAS, Surgeon of the "Earl of Oxford" East Indiaman, and First Baptist Missionary to Bengal. By C. B. LEWIS, Baptist Missionary. 8vo. 10s. 6d.

Thompson.—HISTORY OF ENGLAND. By EDITH THOMPSON. Being Vol. II. of the Historical Course for Schools, Edited by EDWARD A. FREEMAN, D.C.L. New Edition, revised and enlarged, with Maps. 18mo. 2s. 6d.

"*Freedom from prejudice, simplicity of style, and accuracy of statement, are the characteristics of this volume. It is a trustworthy text-book, and likely to be generally serviceable in schools.*"—PALL MALL GAZETTE.
"*In its great accuracy and correctness of detail it stands far ahead of the general run of school manuals. Its arrangement, too, is clear, and its style simple and straightforward.*"—SATURDAY REVIEW.

Todhunter.—THE CONFLICT OF STUDIES; AND OTHER ESSAYS ON SUBJECTS CONNECTED WITH EDUCATION. By ISAAC TODHUNTER, M.A., F.R.S., late Fellow and Principal Mathematical Lecturer of St. John's College, Cambridge. 8vo. 10s. 6d.

Trench (Archbishop).—For other Works by the same Author, see THEOLOGICAL and BELLES LETTRES CATALOGUES, and page 30 of this Catalogue.

GUSTAVUS ADOLPHUS IN GERMANY, and other Lectures on the Thirty Years' War. Second Edition, revised and enlarged. Fcap. 8vo. 4s.

PLUTARCH, HIS LIFE, HIS LIVES, AND HIS MORALS. Five Lectures. Second Edition, enlarged. Fcap. 8vo. 3s. 6d.

LECTURES ON MEDIEVAL CHURCH HISTORY. Being the substance of Lectures delivered in Queen's College, London. Second Edition, revised. 8vo. 12s.

Trench (Maria).—THE LIFE OF ST. TERESA. By MARIA TRENCH. With Portrait engraved by JEENS. Crown 8vo, cloth extra. 8s. 6d.

"*A book of rare interest.*"—JOHN BULL.

Trench (Mrs. R.)—REMAINS OF THE LATE MRS. RICHARD TRENCH. Being Selections from her Journals, Letters, and other Papers. Edited by ARCHBISHOP TRENCH. New and Cheaper Issue, with Portrait. 8vo. 6s.

Trollope.—A HISTORY OF THE COMMONWEALTH OF FLORENCE FROM THE EARLIEST INDEPENDENCE OF THE COMMUNE TO THE FALL OF THE REPUBLIC IN 1831. By T. ADOLPHUS TROLLOPE. 4 Vols. 8vo. Half morocco. 21s.

Uppingham by the Sea.—A NARRATIVE OF THE YEAR AT BORTH. By J. H. S. Crown 8vo. 3s. 6d.

Victor Emmanuel II., First King of Italy.—HIS LIFE. By G. S. GODKIN. 2 vols., crown 8vo. 16s.

"*An extremely clear and interesting history of one of the most important changes of later times.*"—EXAMINER.

Wallace.—THE MALAY ARCHIPELAGO: the Land of the Orang Utan and the Bird of Paradise. By ALFRED RUSSEL WALLACE. A Narrative of Travel with Studies of Man and Nature. With Maps and numerous Illustrations. Sixth Edition. Crown 8vo. 7s. 6d.

"*The result is a vivid picture of tropical life, which may be read with unflagging interest, and a sufficient account of his scientific conclusions to stimulate our appetite without wearying us by detail. In short, we may safely say that we have never read a more agreeable book of its kind.*"—SATURDAY REVIEW.

Ward.—A HISTORY OF ENGLISH DRAMATIC LITERATURE TO THE DEATH OF QUEEN ANNE. By A. W. WARD, M.A., Professor of History and English Literature in Owens College, Manchester. Two Vols. 8vo. 32s.

"*As full of interest as of information. To students of dramatic literature invaluable, and may be equally recommended to readers for mere pastime.*"—PALL MALL GAZETTE.

Ward (J.)—EXPERIENCES OF A DIPLOMATIST. Being recollections of Germany founded on Diaries kept during the years 1840—1870. By JOHN WARD, C.B., late H.M. Minister-Resident to the Hanse Towns. 8vo. 10s. 6d.

HISTORY, BIOGRAPHY, TRAVELS, ETC. 29

Waterton (C.)—WANDERINGS IN SOUTH AMERICA, THE NORTH-WEST OF THE UNITED STATES, AND THE ANTILLES IN 1812, 1816, 1820, and 1824. With Original Instructions for the perfect Preservation of Birds, etc., for Cabinets of Natural History. By CHARLES WATERTON. New Edition, edited with Biographical Introduction and Explanatory Index by the Rev. J. G. WOOD, M.A. With 100 Illustrations. Cheaper Edition. Crown 8vo. 6s.

Wedgwood.—JOHN WESLEY AND THE EVANGELICAL REACTION of the Eighteenth Century. By JULIA WEDGWOOD. Crown 8vo. 8s. 6d.

Whewell.—WILLIAM WHEWELL, D.D., late Master of Trinity College, Cambridge. An Account of his Writings, with Selections from his Literary and Scientific Correspondence. By I. TODHUNTER, M.A., F.R.S. Two Vols. 8vo. 25s.

White.—THE NATURAL HISTORY AND ANTIQUITIES OF SELBORNE. By GILBERT WHITE. Edited, with Memoir and Notes, by FRANK BUCKLAND, A Chapter on Antiquities by LORD SELBORNE, Map, &c., and numerous Illustrations by P. H. DELAMOTTE. Royal 8vo. Cloth, extra gilt. Cheaper Issue. 21s.

Also a Large Paper Edition, containing, in addition to the above, upwards of Thirty Woodburytype Illustrations from Drawings by Prof. DELAMOTTE. Two Vols. 4to. Half morocco, elegant. 4l. 4s.

"*Mr. Delamotte's charming illustrations are a worthy decoration of so dainty a book. They bring Selborne before us, and really help us to understand why White's love for his native place never grew cold.*"—TIMES.

Wilson.—A MEMOIR OF GEORGE WILSON, M.D., F.R.S.E., Regius Professor of Technology in the University of Edinburgh. By his SISTER. New Edition. Crown 8vo. 6s.

Wilson (Daniel, LL.D.)—Works by DANIEL WILSON, LL.D., Professor of History and English Literature in University College, Toronto :—

PREHISTORIC ANNALS OF SCOTLAND. New Edition, with numerous Illustrations. Two Vols. demy 8vo. 36s.

"*One of the most interesting, learned, and elegant works we have seen for a long time.*"—WESTMINSTER REVIEW.

PREHISTORIC MAN : Researches into the Origin of Civilization in the Old and New World. New Edition, revised and enlarged throughout, with numerous Illustrations and two Coloured Plates. Two Vols. 8vo. 36s.

Wilson.—*continued.*

"*A valuable work pleasantly written and well worthy of attention both by students and general readers.*"—ACADEMY.

> CHATTERTON: A Biographical Study. By DANIEL WILSON, LL.D., Professor of History and English Literature in University College, Toronto. Crown 8vo. 6s. 6d.

Yonge (Charlotte M.)—Works by CHARLOTTE M. YONGE, Author of "The Heir of Redclyffe," &c., &c. :—

> A PARALLEL HISTORY OF FRANCE AND ENGLAND: consisting of Outlines and Dates. Oblong 4to. 3s. 6d.
>
> CAMEOS FROM ENGLISH HISTORY. From Rollo to Edward II. Extra fcap. 8vo. Third Edition. 5s.
>
> SECOND SERIES, THE WARS IN FRANCE. Extra fcap. 8vo. Third Edition. 5s.
>
> THIRD SERIES, THE WARS OF THE ROSES. Extra fcap. 8vo. 5s.

"*Instead of dry details,*" says the NONCONFORMIST, "*we have living pictures, faithful, vivid, and striking.*"

> FOURTH SERIES. Reformation Times. Extra fcap. 8vo. 5s.
>
> HISTORY OF FRANCE. Maps. 18mo. 3s. 6d.
> [*Historical Course for Schools.*

POLITICS, POLITICAL AND SOCIAL ECONOMY, LAW, AND KINDRED SUBJECTS.

Anglo-Saxon Law.—ESSAYS IN. Contents: Law Courts—Land and Family Laws and Legal Procedure generally. With Select cases. Medium 8vo. 18s.

Arnold.—THE ROMAN SYSTEM OF PROVINCIAL ADMINISTRATION TO THE ACCESSION OF CONSTANTINE THE GREAT. Being the Arnold Prize Essay for 1879. By W. T. Arnold, B.A. Crown 8vo. 6s.

Ball.—THE STUDENT'S GUIDE TO THE BAR. By WALTER W. BALL, M.A., of the Inner Temple, Barrister-at-Law. Crown 8vo. 2s. 6d.
"*The student will here find a clear statement of the several steps by which the degree of barrister is obtained, and also useful advice about the advantages of a prolonged course of 'reading in Chambers.'*"—ACADEMY.

Bernard.—FOUR LECTURES ON SUBJECTS CONNECTED WITH DIPLOMACY. By MONTAGUE BERNARD, M.A., Chichele Professor of International Law and Diplomacy, Oxford. 8vo. 9s.
"*Singularly interesting lectures, so able, clear, and attractive.*"—SPECTATOR.

Bright (John, M.P.)—Works by the Right Hon. JOHN BRIGHT, M.P.
SPEECHES ON QUESTIONS OF PUBLIC POLICY. Edited by Professor THOROLD ROGERS. Author's Popular Edition. Globe 8vo. 3s. 6d.
"*Mr. Bright's speeches will always deserve to be studied, as an apprenticeship to popular and parliamentary oratory; they will form materials for the history of our time, and many brilliant passages, perhaps some entire speeches, will really become a part of the living literature of England.*"—DAILY NEWS.
LIBRARY EDITION. Two Vols. 8vo. With Portrait. 25s.
PUBLIC ADDRESSES. Edited by J. THOROLD ROGERS. 8vo. 14s.

Bucknill.—HABITUAL DRUNKENNESS AND INSANE DRUNKARDS. By J. C. BUCKNILL, M.D., F.R.S., late Lord Chancellor's Visitor of Lunatics. Crown 8vo. 2s. 6d.

Cairnes.—Works by J. E. CAIRNES, M.A., Emeritus Professor of Political Economy in University College, London.
ESSAYS IN POLITICAL ECONOMY, THEORETICAL and APPLIED. By J. E. CAIRNES, M.A., Professor of Political Economy in University College, London. 8vo. 10s. 6d.
POLITICAL ESSAYS. 8vo. 10s. 6d.
SOME LEADING PRINCIPLES OF POLITICAL ECONOMY NEWLY EXPOUNDED. 8vo. 14s.
CONTENTS :—*Part I. Value. Part II. Labour and Capital. Part III. International Trade.*
"*A work which is perhaps the most valuable contribution to the science made since the publication, a quarter of a century since, of Mr. Mill's 'Principles of Political Economy.'*"—DAILY NEWS.
THE CHARACTER AND LOGICAL METHOD OF POLITICAL ECONOMY. New Edition, enlarged. 8vo. 7s. 6d.
"*These lectures are admirably fitted to correct the slipshod generalizations which pass current as the science of Political Economy.*"—TIMES.

Cobden (Richard).—SPEECHES ON QUESTIONS OF PUBLIC POLICY. By RICHARD COBDEN. Edited by the Right Hon. John Bright, M.P., and J. E. Thorold Rogers. Popular Edition. 8vo. 3s. 6d.

Fawcett.—Works by HENRY FAWCETT, M.A., M.P., Fellow of Trinity Hall, and Professor of Political Economy in the University of Cambridge :—
THE ECONOMIC POSITION OF THE BRITISH LABOURER. Extra fcap. 8vo. 5s.
MANUAL OF POLITICAL ECONOMY. Fifth Edition, with New Chapters on the Depreciation of Silver, etc. Crown 8vo. 12s.
The DAILY NEWS *says:* "*It forms one of the best introductions to the principles of the science, and to its practical applications in the problems of modern, and especially of English, government and society.*"
PAUPERISM: ITS CAUSES AND REMEDIES. Crown 8vo. 5s. 6d.
The ATHENÆUM *calls the work* "*a repertory of interesting and well digested information.*"
SPEECHES ON SOME CURRENT POLITICAL QUESTIONS. 8vo. 10s. 6d.
"*They will help to educate, not perhaps, parties, but the educators of parties.*"—DAILY NEWS.

Fawcett.—*continued.*

FREE TRADE AND PROTECTION: an Inquiry into the Causes which have retarded the general adoption of Free Trade since its introduction into England. Third Edition. 8vo. 7s. 6d.

"*No greater service can be rendered to the cause of Free Trade than a clear explanation of the principles on which Free Trade rests. Professor Fawcett has done this in the volume before us with all his habitual clearness of thought and expression.*"—ECONOMIST.

ESSAYS ON POLITICAL AND SOCIAL SUBJECTS. By PROFESSOR FAWCETT, M.P., and MILLICENT GARRETT FAWCETT. 8vo. 10s. 6d.

"*They will all repay the perusal of the thinking reader.*"—DAILY NEWS.

Fawcett (Mrs.)—Works by MILLICENT GARRETT FAWCETT.

POLITICAL ECONOMY FOR BEGINNERS. WITH QUESTIONS. New Edition. 18mo. 2s. 6d.

The DAILY NEWS *calls it "clear, compact, and comprehensive;" and the* SPECTATOR *says, "Mrs. Fawcett's treatise is perfectly suited to its purpose."*

TALES IN POLITICAL ECONOMY. Crown 8vo. 3s.

"*The idea is a good one, and it is quite wonderful what a mass of economic teaching the author manages to compress into a small space... The true doctrines of International Trade, Currency, and the ratio between Production and Population, are set before us and illustrated in a masterly manner.*"—ATHENÆUM.

Freeman (E. A.), M.A., D.C.L.—COMPARATIVE POLITICS. Lectures at the Royal Institution, to which is added "The Unity of History," being the Rede Lecture delivered at Cambridge in 1872. 8vo. 14s.

"*We find in Mr. Freeman's new volume the same sound, careful, comprehensive qualities which have long ago raised him to so high a place amongst historical writers. For historical discipline, then, as well as historical information, Mr. Freeman's book is full of value.*"—PALL MALL GAZETTE.

Goschen.—REPORTS AND SPEECHES ON LOCAL TAXATION. By GEORGE J. GOSCHEN, M.P. Royal 8vo. 5s.

"*The volume contains a vast mass of information of the highest value.*"—ATHENÆUM.

Guide to the Unprotected, in Every Day Matters Relating to Property and Income. By a BANKER'S DAUGHTER. Fourth Edition, Revised. Extra fcap. 8vo. 3s. 6d.

c

"*Many an unprotected female will bless the head which planned and the hand which compiled this admirable little manual. . . . This book was very much wanted, and it could not have been better done.*"—MORNING STAR.

Hamilton.—MONEY AND VALUE: an Inquiry into the Means and Ends of Economic Production, with an Appendix on the Depreciation of Silver and Indian Currency. By ROWLAND HAMILTON. 8vo. 12s.

"*The subject is here dealt with in a luminous style, and by presenting it from a new point of view in connection with the nature and functions of money, a genuine service has been rendered to commercial science.*"—BRITISH QUARTERLY REVIEW.

Harwood.—DISESTABLISHMENT: a Defence of the Principle of a National Church. By GEORGE HARWOOD, M.A. 8vo. 12s.

Hill.—OUR COMMON LAND: and other Short Essays. By OCTAVIA HILL. Extra fcap. 8vo. 3s. 6d.

CONTENTS:—*Our Common Land. District Visiting. A More Excellent Way of Charity. A Word on Good Citizenship. Open Spaces. Effectual Charity. The Future of our Commons.*

Historicus.—LETTERS ON SOME QUESTIONS OF INTERNATIONAL LAW. Reprinted from the *Times*, with considerable Additions. 8vo. 7s. 6d. Also, ADDITIONAL LETTERS. 8vo. 2s. 6d.

Holland.—THE TREATY RELATIONS OF RUSSIA AND TURKEY FROM 1774 TO 1853. A Lecture delivered at Oxford, April 1877. By T. E. HOLLAND, D.C.L., Professor of International Law and Diplomacy, Oxford. Crown 8vo. 2s.

Hughes (Thos.)—THE OLD CHURCH: WHAT SHALL WE DO WITH IT? By THOMAS HUGHES, Q.C. Crown 8vo. 6s.

Jevons.—Works by W. STANLEY JEVONS, M.A., Professor of Political Economy in University College, London. (For other Works by the same Author, *see* EDUCATIONAL and PHILOSOPHICAL CATALOGUES.)

THE THEORY OF POLITICAL ECONOMY. Second Edition, revised, with new Preface and Appendices. 8vo. 10s. 6d.

"*Professor Jevons has done invaluable service by courageously claiming political economy to be strictly a branch of Applied Mathematics.*"—WESTMINSTER REVIEW.

PRIMER OF POLITICAL ECONOMY. 18mo. 1s.

Laveleye. — PRIMITIVE PROPERTY. By EMILE DE LAVELEYE. Translated by G. R. L. MARRIOTT, LL.B., with an Introduction by T. E. CLIFFE LESLIE, LL.B. 8vo. 12s.

"*It is almost impossible to over-estimate the value of the well-digested knowledge which it contains; it is one of the most learned books that have been contributed to the historical department of the literature of economic science.*"—ATHENÆUM.

Leading Cases done into English. By an APPRENTICE OF LINCOLN'S INN. Third Edition. Crown 8vo. 2s. 6d.

"*Here is a rare treat for the lovers of quaint conceits, who in reading this charming little book will find enjoyment in the varied metre and graphic language in which the several tales are told, no less than in the accurate and pithy rendering of some of our most familiar 'Leading Cases.'*"—SATURDAY REVIEW.

Lubbock.—ADDRESSES, POLITICAL AND EDUCATIONAL. By Sir JOHN LUBBOCK, Bart., M.P., &c., &c. 8vo, pp. 209. 8s. 6d.

The ten speeches given are (1) on the Imperial Policy of Great Britain, (2) on the Bank Act of 1844, (3) on the Present System of Public School Education, 1876, (4) on the Present System of Elementary Education, (5) on the Income Tax, (6) on the National Debt, (7) on the Declaration of Paris, (8) on Marine Insurances, (9) on the Preservation of Ancient Monuments, and (10) on Egypt.

Macdonell.—THE LAND QUESTION, WITH SPECIAL REFERENCE TO ENGLAND AND SCOTLAND. By JOHN MACDONELL, Barrister-at-Law. 8vo. 10s. 6d.

Marshall.—THE ECONOMICS OF INDUSTRY. By A. MARSHALL, M.A., Principal of University College, Bristol, and MARY PALEY MARSHALL, late Lecturer at Newnham Hall, Cambridge. Extra fcap. 8vo. 2s. 6d.

Martin.—THE STATESMAN'S YEAR-BOOK: A Statistical and Historical Annual of the States of the Civilized World, for the year 1880. By FREDERICK MARTIN. Seventeenth Annual Publication. Revised after Official Returns. Crown 8vo. 10s. 6d.

The Statesman's Year-Book is the only work in the English language which furnishes a clear and concise account of the actual condition of all the States of Europe, the civilized countries of America, Asia, and Africa, and the British Colonies and Dependencies in all parts of the world. The new issue of the work has been revised and corrected, on the basis of official reports received direct from the heads of the leading Governments of the world, in reply to letters sent to them by the Editor. Through the valuable assistance thus given, it has been possible to collect an amount of information, political, statistical, and commercial, of the latest date, and of unimpeachable trustworthiness, such as no publication of the same kind has ever been able to furnish. "As indispensable as Bradshaw."—TIMES.

Monahan.—THE METHOD OF LAW: an Essay on the Statement and Arrangement of the Legal Standard of Conduct. By J. H. MONAHAN, Q.C. Crown 8vo. 6s.

"*Will be found valuable by careful law students who have felt the importance of gaining clear ideas regarding the relations between the parts of the complex organism they have to study.*"—BRITISH QUARTERLY REVIEW.

Paterson.—THE LIBERTY OF THE SUBJECT AND THE LAWS OF ENGLAND RELATING TO THE SECURITY OF THE PERSON. Commentaries on. By JAMES PATERSON, M.A., Barrister at Law, sometime Commissioner for English and Irish Fisheries, etc. Cheaper issue. Two Vols. Crown 8vo. 21s.

"*Two or three hours' dipping into these volumes, not to say reading them through, will give legislators and stump orators a knowledge of the liberty of a citizen of their country, in its principles, its fulness, and its modification, such as they probably in nine cases out of ten never had before.*"—SCOTSMAN.

Phillimore.—PRIVATE LAW AMONG THE ROMANS, from the Pandects. By JOHN GEORGE PHILLIMORE, Q.C. 8vo. 16s.

Rogers.—COBDEN AND POLITICAL OPINION. By J. E. THOROLD ROGERS. 8vo. 10s. 6d.

"*Will be found most useful by politicians of every school, as it forms a sort of handbook to Cobden's teaching.*"—ATHENÆUM.

Stephen (C. E.)—THE SERVICE OF THE POOR; Being an Inquiry into the Reasons for and against the Establishment of Religious Sisterhoods for Charitable Purposes. By CAROLINE EMILIA STEPHEN. Crown 8vo. 6s. 6d.

"*The ablest advocate of a better line of work in this direction that we have ever seen.*"—EXAMINER.

Stephen.—Works by Sir JAMES F. STEPHEN, K.C.S.I., Q.C.

A DIGEST OF THE LAW OF EVIDENCE. Third Edition with New Preface. Crown 8vo. 6s.

A DIGEST OF THE CRIMINAL LAW. (Crimes and Punishments.) 8vo. 16s.

"*We feel sure that any person of ordinary intelligence who had never looked into a law-book in his life might, by a few days' careful study of*

Stephen.—*continued.*

this volume, obtain a more accurate understanding of the criminal law, a more perfect conception of its different bearings, a more thorough and intelligent insight into its snares and pitfalls, than an ordinary practitioner can boast of after years of study of the ordinary textbooks and practical experience of the Courts unassisted by any competent guide."—SATURDAY REVIEW.

    A GENERAL VIEW OF THE CRIMINAL LAW OF ENGLAND. Two Vols. Crown 8vo. [*New edition in the press.*

Stubbs.—VILLAGE POLITICS. Addresses and Sermons on the Labour Question. By C. W. STUBBS, M.A., Vicar of Granborough, Bucks. Extra fcap. 8vo. 3s. 6d.

Thornton.—Works by W. T. THORNTON, C.B., Secretary for Public Works in the India Office :—

    ON LABOUR : Its Wrongful Claims and Rightful Dues; Its Actual Present and Possible Future. Second Edition, revised, 8vo. 14s.

    A PLEA FOR PEASANT PROPRIETORS : With the Outlines of a Plan for their Establishment in Ireland. New Edition, revised. Crown 8vo. 7s. 6d.

    INDIAN PUBLIC WORKS AND COGNATE INDIAN TOPICS. With Map of Indian Railways. Crown 8vo. 8s. 6d.

Walker.—Works by F. A. WALKER, M.A., Ph.D., Professor of Political Economy and History, Yale College :—

    THE WAGES QUESTION. A Treatise on Wages and the Wages Class. 8vo. 14s.

    MONEY. 8vo. 16s.

"*It is painstaking, laborious, and states the question in a clear and very intelligible form. . . . The volume possesses a great value as a sort of encyclopædia of knowledge on the subject.*"—ECONOMIST.

    MONEY IN ITS RELATIONS TO TRADE AND INDUSTRY. Crown 8vo. [*Shortly.*

Work about the Five Dials. With an Introductory Note by THOMAS CARLYLE. Crown 8vo. 6s.

"*A book which abounds with wise and practical suggestions.*"—PALL MALL GAZETTE.

WORKS CONNECTED WITH THE SCIENCE OR THE HISTORY OF LANGUAGE.

Abbott.—A SHAKESPERIAN GRAMMAR: An Attempt to illustrate some of the Differences between Elizabethan and Modern English. By the Rev. E. A. ABBOTT, D.D., Head Master of the City of London School. New and Enlarged Edition. Extra fcap. 8vo. 6s.

"*Valuable not only as an aid to the critical study of Shakespeare, but as tending to familiarize the reader with Elizabethan English in general.*"—ATHENÆUM.

Breymann.—A FRENCH GRAMMAR BASED ON PHILOLOGICAL PRINCIPLES. By HERMANN BREYMANN, Ph.D., Professor of Philology in the University of Munich late Lecturer on French Language and Literature at Owens College, Manchester. Extra fcap. 8vo. 4s. 6d.

Ellis.—PRACTICAL HINTS ON THE QUANTITATIVE PRONUNCIATION OF LATIN, FOR THE USE OF CLASSICAL TEACHERS AND LINGUISTS. By A. J. ELLIS, B.A., F.R.S., &c. Extra fcap. 8vo. 4s. 6d.

Fleay.—A SHAKESPEARE MANUAL. By the Rev. F. G. FLEAY, M.A., Head Master of Skipton Grammar School. Extra fcap. 8vo. 4s. 6d.

Goodwin.—Works by W. W. GOODWIN, Professor of Greek Literature in Harvard University.

SYNTAX OF THE GREEK MOODS AND TENSES. New Edition. Crown 8vo. 6s. 6d.

AN ELEMENTARY GREEK GRAMMAR. Crown 8vo. 6s.

"*It is the best Greek Grammar of its size in the English language.*"—ATHENÆUM.

Hadley.—ESSAYS PHILOLOGICAL AND CRITICAL. Selected from the Papers of JAMES HADLEY, LL.D., Professor of Greek in Yale College, &c. 8vo. 16s.

Hales.—LONGER ENGLISH POEMS. With Notes, Philological and Explanatory, and an Introduction on the Teaching of English. Chiefly for use in Schools. Edited by J. W. HALES, M.A., Professor of English Literature at King's College, London, &c. &c. Fifth Edition. Extra fcap. 8vo. 4s. 6d.

Helfenstein (James).—A COMPARATIVE GRAMMAR OF THE TEUTONIC LANGUAGES : Being at the same time a Historical Grammar of the English Language, and comprising Gothic, Anglo-Saxon, Early English, Modern English, Icelandic (Old Norse), Danish, Swedish, Old High German, Middle High German, Modern German, Old Saxon, Old Frisian, and Dutch. By JAMES HELFENSTEIN, Ph.D. 8vo. 18s.

Masson (Gustave).—A COMPENDIOUS DICTIONARY OF THE FRENCH LANGUAGE (French-English and English-French). Followed by a List of the Principal Diverging Derivations, and preceded by Chronological and Historical Tables. By GUSTAVE MASSON, Assistant-Master and Librarian, Harrow School. Fourth Edition. Crown 8vo. Half-bound. 6s.

"*A book which any student, whatever may be the degree of his advancement in the language, would do well to have on the table close at hand while he is reading.*"—SATURDAY REVIEW.

Mayor.—A BIBLIOGRAPHICAL CLUE TO LATIN LITERATURE. Edited after Dr. E. HUBNER. With large Additions by JOHN E. B. MAYOR, M.A., Professor of Latin in the University of Cambridge. Crown 8vo. 6s. 6d.

"*An extremely useful volume that should be in the hands of all scholars.*"—ATHENÆUM.

Morris.—Works by the Rev. RICHARD MORRIS, LL.D., Member of the Council of the Philol. Soc., Lecturer on English Language and Literature in King's College School, Editor of "Specimens of Early English," etc., etc. :—

HISTORICAL OUTLINES OF ENGLISH ACCIDENCE, comprising Chapters on the History and Development of the Language, and on Word-formation. Sixth Edition. Fcap. 8vo. 6s.

ELEMENTARY LESSONS IN HISTORICAL ENGLISH GRAMMAR, containing Accidence and Word-formation. Third Edition. 18mo. 2s. 6d.

Oliphant.—THE OLD AND MIDDLE ENGLISH. By T. L. KINGTON OLIPHANT, M.A., of Balliol College, Oxford. A New Edition, revised and greatly enlarged, of "The Sources of Standard English." Extra fcap. 8vo. 9s.

"*Mr. Oliphant's book is to our mind, one of the ablest and most scholarly contributions to our standard English we have seen for many years.*"—SCHOOL BOARD CHRONICLE. "*The book comes nearer to a history of the English language than anything we have seen since such a history could be written, without confusion and contradictions.*"—SATURDAY REVIEW.

Peile (John, M.A.)—AN INTRODUCTION TO GREEK AND LATIN ETYMOLOGY. By JOHN PEILE, M.A., Fellow and Tutor of Christ's College, Cambridge. Third and revised Edition. Crown 8vo. 10s. 6d.

"*The book may be accepted as a very valuable contribution to the science of language.*"—SATURDAY REVIEW.

Philology.—THE JOURNAL OF SACRED AND CLASSICAL PHILOLOGY. Four Vols. 8vo. 12s. 6d. each.

THE JOURNAL OF PHILOLOGY. New Series. Edited by JOHN E. B. MAYOR, M.A., and W. ALDIS WRIGHT, M.A. 4s. 6d. (Half-yearly.)

Roby (H. J.)—A GRAMMAR OF THE LATIN LANGUAGE, FROM PLAUTUS TO SUETONIUS. By HENRY JOHN ROBY, M.A., late Fellow of St. John's College, Cambridge. In Two Parts. Second Edition. Part I. containing:—Book I. Sounds. Book II. Inflexions. Book III. Word Formation. Appendices. Crown 8vo. 8s. 6d. Part II.—Syntax, Prepositions, &c. Crown 8vo. 10s. 6d.

"*The book is marked by the clear and practical insight of a master in his art. It is a book which would do honour to any country.*"—ATHENÆUM. "*Brings before the student in a methodical form the best results of modern philology bearing on the Latin language.*"—SCOTSMAN.

Schmidt.—THE RYTHMIC AND METRIC OF THE CLASSICAL LANGUAGES. To which are added, the Lyric Parts of the "Medea" of Euripides and the "Antigone" of Sophocles; with Rhythmical Scheme and Commentary. By Dr. J. H. SCHMIDT. Translated from the German by J. W. WHITE, D.D. 8vo. 10s. 6d.

Taylor.—Works by the Rev. ISAAC TAYLOR, M.A.:—

ETRUSCAN RESEARCHES. With Woodcuts. 8vo. 14s.

The TIMES *says:*—"*The learning and industry displayed in this volume deserve the most cordial recognition. The ultimate verdict of science we shall not attempt to anticipate; but we can safely say this, that it is a learned book which the unlearned can enjoy, and that in the descriptions of the tomb-builders, as well as in the marvellous coincidences and unexpected analogies brought together by the author, readers of every grade may take delight as well as philosophers and scholars.*"

WORDS AND PLACES; or, Etymological Illustrations of History, Ethnology, and Geography. By the Rev. ISAAC TAYLOR. Third Edition, revised and compressed. With Maps. Globe 8vo. 6s.

GREEKS AND GOTHS: a Study on the Runes. 8vo. 9s.

Trench.—Works by R. CHENEVIX TRENCH, D.D., Archbishop of Dublin. (For other Works by the same Author, *see* THEOLOGICAL CATALOGUE.)

SYNONYMS OF THE NEW TESTAMENT. Eighth Edition, enlarged. 8vo, cloth. 12s.

"*He is,*" *the* ATHENÆUM *says,* "*a guide in this department of knowledge to whom his readers may entrust themselves with confidence.*"

ON THE STUDY OF WORDS. Lectures Addressed (originally) to the Pupils at the Diocesan Training School, Winchester. Seventeenth Edition, enlarged. Fcap. 8vo. 5s.

ENGLISH PAST AND PRESENT. Tenth Edition, revised and improved. Fcap. 8vo. 5s.

A SELECT GLOSSARY OF ENGLISH WORDS USED FORMERLY IN SENSES DIFFERENT FROM THEIR PRESENT. Fifth Edition, enlarged. Fcap. 8vo. 5s.

Vincent and Dickson.—A HANDBOOK TO MODERN GREEK. By EDGAR VINCENT and T. G. DICKSON. Extra fcap. 8vo. 5s.

Whitney.—A COMPENDIOUS GERMAN GRAMMAR. By W. D. WHITNEY, Professor of Sanskrit and Instructor in Modern Languages in Yale College. Crown 8vo. 6s.

"*After careful examination we are inclined to pronounce it the best grammar of modern language we have ever seen.*"—SCOTSMAN.

Whitney and Edgren.—A COMPENDIOUS GERMAN AND ENGLISH DICTIONARY, with Notation of Correspondences and Brief Etymologies. By Professor W. D. WHITNEY, assisted by A. H. EDGREN. Crown 8vo. 7s. 6d.

The GERMAN-ENGLISH Part may be had separately. Price 5s.

Yonge.—HISTORY OF CHRISTIAN NAMES. By CHARLOTTE M. YONGE, Author of "The Heir of Redclyffe." Cheaper Edition. Two Vols. Crown 8vo. 12s.

Now publishing, in crown 8vo, price 2s. 6d. each.

ENGLISH MEN OF LETTERS.

Edited by JOHN MORLEY.

A Series of Short Books to tell people what is best worth knowing to the Life, Character, and Works of some of the great English Writers.

ENGLISH MEN OF LETTERS.—JOHNSON. By LESLIE STEPHEN.

"The new series opens well with Mr. Leslie Stephen's sketch of Dr. Johnson. It could hardly have been done better, and it will convey to the readers for whom it is intended a juster estimate of Johnson than either of the two essays of Lord Macaulay."—*Pall Mall Gazette.*

ENGLISH MEN OF LETTERS.—SCOTT. By R. H. HUTTON.

"The tone of the volume is excellent throughout."—*Athenæum.*

"We could not wish for a more suggestive introduction to Scott and his poems and novels."—*Examiner.*

ENGLISH MEN OF LETTERS.—GIBBON. By J. C. MORISON.

"As a clear, thoughtful, and attractive record of the life and works of the greatest among the world's historians, it deserves the highest praise."—*Examiner.*

ENGLISH MEN OF LETTERS.—SHELLEY. By J. A. SYMONDS.

"The lovers of this great poet are to be congratulated on having at their command so fresh, clear, and intelligent a presentment of the subject, written by a man of adequate and wide culture."—*Athenæum.*

ENGLISH MEN OF LETTERS.—HUME. By Professor HUXLEY.

"It may fairly be said that no one now living could have expounded Hume with more sympathy or with equal perspicuity."—*Athenæum.*

ENGLISH MEN OF LETTERS.—GOLDSMITH. By WILLIAM BLACK.

"Mr. Black brings a fine sympathy and taste to bear in his criticism of Goldsmith's writings, as well as in his sketch of the incidents of his life."—*Athenæum.*

ENGLISH MEN OF LETTERS.—DEFOE. By W. MINTO.

"Mr. Minto's book is careful and accurate in all that is stated, and faithful in all that it suggests. It will repay reading more than once."—*Athenæum.*

ENGLISH MEN OF LETTERS—*Continued.*

ENGLISH MEN OF LETTERS.—BURNS. By Principal SHAIRP, Professor of Poetry in the University of Oxford.

"It is impossible to desire fairer criticism than Principal Shairp's on Burns's poetry. . . . . None of the series has given a truer estimate either of character or of genius than this little volume. . . . and all who read it will be thoroughly grateful to the author for this monument to the genius of Scotland's greatest poet."—*Spectator.*

ENGLISH MEN OF LETTERS.—SPENSER. By the Very Rev. the DEAN OF ST. PAUL'S.

"Dr. Church is master of his subject, and writes always with good taste."—*Academy.*

ENGLISH MEN OF LETTERS.—THACKERAY. By ANTHONY TROLLOPE.

"Mr. Trollope's sketch is exceedingly adapted to fulfil the purpose of the series in which it appears."—*Athenæum.*

ENGLISH MEN OF LETTERS.—BURKE. By JOHN MORLEY.

"Perhaps the best criticism yet published on the life and character of Burke is contained in Mr. Morley's compendious biography. His style is vigorous and polished, and both his political and personal judgment and his literary criticisms are just, generous, subtle, and in a high degree interesting."—*Saturday Review.*

Just ready.

MILTON. By MARK PATTISON.

In preparation.

HAWTHORNE. By HENRY JAMES.

SOUTHEY. By Professor DOWDEN.

CHAUCER. By Professor WARD.

COWPER. By GOLDWIN SMITH.

BUNYAN. BY J. A. FROUDE.

WORDSWORTH. By F. W. H. MYERS.

Others in preparation.

MACMILLAN AND CO., LONDON.

LONDON:
R. CLAY, SONS, AND TAYLOR, PRINTERS,
BREAD STREET HILL.

www.ingramcontent.com/pod-product-compliance
Lightning Source LLC
Chambersburg PA
CBHW032141230426
43672CB00011B/2417